Verdun 1916

Verdun 1916
The Deadliest Battle of
the First World War

William F. Buckingham

AMBERLEY

First Published 2016

Amberley Publishing
The Hill, Stroud
Gloucestershire, GL5 4EP

www.amberley-books.com

Copyright © William F. Buckingham, 2016

The right of William F. Buckingham to be
identified as the Author of this work has been
asserted in accordance with the Copyrights,
Designs and Patents Act 1988.

ISBN 978 1 4456 4108 9 (hardback)
ISBN 978 1 4456 4117 1 (ebook)

British Library Cataloguing in Publication Data.
A catalogue record for this book is available
from the British Library.

Typesetting and Origination by Amberley
Publishing
Printed in the UK.

CONTENTS

INTRODUCTION

The 1916 Battle of Verdun is widely regarded as a uniquely awful low point in a conflict that was by no means short of such woeful milestones. The very name has become synonymous with Pyrrhic victory, as exemplified by the tag 'Verdun on the Volga' applied to the Battle of Stalingrad twenty-six years later in a different war. This reputation is not simply due to casualty figures, which are notoriously difficult to pin down with certainty. The combined figure of around 681,000 French and German killed, wounded and missing at Verdun is only around half that for the 1916 Battle of the Somme, which racked up a combined British, French and German casualty toll of somewhere between 1.1 and 1.3 million. Despite this, Verdun's reputation as the worst of the worst is well deserved. The Battle of the Somme lasted for just over four months, while Verdun ground on for just over five months before the Germans finally abandoned their offensive, and nine months if the French counter-offensives that restored their line to something like the pre-battle status quo are included. The nearest British equivalent to this longevity was the dogged occupation of the Ypres Salient, but that particular trial was overwhelmingly a matter of sitting and taking whatever the Germans chose to dish out rather than withstanding months of heavy and sustained attack followed by heavy and sustained counter-attack. Unlike its British counterparts the battle for Verdun also had the potential to make or break the Allied war effort. Had the Germans succeeded in breaking through to Verdun, as they almost did in February and July 1916, there would be little between them and Paris and the morale impact of losing Verdun might well have been sufficient to knock France out of the war, as the architect of the German plan and some of his French opponents predicted.

Be that as it may, the intensity of the fighting at Verdun was also more tightly focussed. The original attack frontage at Verdun was approximately 7 miles wide, only half that of the Somme, and in the later climactic stages of the German offensive at Verdun in July 1916 entire corps were being compressed into attack frontages of 3 miles or less. By that time the Germans had abandoned any pretence of tactical finesse and were simply trying to bludgeon through the French defence by sheer weight of numbers, with an attack density of up to two men for every metre of front. The result of such 'tactics' in the face of modern weaponry can be easily imagined, and the battle left an indelible mark on the French too. Their *noria* replacement system meant that seventy of the ninety-six French divisions on the Western Front passed through what became dubbed 'the mill on the Meuse', and the deleterious effects of this exposure lay at the root of the widespread mutiny that gripped the French army from April 1917 and arguably underlay the French defeat in 1940.

However, the most graphic evidence to support Verdun's unenviable status are the physical scars the battle has left on the ground over which it was fought. With the exception of a handful of fragments, such as Sanctuary Wood near Ypres, the Memorial Parks at Vimy and Beaumont Hamel on the Somme, there is little trace of the monumental struggle that took place along a 400-mile strip of Belgium and France. Without the immaculately maintained military graveyards, memorials and occasional museum there would be little to no clue at all. The exception to this is Verdun, where, with the addition of large-scale conifer planting and the erection of memorials, almost 200 square kilometres have been left largely in the state they were in in 1918. This was not generally a deliberate policy to preserve the battlefield for posterity, but was obliged by the fact that the intensity of the fighting had literally blasted away the topsoil and poisoned the ground to an extent that defied post-war attempts to return it to former use. Thus the conifer plantations that blanketed the battlefield have preserved a moonscape of shell craters, trenches and the sedately crumbling remains of permanent fortifications like Fort Douaumont and Fort Vaux, the latter being the scene of hellish underground fighting of a scale and intensity that occurred nowhere else on the Western Front.

The following work begins with a brief examination of Verdun's historical background as a religious and cultural centre alongside its importance as a strategic location, augmented by a detailed account of Verdun's evolution as a key fortified location on France's eastern border and the parallel development of the French army's strategic and operational doctrine; both the latter were to play a crucial role in the battle. Along with the examination of the course of French operations from 1914, this provides the background necessary to put the account of the Battle of Verdun that follows into its proper context, and explains how and why the titanic struggle in 1916 developed in the way that it did. The account of the battle is supported with material from English-language sources, French official records, the words of participants, and contemporary and modern photographs and maps. After reading Alistair Horne's classic *The Price of Glory* as a teenager, the author has been inspired to visit Verdun and the surrounding battlefields on a score of occasions since 1989. Hopefully this work will inspire others to visit this small corner of north-eastern France, which still provides a unique insight into the reality of combat during the First World War. Finally, I would like to thank Jonathan Reeve at Amberley Publishing for once again tolerating my sometimes elastic approach to deadlines, and my partner Aileen for her patience and forbearance while normal life has been placed on hold for the last several months.

William F. Buckingham
Bishopbriggs, Glasgow
September 2015

'VIRODUNUM: THE FORTRESS THAT CONTROLS THE RIVER CROSSING', VERDUN 450 BC – AD 1873

Verdun today is a typical small French provincial town located astride the River Meuse 140 miles east of Paris. Built around a steep rocky bluff on the west bank of the Meuse occupied by the *Cathédrale Notre-Dame de Verdun*, the bluff rises from the wooded ridges of the Argonne which in turn subside into the chalk plain dominated by the cathedral city of Reims 75 miles to the west. On the east bank of the river the heavily wooded ridge of the Meuse Heights looms menacingly over the town before sloping gradually eastward into the low-lying Woëvre Plain that stretches the 30 miles to Metz on the River Moselle, cut by numerous small watercourses and dotted with woods, villages and small lakes. The Meuse Heights run north paralleling the wide loops and oxbow lakes of the River Meuse, rumpling into a series of ridges intercut with steep ravines running down to the river that undulate for 40 miles or so before merging into the semi-mountainous Ardennes. The town's name originated with the Celtic tribesmen who occupied the site from 450 BC and dubbed it Virodunum, roughly 'the fortress that controls the river crossing'. In 57 BC the Celts were supplanted by the Romans and by the fourth century AD the strategic military outpost had developed into the prosperous civil settlement of Virodunensium, thanks to its key location on the road linking Reims and Metz. The town was sacked by Attila's Huns in AD 450 and four centuries later gave its name to the 843 Treaty of Verdun that saw the Carolingian Empire divided between Emperor Louis I's three sons after Charles and Louis refused to accept Lothair I as sole successor to the Imperial throne.

The treaty saw Verdun initially assigned to the Central Frankish Realm under Emperor Lothair, but in 923 the city was incorporated into the Germanic Eastern Empire during another bout of border reframing, which saw its name Germanised to Wirten. There it remained for the next six centuries, during which time the construction of the *Cathédrale Notre-Dame de Verdun* began in 990 amid the Roman ruins atop the bluff. In conjunction with the cathedral cities of Metz and Toul, Verdun became part of the Holy Roman province dubbed The Three Bishoprics. Elevated to Free Imperial City status in 1374, Verdun also gained fame for two diverse trading activities in this period. First, it served as a major hub for the Europe-wide trade supplying young boys to Islamic Spain to become enslaved eunuchs. Second, and less controversially, Verdun became a production centre for sugared almonds or *dragées*. Likely building on the Roman practice of eating honey-dipped almonds at festivals, *dragée* production was initially at the behest of the local apothecary's guild who used them to offset the bitter taste of medicinal concoctions. The sugary treats were also distributed at noble christenings and later became a popular wedding staple, representing the bitterness of life and sweetness of love.

Verdun returned to the Gallic fold in the middle of the sixteenth century. In 1551 Henri II of France declared war on Emperor Charles V, sparking the Valois-Habsburg War and his troops annexed Verdun and the remainder of the Three Bishoprics the following year, although the Germanic claim was not abandoned until the 1648 Treaty of Münster formally acknowledged French sovereignty at the end of the Thirty Years War. Verdun's medieval defences were the standard vertical curtain wall interspersed with round towers, the curtain wall running around the *Abbaye de St. Vanne* atop the bluff west of the *Cathédrale Notre-Dame de Verdun* and bounded the old *Haute Ville* to the east up to and along the left bank of the River Meuse; another appendix-shaped circuit of curtain wall projected from the south-east corner of the main defences, backing onto the right bank of the Meuse river and extending south to enclose the Saint Victor Heights to prevent the walls being overlooked from higher ground.

The existing works were strengthened between 1567 and 1591 in expectation of a Germanic riposte, and in 1624 Verdun's new governor, future *Maréchal de France* Louis de Marillac, set in motion a large-scale modernisation and reworking of the city's defences. The western end of the rocky bluff was razed including the *Abbaye de Saint-Vanne* to permit construction of a fortified citadel atop the bluff. Inspired by the work of Jean Errard de Bar-le-Duc, dubbed the father of French fortifications for putting a Gallic slant on the geometric *trace italienne* defence works, the citadel was an irregular pentagon in shape with four integral and two semi-detached bastions. Three of the integral bastions projected beyond the line of the medieval curtain wall, one to the west and two to the north, while the fourth overlooked the cathedral and *Haute Ville* to the east. The citadel was completed in 1636, although it is unclear if this included six triangular outer works called ravelins, which were intended to channel attackers into the fields of fire from the bastions and to protect the sections of curtain wall running between them from interference. Four ravelins fronted the west, north and eastern faces of the citadel, while the remaining two were constructed to protect the northern stretch of the medieval defences, one at the north-east corner overlooking the River Meuse. The east and southern sections of the city's defences appear to have been left as they were, including the appendix enclosing the Saint Victor Heights.[1] For his part, de Marillac was promoted to *Maréchal de France* in 1626 and rose to command the French army in Italy before inadvertently incurring Louis XIII's displeasure. He was executed on 10 May 1632 after a politically manipulated eighteen-month trial which found him guilty of 'embezzling funds when building ... the Citadel of Verdun, and that his subordinates had been guilty of perpetrating various outrages upon the local population'.[2]

De Marillac's work marked the beginning of Verdun's connection with state-of-the-art military defence works and that connection went up several notches in 1664 when the city's defences were inspected by Sebastien Le Prestre, better known as *Maréchal* Vauban, Louis XIV's most eminent military engineer. Born in Burgundy in 1633, Vauban was educated in a Carmelite priory after being orphaned and served briefly in the army of the Prince of Condé during the *Fronde des nobles* civil war before switching allegiance and fighting in the Franco-Spanish War on the Royalist side. After participating in a number of sieges and incurring wounds in the process, Vauban served an apprenticeship under Louis Nicolas de Clerville, one of the leading engineers of the time, and was awarded a commission as *ingénieur du roi* in May 1655. Over the next four years he participated in ten separate sieges, being wounded numerous times in the process, and after hostilities ceased he turned his hand from reducing to creating defence works for Louis XIV, in line with the idea of a *pré carré* (enclosed domain) envisioned by Cardinal Richelieu during the reign of Louis XIII. By 1707 Vauban had overseen the construction of thirty-seven new fortresses and fortified ports across Louis' kingdom, and had overseen the modernisation of 300 towns and cities as far flung as La Rochelle, Saarlouis, Perpignan and Lille. Back at Verdun, over the three decades to 1692 the whole of the city's defensive perimeter was remodelled in Vauban's standard geometric design with the curtain wall being replaced by an enceinte cordon protected by bastions and ravelins, some protected by moats filled by diverting the course of the River Meuse, using specially designed sluice gates to maintain the necessary depth. The new perimeter included the St Victor appendix to the south-east, which received specially designed works to allow all-round defence of the Heights and a gateway accessing the Nancy road. All the outer works were sited to provide mutual support with interlocking fields of fire, and the whole perimeter was girdled by a sloping, grass-covered glacis intended to deflect artillery shot and slow the pace of an attacking troop. The glacis followed the geometric outline of the bastions and ravelins, and concealed a wide moat, some sections of which were filled with water redirected from the River Meuse via a series of specially constructed lock gates. Verdun's transformation into a fully-fledged military garrison town was arguably complete with the construction of a barracks to house a permanent garrison in 1739, thirty-two years after Vauban's death.[3]

However, Vauban's state-of-the-art defences could only be as good as the troops manning them and this proved to be the weak link in their first encounter with a live enemy. The French Revolution of 1789 provoked alarm from the crowned heads of Europe and in July 1792 Emperor Leopold II of Austria and King Frederick Wilhelm II ordered Karl Wilhelm Ferdinand, Duke of Brunswick-Wolfenbüttel, to invade France with a Prussian army augmented with Austrian and Hessian troops and a Royalist French force commanded by the Bourbon Prince de Condé. The French border town of Longwy, 60 miles north-east of Verdun, was swiftly besieged. Longwy capitulated on 23 August and six days later the Duke of Brunswick-Wolfenbüttel arrived at Verdun with a force of around 60,000 men and forty guns. The city's garrison had been commanded since 2 June by Lieutenant-Colonel Nicolas-Joseph Beaurepaire, a fifty-two-year-old former Royalist officer who had come out of retirement to serve the Revolution and was duly elected to command a *bataillon*, the 1st *Régiment de Volontaires de Mayenne-et-Loire*. Beaurepaire had been despatched to Verdun with his unit at the beginning of May 1792, although the move proved to be less than auspicious as around a quarter of his men deserted en route; by the time the siege commenced the garrison could only muster forty-four men to man Verdun's thirty-two artillery pieces.

After a day of bombardment Brunswick offered the city a chance to surrender. Beaurepaire publicly and volubly refused to contemplate surrender but Verdun's citizenry showed rather less revolutionary zeal, not least because no relief could be expected from Paris for at least two days. The city's Council for Defence convened on 2 September and, despite impassioned argument from Beaurepaire, voted to surrender, after which the Town Commandant retired to his quarters. He was subsequently found dead from a gunshot wound with a discharged pistol nearby. The circumstances of the shooting remain unclear but the Revolutionary propaganda machine quickly swung into action. An assembly deputy from Beaurepaire's Loire constituency, named Joseph Delauney, declared the Town Commandant had committed suicide rather than face the ignominy of surrender, although a plan to entomb him in the *Panthéon* in Paris was stymied when Beaurepaire's body went missing as his men were withdrawing 30 miles west to St Menehould. Beaurepaire's alleged sacrifice was nonetheless celebrated in Revolutionary theatre and literature. More permanently his name was added to the *Arc de Triomphe* and a dramatic statue was also erected and remains in place on the *Pont de Verdun* across the River Loire in Angers. The speed and scale of the Revolutionary response, in conjunction with the mysterious disappearance of Beaurepaire's body, raised suspicions that his death was rather less praiseworthy, possibly at the hands of one of Verdun's citizens. Be that as it may, Verdun surrendered to the Duke of Brunswick on 3 September and remained in Prussian hands for just over a month. The Prussian-led invasion force began to withdraw after Brunswick's army was defeated by a French force commanded by *Général* Charles Dumouriez and *Général* François Kellerman at Valmy, 35 miles west of Verdun, on 20 September. Verdun was liberated by a force led by Kellerman in person on 14 October. With that the city seems to have returned to being a backwater, with the citadel being used to house British prisoners of war during the Napoleonic War. The defences also appear to have been allowed to deteriorate over the period. Future Royal Navy Admiral Norwich Duff, who visited Verdun in 1819 in the course of a European tour between appointments, referred to the citadel and outer works being 'a good deal out of repair' and to renovations being underway during his stay.

Verdun's defences do not appear to have been upgraded in the half-century following Duff's visit, presumably because the distance from the border rendered the city a secondary position at best. They nonetheless proved sufficient for Verdun's second encounter with a live Prussian enemy which proved to be a rather more drawn out and honourable affair, albeit with the same ultimate outcome. Following a manufactured diplomatic dispute over succession to the vacant Spanish throne orchestrated by the Prussian Chancellor Otto von Bismarck, Napoleon III's Second Empire allowed itself to be provoked into declaring war on the Prussian-led North German Confederation on 19 July 1870. By the end of the month the French army had gathered a force in excess of 200,000 men, around half its total peacetime strength, on its eastern border and on 28 July Napoleon III moved to Metz to take command of this host, which had been optimistically named the *Armée du Rhin* (Army of the Rhine). The outbreak of war was generally greeted with enthusiasm by civilians and military alike. In Paris,

> something like hysteria reigned; mobs in the street sang the banned Marseillaise and shouted '*Vive le guerre!*' endlessly … Zouaves paraded a parrot that had been taught to screech '*A Berlin!*' [and] *Le Figaro* opened a subscription fund to present every soldier in the Army with a glass of brandy and a cigar.[4]

Lieutenant Léonce Patry and his fellow officers serving with the 6ᵉ *Régiment d'Infanterie* based at Mézières just west of Sedan expressed similar enthusiasm after his garrison

> was brusquely disturbed by the events of early July. Thenceforward our minds turned to war and … we expressed the ardent wishes for affairs to become more embroiled and for a short and brilliant campaign … to put an end to Prussian bluster … I was in a state of the highest enthusiasm, and so were the rest of my young comrades who, having left Saint-Cyr after the Italian War of 1859, had not had the chance of a serious campaign in Europe.[5]

In the event Patry and his comrades were to get their short and serious European campaign, although not quite in the way they had envisaged. The outbreak of war caught the French army in the middle of reforming its conscription system and this was exacerbated by the routine problems attached to mobilising a quarter of a million men along with plain old-fashioned incompetence. For example, according to Patry, the colonel serving as chief of staff of the division to which the 6ᵉ *Régiment d'Infanterie* was assigned had no idea of which regiments his HQ was responsible for.[6]

French strategy was also in a state of flux. The original plan had been to concentrate in the vicinity of Thionville, 50 miles north-east of Verdun, prior to launching an attack toward Trier in the Prussian Rhineland but this scheme was abandoned in favour of a maintaining a defensive posture just inside the French border; the resultant operational hiatus was to be used to persuade Austria and the South German states to join the fray against Prussia but this proved to be wishful thinking. Perhaps more surprisingly, given the rapid and decisive defeats inflicted on Denmark and Austria by the Prussians in 1864 and 1866 respectively, the French not only seriously underestimated the Prussian's operational prowess but also the speed and efficiency of their mobilisation. By the time the fighting began in earnest the Prussians had a force in excess of 400,000 men in the field, compared to a French total of around half that number.[7]

The full extent of French miscalculation rapidly became apparent after the battle was joined. Driven by popular demands for action Napoleon III reversed the stand fast strategy and on 31 July 1870 ordered an advance to seize Saarbrücken (just over the border on the River Saar). The German town was secured on 2 August giving the French their first and arguably only significant victory of the war, but was abandoned two days later after the French were defeated in a day-long battle at Wissembourg, 30 miles to the south-east. The battles at Spicheren and Woerth on 5 and 6 August respectively saw the *Armée du Rhin* split in two. One half, under *Maréchal* Marie Edmé Patrice de MacMahon and accompanied by Napoleon III, withdrew around 200 miles west to the military depot town of Châlons-sur-Marne, where it linked up with a reserve army and became the *Armée du Châlons*.[8] The remainder of the *Armée du Rhin*, over 140,000 strong and commanded by *Maréchal* Achille Bazaine, withdrew south toward the depot city of Metz. Bazaine's force included Lieutenant Patry and the 6e *Régiment d'Infanterie*, which was located near Bouzonville, 25 miles west of Saarbrücken, when a French defeat at Spicheren sparked the general withdrawal; Patry and his *Régiment* then spent a week marching in a 25 mile semicircle before arriving in the vicinity of Metz on 12 August.[9] After four days of rest and reorganisation Bazaine attempted to move west toward Verdun with the intention of linking up with MacMahon at Châlons but was stymied by a Prussian force astride the Metz–Verdun road at Mars-la-Tour, 15 miles west of Metz. A second attempt on 18 August sparked the largest battle of the war at Gravelotte, just 3 miles or so west of Metz, after which Bazaine and his 180,000 men were bottled up in the city; Verdun also came under attack from the Prussian force investing Metz at around the same time.

An attempt to lift the siege by outflanking the Prussians from the north was similarly stymied on 29 August when the *Armée du Châlons* ran into a Prussian blocking force at Beaumont-en-Argonne, provoking a two-day battle that ended with a French withdrawal to the fortress city of Sedan, 15 miles to the north-west. Sedan proved to be a rapidly surrounded trap, as colourfully pointed out at the time by French corps commander *Général* Auguste-Alexandre Ducrot in his oft quoted comment 'Nous sommes dans un pot de chamber et nous y serons emmerdés!'[10] The accuracy of Ducrot's assessment became clear when the Prussians attacked on 1 September, employing 606 artillery pieces that fired 33,134 shells in the course of the battle.[11] Unable to break out of the Prussian trap the *Armée du Châlons* surrendered the following day and a wounded MacMahon, Napoleon III and around 104,000 men passed into captivity. With one French field army destroyed and the other bottled up in Metz the Prussians pushed west to besiege Paris and its newly formed Government of National Defence from 19 September. The fighting continued via the newly-raised *Armée de l'Est, Armée de la Loire, Armée du Nord* and *Armée de la Vosges* until Paris was starved and bombarded into accepting an armistice on 28 January 1871; the field armies followed suit on 5 February. Starvation had also obliged Bazaine to surrender Metz on 27 October 1870 but Verdun, which had also been besieged for fourteen days at that point, continued to hold out until 8 November before accepting a Prussian offer of surrender with full military honours.

The armistice brought hostilities between the French and Prussian militaries to a halt, but the French army was then almost instantly pitched into an internecine conflict with its own citizens. The defence of Paris had been hastily arranged by the Governor of Paris, *Général* Louis Jules Trochu, employing around 60,000 regular troops, approximately 10,000 of which had escaped the Prussians at Sedan or elsewhere, augmented with 13,000 naval personnel equipped for ground operations and around 100,000 members of the *Garde Mobile*, an unpopular territorial force formed in 1868 as a stopgap equivalent to the Prussian *Landwehr* reserve force.[12] However, the bulk of the defensive manpower was provided by the Paris *Garde National*, a bourgeois citizen militia originally raised to safeguard public safety just prior to the 1789 Revolution, raised on a district basis. By 1870 the strength of the Paris *Garde National* stood at just 24,000, largely due to Napoleon III's suspicion of the liberal and republican sympathies within its ranks. This rose to 90,000 at the outbreak of war and again to 350,000 when the newly formed Government of National Defence widened the recruitment criteria and added the inducement of a payment of 1.5 francs per day in order to fully man the 40-mile perimeter of the city; the newly raised units were also permitted to elect their officers.[13]

However, the widening of the recruiting criteria also brought a large number of left-wing radicals and politicised members of the working class into the ranks from districts such as Belleville, Buttes-Chaumont and Montmartre, an act aptly described as sowing dragon's teeth by one source.[14] Politically radical elements of the *Garde National* unsuccessfully attempted to seize power on 31 October 1870 and 22 January 1871 but matters came to a head on 18 March 1871 when Adolphe Thiers, head of the newly elected national government, ordered army units to secure the guns gathered in artillery parks controlled by the *Garde National*. The troops despatched to carry out the mission were subsumed in a widespread popular insurrection, during which the commander of one of the Brigades tasked to secure the guns, *Général* Claude Lecomte and the retired commander of the Paris *Garde National*, *Général* Clément Thomas, were seized and murdered in cold blood. This prompted the national government and army to make a hasty withdrawal to Versailles where Thiers set about gathering army reinforcements to allow him to impose the government's will on the Commune. The radicals meanwhile replaced the tricolour with the Red flag, declared a Commune in imitation of the Commune of Paris that had dominated Revolutionary France in the 1790s and held elections for their new government on 26 March. The newly elected Committee of Public Safety also took time out from running the city and prosecuting the fight against the national government to officially loot Thiers grand house in the Place Saint-Georges before literally razing it to the ground.[15]

In the meantime Thiers had gathered in excess of 100,000 men, many of them drawn from the 400,000 regular army troops recently released from Prussian captivity, who were channelled through special camps in preparation for joining the *Armée du Versailles* commanded by the also newly returned *Maréchal* MacMahon.[16] MacMahon's force entered the city via an unmanned section of the defensive wall at Point-du-Jour at the south-western tip of the city's defences in the early morning of Sunday 21 May 1871 and crushed the insurrection in seven days of intense fighting which became known as *La Semaine Sanglante* or Bloody Week. The army enhanced the bitterness of the conflict from the outset by summarily executing any Communards captured carrying weapons or with gunpowder residue on their hands. The latter's ability to resist was weakened further by the district-specific nature of its *Garde National* units, which precluded effective cooperation while their traditional preference for fighting from barricades was undermined by Haussman's redevelopment of some areas into wide boulevards and open spaces between 1853 and 1870, and the army's tactic of bypassing them by burrowing through adjacent buildings. The Tuileries Palace was burned by its *Garde National* garrison on 23 May, followed by the Hotel de Ville the following day, and the Place de la Bastille was recaptured on 26 May. The *Cimetière Père-Lachaise* in Belleville, one of the last Communard strongholds, was taken on 27 May after a day-long fight among the tombstone. The following day 147 members of the *Garde National* surrendered and were shot against the cemetery wall after the victors discovered the body of the Archbishop of Paris, Georges Darboy, who had been murdered with several priests in retaliation for the army's execution of captured Communards.[17] The final Communard positions were mopped up the following day, Whit Sunday. The campaign cost the *Armée du Versailles* 877 dead and 6,454 wounded. Communard losses are unclear but appear to have been around 10,000 with a further 40,000 arrested; trials of the latter went on until 1875.[18] The *Garde National* was formally disbanded on 14 March 1872.

The wider war against Prussia that had spawned the Commune was formally ended while all this was going on, via the Treaty of Frankfurt signed on 10 May 1871. This obliged the French to surrender the eastern province of Alsace, part of Lorraine, and to pay reparations of five billion francs within three years; the amount appears to have been deliberately tailored to mirror the indemnity demanded by Napoleon Bonaparte after his defeat of Prussia in 1807. The Prussians also continued to occupy a large area of north-eastern France extending west of Paris and almost as far south as Lyon in order to guarantee payment, although the French Government made the final instalment of the indemnity at the beginning of September 1873, two years ahead of schedule. The Prussian occupation army then withdrew from French territory with the last element to retire being the garrison of Verdun, which marched out of the city on 13 September 1873. They left behind a rather different France and a radically different military place for Verdun within it.

2

FORTRESSES AND *PANTALON ROUGE*: VERDUN AND THE FRENCH ARMY, 1873–1914

The final departure of the last Prussian occupation troops from Verdun on 13 September 1873 left France facing very different political and military circumstances than before. Domestically France was again a republic led by the man who had lost Sedan and crushed the Paris Commune, former *Maréchal* Marie Edmé Patrice de MacMahon. He succeeded Adolphe Thiers as president on 24 May 1873. In foreign policy terms France was facing an even more formidable foe on her eastern border than she had faced in 1870. Bismarck had succeeded in bringing together the twenty-five assorted kingdoms, duchies, principalities and free cities that made up the North German Confederation into a politically and administratively unified nation state shortly before the end of the war against France, and on 18 January 1871 Wilhelm I of Prussia was crowned Emperor of Germany in the Hall of Mirrors at the Palace of Versailles. Perhaps most seriously the German acquisition of Alsace and part of Lorraine shifted the French border west from the River Rhine and at a stroke robbed the French army of virtually all the military infrastructure it had employed in 1870, including the depot city of Metz and its four newly completed forts that had permitted *Maréchal* Bazaine's portion of the *Armée du Rhin* to withstand Prussian siege for three months. At the widest point the border moved 80 miles closer to Nancy and to within 10 miles or so of the city, while in the north the border shifted from 60 miles east of Verdun to around 25 miles. The urgent problem facing the French army in 1873 was therefore how to render this new 140-mile long border defensible, and the task was entrusted to an engineer *Général* named Séré de Rivières.[1]

Raymond Adolphe Séré de Rivières was born in Albi in south-west France on 20 May 1815. After graduating in law at the *École Polytechnique* in Paris in 1837 he entered the *École d'Application de Artillerie et du Génie* (School of Applied Artillery and Military Engineering) in Metz and joined the 2ᵉ *Régiment du Génie* at Arras in northern France in 1839. Promoted to *Capitaine* and posted to Toulon in 1843, he worked on a number of defence works before being posted to Perpignan in 1848 and thereafter served in seven separate posts over the following twenty years. This included stints in Carcassonne, Paris, Nice and Metz, during which he developed his own ideas while working on a number of defensive works. These included the *Tête du Chien* and *Drette et de la Revère* works protecting Nice and four of a planned eight new forts protecting the depot city of Metz; the outbreak of war in 1870 brought the programme to turn the city into a modern *camp retranché* (literally entrenched camp) to a halt. Séré de Rivières built upon the theory of distance defence developed by *Général* Casimir-Charles de Poitevin, *Vicomte* de Maureilhan and *Général Vicomte* Joseph Rogniat, which was intended to nullify the effects of enemy artillery by constructing outer works at sufficient distance to keep the defended location beyond the range of enemy artillery. With the outbreak of war in 1870 Séré de Rivières was promoted to the rank of *Général de Brigade* for preparing Lyon for defence and suppressing an insurrection in the city before being promoted to command corps and army-level engineer units with the *Armée de l'Est*. He was then posted to Paris with the *Armée du Versailles* where he supervised the siege and capture of the Commune-held forts d'Issy, de Vanvres and de Montrouges in May 1871.

With the cessation of hostilities Séré de Rivières was tasked to carry out a review of the defences on the Italian border in the latter half of 1871 and the following year prepared a study of the fall of Metz on behalf of *Maréchal* MacMahon, which was published on 6 March 1873. In the meantime *Président* Thiers created a *Comité de Défense* on 28 July 1872, chaired by MacMahon and made up of nine members of the *Minstère de la Guerre* augmented with representatives from the army's artillery and engineering branches. It is unclear if Séré de Rivières was included in the original line up but he was appointed Secretary to the *Comité* in June 1873, possibly as a result of his studies of the Franco-Italian frontier defences and the fall of Metz. Between 1871 and 1877 he produced a number of reports on France's border defences, and two in particular were key in laying out his theories on distance defence: *Considérations sur la reconstitution de la frontière de l'Est* (Considerations on the Reconstitution of the Eastern Frontier) submitted on 21 June 1873, and *Exposé sur la système défensif de la France* (Presentation on the Defensive System for France) submitted on 20 May the following year. The opportunity to translate his ideas into reality came in 1874. In February that year Séré de Rivières was appointed *Directeur du Service du Génie au ministére de la Guerre* (Director of the Military Engineer Service at the Ministry of War), and on 17 July the *Comité de Défense* unanimously approved his scheme for the defence of France's eastern border from the Channel coast to the Mediterranean.[2]

Although it included the whole of the eastern French border from the Channel to the Mediterranean, the primary focus of Séré

27

de Rivières' plan was the new frontier with Germany running for around 190 miles between Longwy on the Belgian border to the Swiss border just south of Belfort. The southern end was anchored in the foothills of the Alps and dropped to a flat area called the *Trouée de Belfort* (Belfort Gap) before rising up and over the western edge of the Vosges Mountains and then descending again across the low-lying Woëvre plain and on into the broken wooded uplands of the Ardennes. The plan envisaged a line of fortifications just inside the border to slow any German invasion and to provide a protective curtain for the French army to mobilise behind. The northern section of the curtain, dubbed the *le Groupe de la Meuse*, ran south-east for 50 miles from Verdun to Toul; both cities were designated *camps retranché*, as were Épinal and Belfort, the northern and southern anchors of the 60-mile-long southern section of the curtain, dubbed *le Groupe Vosges*. The curtain was intended to block the German lines of advance into French territory where the German road and railway network were capable of supporting the transit of hundreds of thousands, if not millions, of men with their guns, ammunition and other equipment. The line also included a 40-mile gap between Épinal and Toul facing the Vosges Mountains, nicknamed the *Trouée de Charmes*, a play on the town of Charmes located in the centre of the gap. Although the latter was later employed as a ruse intended to draw any German advance onto terrain favourable for a French counter-attack, its origins were more prosaic; as communications in the Vosges region were primitive to non-existent Séré de Rivières concluded the Germans would be unable to pass large numbers of troops through the region, and that any that did penetrate could be dealt with by French troops stationed in the area without recourse to sophisticated defence works. The same rationale presumably lay behind the *Trouée de Stenay* spanning the 50 miles of wooded, broken country running north from Verdun to Sedan on the Belgian border.[3]

Work commenced on Séré de Rivières' overall scheme for the eastern border in 1874, although it was not officially accepted and published until 1880 and he was not destined to guide it to completion. Séré de Rivières was ousted from his post as *Directeur du Service du Génie* the same year in a bout of political infighting, sparked in part by the initial construction programme running hugely over budget due to uncosted modifications. The initial 1874 estimate of 88 million francs had ballooned to 400 million francs by 1879 for example, and by the time the programme was completed in 1885 the cost had risen to 564 million francs, with armaments for the new works requiring an additional 229 million. For his part, Séré de Rivières spent fifteen years in quiet retirement in Paris before passing away peacefully on 16 February 1895. He was buried in the *Cimetière Père-Lachaise*, where the *Armée du Versailles* had finally crushed the Paris Commune in May 1871. By that time France's eastern border was protected by 105 forts, 25 smaller fortifications called *ouvrages* and 162 fortified artillery batteries spread along *le Groupe Vosges*, *le Groupe de la Meuse* and *le Groupe Nord*, the latter linking the fortified cities of Dunkerque, Lille, Maubeuge and Reims.[4] Some of these works were integrated into the *camps retranché*, while others were sited in clusters or individually to protect strategic points such as river crossings, terrain features, railway lines and roads. The defensive underpinning of Séré de Rivières' scheme was also retained until *Plan X* of 1889, when it was revised to include a limited offensive toward Metz and Strasbourg given favourable conditions. The offensive element was expanded again in *Plan XIII* of 1896 which envisaged deliberately enticing any German attacks into the *Trouée de Charmes* and/or the *Trouée de Stenay* to be eliminated by pincer attacks from the mobilised French forces concentrated behind the fixed defences; the latter were then to act as launch pads for counter-attacks to liberate Alsace and Lorraine from German occupation. This dual stance remained in place until 1913, when

Plan XVII jettisoned the defensive requirement altogether for *le Groupe Vosges* and *le Groupe de la Meuse.*[5]

All this lay in the future however, and it soon became apparent that the cost of the initial construction programme of 1874–89 was merely the beginning of an ongoing expenditure, as the defence works had to be updated and modified to keep pace with advances in technology, in particular, increases in the range and penetrating power of artillery. Fortuitously a parallel development permitted the French military to hold its own in this arms race in the shape of the *Commission des Cuirassements* (Commission for Armouring) set up by MacMahon's *Comité de Défense* on 9 May 1874. Initially headed by a *Général* Cadart, the *Commission* then came under control of *Capitaine* Henri Mougin, an engineer officer who had served as Séré de Rivières' aide-de-camp. Subsequent promotion to *Commandant* permitted Mougin to explore different methods and materials to protect emplaced guns and their crews, and to this end he oversaw the establishment of the *Polygone d'Essais de Gâvres* (Gâvres Testing Ground) near Lorient on the French Atlantic coast. The *Polygone* subsequently became the home of the *Commission* which then became known as the *Commission de Gâvres,* although it is unclear if this were an official redesignation. A clear example of the incremental development of the French defences was Fort Manonviller, located in the *Trouée de Charmes* overlooking the major road and railway linking Nancy and Strasbourg that ran to the south and north of the fort respectively.

Located 10 miles east of Lunéville and just 6 miles west of the German border, construction of Fort Manonviller commenced on 15 July 1879 and was completed in 1882 at a cost of 3.5 million francs. An irregular polygon girdled by a twelve-metre wide dry moat, the fort boasted a bakery, separate kitchens for the officers and other ranks, an infirmary with ninety beds and stables for fourteen horses, and was garrisoned by twenty-four officers and 892 of other ranks. Primary armament initially consisted of two revolving Mougin turrets mounting twin 155 mm guns weighing 160 tons and costing 205,000 francs apiece. This was augmented with five 84 mm pieces and five multi-barrelled guns mounted in counterscarp casemates built into the outer walls of the moat and linked to the fort proper by tunnels.[6] There then followed a host of upgrades spanning the following three decades. The fort's masonry fabric was hardened with a sheathing of concrete and its armament was modified and improved in the years running up to 1896, with the Mougin turrets being enhanced with two Galopin eclipsing turrets between 1892 and 1894. Each mounting twin 155 mm gun, the Galopin turrets were fully retractable via two 40-ton counterweights, weighed 200 tons in total and cost 850,000 francs apiece. The following year, two slightly smaller Bussière eclipsing turrets mounting 57 mm quick-firing guns were added, followed by a smaller turret mounting a Gatling gun at the south-east corner of the fort. By 1914, all this firepower had been supplemented with seven armoured artillery observation posts, two turret-mounted searchlights capable of illuminating targets out to almost 2 miles, and an electricity generating plant to provide power for lighting and ventilation. [7] Fort Manonviller was thus undergoing a near constant round of upgrades and modifications from the early 1880s to 1914, and the process clearly illustrates the longevity of the defensive arms race in which the French army became enmeshed.

The redrawing of the Franco-German border propelled Verdun from a military backwater into a critical, defensive location. Lying just 25 miles from the new boundary, Verdun not only straddled the shortest and most direct route from German territory to Paris, but more importantly commanded the only easily defensible feature on that route, the River Meuse and the Heights overlooking it. The result was what was to become *Le camp retranché de Verdun*, which began in 1874 with a scheme for five forts supported by an equal number of supplementary redoubts and nine fortified artillery battery positions. The scheme was drawn up by the *Chef du Génie de Verdun* (Chief Engineer of Verdun), a Lieutenant-Colonel Marchand, at a cost of 18 million francs.[8] The plan was modified by increasing the number of forts to six, five located on the east bank of the Meuse east and south-east of Verdun facing the main direction of threat, and one on the west bank to the north-west of the city covering the river valley to the north. Construction of Fort Tavannes, overlooking the Verdun–Metz railway line 4 miles east of Verdun, began in December 1874, along with a supporting programme of road and narrow gauge railway construction initially intended to permit the movement of construction materials, plant and other equipment from the mainline railway and local quarries to the construction sites – in some instances utilising specially-constructed planes linked to steam engines or pulley systems to climb steep slopes.[9] However, work had barely commenced when a dip in Franco-German diplomatic relations threatened the resumption of hostilities and an emergency defensive construction programme was hastily implemented. Six trapezoid artillery *redoutes*, subsequently dubbed the *Forts de la Panique* (panic forts) were constructed on hurriedly surveyed sites between December 1874 and February 1875. Girded with a dry ditch containing two-storey defensive casemates, the gun batteries were emplaced in ramparts atop the *redoutes* while the infantry garrison were provided with a defensive parapet and underground shelters. Three *redoutes* were located on the east bank of the Meuse; one at Belleville; one at Saint-Michel, 2 miles north-east of Verdun; and the last at Belrupt, 3 miles to the south-east. The remaining three were located on the west bank at La Chaume, 2 miles due west of the city, Regret, the same distance to the south-west, and Dugny, 3 miles to the south. Unsurprisingly given the principle of keeping enemy artillery at arm's length, some of these sites had been occupied by Prussian siege guns in 1792 and 1870.[10] All six were subsequently expanded into fully fledged forts.

The original building programme was resumed in 1875 with work on Forts Tavannes and Souville on the east bank of the Meuse and Fort Marre on the west, followed by Fort Haudainville in 1876, Rozelier the following year and Bois-Réunis in 1878. All were completed in two years (apart from Haudainville which took three), and all were complete by 1880. The formation of what was to become the Triple Alliance between Germany and the Austro-Hungarian Empire in 1879 sparked a second wave of construction beginning in 1881 that extended Verdun's defensive perimeter out to around 6 miles. The west bank defences were augmented with an additional six new forts between 1881 and 1883, and work began on a further four, Forts Croix-Brandier, Douaumont, Moulainville and Vaux, on the east bank between 1883 and 1885; all ten were complete by the following year. The new east bank works formed an outer ring in relation to the original scheme forts, while those on the less broken western side were distributed in a more linear manner; Fort Marre was flanked to the east and west by Fort Bell-Épine and Fort Bois-Bourrus respectively, for example. Whatever their precise positioning, the new works were deliberately sited to provide mutual support and were within range of the guns mounted in the original scheme forts. Forts Douaumont and Vaux in the eastern outer ring were around 2 miles apart for example, and both were approximately the same distance from Fort Souville in the inner ring.[11]

In just over a decade Verdun's defences had grown from a Vauban fortress to twenty-two separate defensive works costing 45 million francs and garrisoned by over 6,000 men.[12] At this point, however, two coincidental scientific and technical advances conspired to nullify the French effort and expenditure. The first was the development of steel-rifled barrels for guns from the 1850s by the German company Krupp, based in Essen, which extended the range, accuracy and penetrating power of artillery beyond that of the weapons installed in Verdun's fortifications. The second was the patenting of a picric acid-based explosive by Eugène Turpin in 1885, christened *mélinite* on adoption by the French military two years later, which gave a tremendous increase in destructive power. Modern artillery was thus able to target the new French defensive works from beyond the range of their emplaced guns with streamlined, explosive-filled projectiles capable of penetrating earth overhead cover and inflicting severe damage on the brick and stone masonry beneath. The French defences were thus rendered obsolete at a stroke by what became known as the *Crise de l'Obus-torpille* (Torpedo-shell Crisis).[13]

The French responded by conducting tests to ascertain the resilience of concrete as an alternative to masonry beginning in December 1886. These tests, completed by May 1887, involved firing 155 mm and 220 mm guns at structures cast in various configurations and thicknesses from a variety of aggregate mixes. The most resilient mix, dubbed *bétonné spécial* (special concrete), was then adopted for the construction of new fortifications augmented with steel reinforcement bars from 1898. The latter was used exclusively in new works constructed after that date and for particularly exposed overhead protection and walls in a hardening and modernisation programme carried out on the existing forts, beginning in 1888 with Forts Marre and Souville. The modernisation involved redeploying the rampart gun batteries located atop the forts to other locations, stripping away the earth covering, and either pouring 4 to 6 metres thickness of *bétonné spécial* onto the existing vaulted masonry roof or simply removing the latter and casting a new roof before replacing the earth for camouflage. Both methods included placing a layer of sand up to a metre and a half thick under the concrete carapace to act as a buffer, and the masonry facing the central barrack blocks, external walls, gateways and ditch sides was also sheathed in concrete.[14] The modernisation programme also involved adding flanking works mounting two field guns known as *Casemates de Bourges* to some forts and smaller works, and installing retracting turrets mounting 155 mm or 75 mm artillery pieces or machine guns for close defence in others. The prefabricated sections of retracting turrets, observation cupolas, armour plating and other equipment was hauled from the mainline railway to their destinations by steam traction engines, using the network of *routes militaire* (military roads) constructed to complement the narrow gauge railway linking the forts and other works across the whole of the *camp retranché de Verdun*.[15]

The modernisation programme was paralleled by another round of construction with work commencing on a total of twenty new installations between 1887 and 1889, seven on the west bank of the Meuse and thirteen on the east. All were smaller infantry defence works, some with *Casemate de Bourges* and/or retractable turrets for 75 mm cannon or machine guns. Eleven were begun in 1887, six more the following year and a further three in 1889. Some were intended to be protective outposts for the larger forts. The *Ouvrage* de Bezonvaux for example, located 2 miles north-east of Forts Douaumont and Vaux, consisted of two infantry shelters and an ammunition bunker constructed from *bétonné spécial* inside an earth rampart armed with machine guns, and was intended to break up any infantry assaults on the forts. Others were sited to fill gaps or dead ground between the forts and were both larger and more heavily armed. *Ouvrage* de Thiaumont and *Ouvrage* de Froidterre were located 1 mile and 2 miles respectively south-west of Fort Douaumont in order to fill the gap between the fort and the River Meuse, for example. The former was equipped with a *Casemate de Bourges* and a retracting machine gun turret, while Froidterre had a *Casemate de Bourges* sited to cover the slope down to the river interlocking with the *Ouvrage* de Charny on the west bank and three retracting turrets covering the north and east, one mounting twin 75 mm gun and the others machine guns. The final two works in Verdun's defensive network were the *Ouvrage* de la Falouse, sited 2 miles south of Verdun overlooking the west bank of the Meuse and Fort Vacherauville, 3 miles north-west of the city. Begun in 1906 and 1910 respectively, both were constructed entirely from reinforced concrete. The *ouvrage* was garrisoned by eighty men and armed with a 75 mm retracting turret and two retracting machine gun turrets. Fort Vacherauville was not completed until 1915, had a garrison of 195 men and boasted two single-gun 155 mm Galopin turrets, a twin-gun 75 mm turret and two machine gun turrets.[16]

By the outbreak of war in August 1914 the *camp retranché de Verdun* was thus the most modern and heavily defended military location in France if not the world, albeit one that was not quite complete; Fort Vacherauville was awaiting the installation of a retracting machine gun turret, while Forts Bois-Bourrus and Douaumont were awaiting installation of a twin-75 mm retracting turret apiece. In the event the latter two installations were abandoned, with at least one of the two turrets being employed in the Maginot Line fortifications in the 1930s.[17] At the centre of a perimeter just over 30 miles in circumference the Vauban citadel in the centre of Verdun had been expanded with 4,000 metres of tunnels, two thirds of them over 4 metres wide, carved into the rock 50 feet or more below the surface supporting the cathedral. The tunnel system was equipped with a bakery, kitchens, a telephone exchange, an infirmary, water cisterns and accommodation for 2,000 men; according to one source it was also intended to provide shelter for many thousands more including Verdun's civilian population.[18] The fortified zone stretching up to 6 miles from the city contained nine forts, eight *redoutes*, four *postes* and eleven *ouvrages* manned by 4,865 men, 114 protected artillery battery positions deploying a total of 407 field guns, eight protected ammunition magazines, twenty-five supply depots, an airfield, a *parc à dirigeables* for observation balloons, three protected command posts and numerous protected infantry shelters, all linked with a specially constructed network of roads and *système* Péchot narrow gauge railway lines.[19] The total cost of all this is unclear. According to one source France spent 820 million francs on Verdun's defences between 1874 and 1914, while another more detailed account cites figures that add up to between 60 and 78 million francs.[20]

The showpiece of Verdun's defences was Fort Douaumont. Located atop a 390-metre ridge just over 4 miles north-east of Verdun, Fort Douaumont was the highest work in the *camp retranché de Verdun* and was also the largest at 400 metres wide across the base of its elongated polygon shape and covering an area of 30,000 square metres. Constructed between 1884 and 1886 at an initial cost of just under 1.5 million francs and armed with a total of sixteen 155 mm, 120 mm and 95 mm guns, the *Crise de l'Obus-torpille* rendered the fort's masonry construction obsolete almost the moment it was completed. Douaumont was therefore the first of Verdun's forts to undergo hardening modification, and between 1887 and 1890 a new 12-metre thick concrete roof resting on a metre-thick sand buffering layer was added over the existing structure, using 280,000 cubic metres of *bétonné spécial*. During the same period the ditch and its three protective casemates were reworked in *bétonné spécial*, and the barracks' façade and the fort's main ammunition magazine were also reinforced with the same material.

The 1890s saw Fort Douaumont integrated into the military narrow gauge railway network, followed by two major modification programmes in 1900 and 1908. The first involved the fort being equipped with two retracting machine gun turrets, two *Casemates de Bourges* mounting two 75 mm guns apiece at the south-west and south-east corners, a single-gun 155 mm Galopin turret, the first turret of this type to be installed, and two armoured observation posts for fire control; it also involved lining the edge of the moat with 3-metre-high steel railings, a measure adopted from Russian experience during the Russo-Japanese War. The second programme envisaged adding a second external 155 mm Galopin turret and two twin-gun 75 mm retracting turrets to the fort proper, along with two non-retracting 155 mm turrets in an adjacent subsidiary work. In the event only one 75 mm turret was installed between 1911 and 1913 and the shaft prepared for the second was plugged with concrete and later adapted to house a fixed machine gun post in 1915. Work on the external 155 mm turrets, an additional machine gun turret and plans to provide the fort with electric lighting and ventilation were all abandoned at the outbreak of war. At that point Douaumont was garrisoned by seven officers and 477 of other ranks, reinforced by an additional two officers and 334 men in the event of mobilisation, housed in two-level barracks running east to west through the centre of the fort; the central corridor was decorated with the motto *S'ensevelir sous les ruines du fort plutôt que de le rendre* (rather be buried beneath the ruins of the fort than surrender) to stiffen the resolve of the garrison.[21] Other amenities included kitchens with a separate bakery manned by six bakers, an infirmary with a doctor and two assistants, a telegraph station manned by four signallers, a water reservoir, an armoury and numerous ammunition magazines and storerooms.[22] The total cost of all this was 6.1 million francs, almost 2 million francs more expensive than Fort du Rozellier and over double the cost of the other Verdun forts.[23]

However, while Verdun may have been girdled by an integrated network of state-of-the-art defence works by 1914, the example of 1792 showed that defences were only as good as the troops manning them, and by the outbreak of the First World War the French army's prevailing orthodoxy had moved away from fixed defences. The politicians of the Third Republic quickly identified the root causes of the debacle of 1870–71 which, with the arguable exception of the reference to numbers, tied in with the experience of participants like Lieutenant Patry cited above: 'We were beaten by the absence of preparation, organisation, and direction, and by the small number of our soldiers more than by the arms of our enemies.'[24] Achieving the necessary reforms was less than straightforward however, at least at the top of the army because the creation of a general staff on the German model ran counter to French Republican political establishment's wariness if not outright suspicion of the army's loyalties. The latter was arguably justified given that the army had backed Louis-Napoleon's December 1851 coup that created the Second Empire and the apparent threat of a Royalist coup by *Général* Georges Boulanger's Populist Party in the late 1880s, and tension was maintained thereafter by scandals such as the Dreyfus Affair of 1894 and the 1904 *Affaire des Fiches*. The latter broke when it was discovered that *Premier Ministre* Émile Combles' *Ministre de la Guerre* (Minister of War), *Général* Louis André, was actively blocking the promotion of officers and civil servants identified as Roman Catholics via an extensive secret card index.

The civilian government maintained control of the army via a deliberately cumbersome system that placed a short-appointment *Ministre de la Guerre* with a small dedicated staff in overall charge, but appointed by and answerable to the *Assemblée Nationale* (National Assembly), augmented by a subordinate *Chef d'Etat-Major Général de l'Armee* (Chief of Staff of the Army), a *Conseil Supérieur de la Guerre* (Superior Council of War) whose vice president was to head the army in the event of mobilisation and, from 1906, a *Conseil Supérieur de la Défense Nationale* (Superior Council for National Defence).[25] It was not until 1911 that an organisation akin to the German general staff was created, and then only as a wartime equivalent to the *Conseil Supérieur de la Guerre*. Dubbed the *Grand Quartier Général*, the new organisation was maintained by a skeleton staff during peacetime and had four separate sections. The *Première Bureau* was responsible for organisation, personnel and equipment, the *Deuxième Bureau* was tasked with intelligence and political affairs, the *Troisième Bureau* dealt with planning and operations, and the *Quatrième Bureau* was responsible for communications, transport and supply. The *Grand Quartier Général* was to be activated and fully manned on mobilisation, headed by the *Chef d'Etat-Major Général de l'Armee* who then became *Commandant en Chef des Armées* (Commander-in-Chief of the Armies) with wide-ranging powers within a specified zone of operations. The location and extent of this zone was the sole responsibility of the *Assemblée Nationale* however, along with the power to activate the *Grand Quartier Général*, and control of the army outside the operational zone also remained firmly in the hands of the *Ministre de la Guerre*.

Matters lower down the chain of command ran rather more smoothly. With regard to manpower, the Second Empire had relied on a long-service volunteer force reinforced with limited conscription by lot, from which the monied classes were able to purchase exemptions. The Third Republic dispensed with this in favour of conscription by ballot for three years under the Law of 24 July 1873 which divided France into eighteen geographical regions, each of which was to provide lot-selected manpower for an associated army corps. The intention was to provide a unifying 'school of the nation', but this was undermined by the lot system, the modified service terms and other exemptions provided for some groups. This ceased with the Two Year Law of 1905 which tightened the regulations to remove all exemptions except on medical grounds, including convicted felons, who were despatched to the colonies to serve in penal units called *Bataillons d'Infanterie Légère d'Afrique* (African Light Infantry Battalions). The term of conscription was put back up to three years in 1913 for men over the age of twenty, with conscripts being called up in October, and was extended to the Moslem inhabitants of France's colony in Algeria, where recruiting had been voluntary hitherto. The change was in response to a German military law ratified on 30 June

1913 which increased the German peacetime standing army from 628,000 men to 760,000, with a further rise to 820,000 planned for October the following year. This was possible for the Germans because, at 60 million, the German population was one-third larger than the French, and thus provided a larger recruiting pool. The French Three Year Law of July 1913 was intended as a short-term remedy to counter this imbalance. The average French conscription intake between 1906 and 1913 was approximately 223,000 and the Three Year Law expanded this fourfold to over 800,000 by extending the intakes of 1911 and 1912 service by an additional year, and calling up the October 1913 intake and the following year's in November 1913.[26]

Equipping the field army involved the same harnessing of new technology as the construction of the fixed defence works guarding France's borders; as future *Général* and *Président* Charles de Gaulle put it, 'There was not a tool, a wagon or a boat, for which new models were not adopted between 1897 and 1900.'[27] The invention of *Poudre B* smokeless propellant by Paul Vieille in 1884 sparked a small-arms revolution and the adoption of the 8 mm Lebel cartridge two years later allowed the French to develop a range of small arms comparable to those of the other Great Powers. The *St. Étienne Modèle 1907* machine gun, although more complicated, was twenty-pounds lighter and thus easier to handle than its Maxim-based German equivalent for example, while the Mauser *Gewehr 71* rifle was outclassed by the nine-shot *Fusil Modèle 1886* weapon developed by a commission headed by *Colonel* Nicolas Lebel. Reworked in 1893 and mated with a pointed boat-tail projectile dubbed the *Balle D* in 1898, the Lebel rifle had an effective range to 457 yards and a maximum range of approximately ten times that and remained a viable weapon in comparison with its contemporaries.

The *Canon de 75 Modèle 1897* field gun was similarly groundbreaking. Nicknamed the *Soixante-Quinze* (seventy-five), the gun was the first in the world to employ a hydro-pneumatic recoil system which kept the gun stationary when fired and thus dispensed with the need for re-laying after every shot, while its Nordenfeldt rotating screw-breech permitted a sustained rate of fire of fifteen rounds per minute or a shot every four seconds; a well-drilled crew could almost double that for short periods. Perhaps unsurprisingly given the prominence of French aviation pioneers such as Louis Blériot and Henri Farman, the French military were also swift to appreciate the potential of aviation for military reconnaissance. The army began sending officers and NCOs for flying training at civilian establishments at locations including Reims, Bron and Pau from December 1909 and aircraft participated in French annual manoeuvres the same year. An experimental *Établissement Militaire d'Aviation* (Establishment for Military Aviation) was set up on 10 March 1910 and on 2 October 1910 a semi-official *Aéronautique Militaire* (Military Aviation) branch was set up under the army's engineering branch commanded by *Général* Pierre Roques. The latter was appointed *Inspecteur Permanent de l'Aéronautique Militaire* (Permanent Inspector of Military Aeronautics) the same year, although the *Aéronautique Militaire* was not officially incorporated into the army until 29 March 1912 and did not come under the auspices of the *Ministére de la Guerre* until 21 February 1914. France is nonetheless routinely credited with creating the world's first true air force rather than an aviation unit under Roques guidance and by the outbreak of war in 1914 had twenty-one *Escadrilles* (squadrons) fielding over 130 aircraft.[28]

The French army may have been swift to adopt cutting edge technology but this was not totally at the expense of tradition. Harking back to the military glories of the First Empire helped to restore the army's self-confidence which had been badly dented in the war with Prussia, along with its standing in wider society, and did the same for France as a whole. Even the political left viewed the army as an honourable bulwark and conduit for *revanche* (revenge) against the German foe. Much of the revanchist Boulangist Party's support was drawn from the Parisian working classes despite the fact that *Général* Boulanger had been involved in the ruthless suppression of the Paris Commune in 1871, and the modifications to the conscription system in 1873, 1905 and 1913 were widely viewed as an adjunct to national honour and a move back toward the Revolutionary *levée en masse* that had safeguarded the 1792 Revolution. The acceptance of modernity over tradition had its limits however, as illustrated by the saga over the adoption of a less visible uniform for the French army in the run up to 1914. The Boer and Russo-Japanese wars clearly showed that concealment was necessary to offset the increasing lethality of the modern battlefield wrought by advances in the range and accuracy of small arms and artillery fire. The British Army, which had utilised a pale khaki uniform for overseas troops from the mid-nineteenth century, adopted a Service Dress uniform for issue to home-based troops in a darker brown shade of khaki from 1902 for example, while the German *Heer* (army) adopted a universal drab *feldgrau* (field grey) uniform to replace the wide variety of pre-unification uniforms in 1910.

The French army followed this trend in part on the recommendation of officers who had served in France's African territories, with blue-grey and beige-grey uniforms being trialled in 1902 and 1903, and another in a grey-green shade in 1911; the first two were rejected as being too similar to contemporary German uniform, while the latter was deemed too similar to contemporary Italian outfits. These rejections were politically motivated rather than based on practical or tactical considerations however, and were part of an ongoing French debate on the shape, nature and role of the army that went back to the Revolution of 1789. With the French political left in the ascendant following the Dreyfus and *Affaire des Fiches* scandals, the political right interpreted any attempt to interfere with the army as a ploy to replace it with a citizen's militia. The *pantalon rouge* (red trousers) of the existing uniform became a particular bone of contention, with the right viewing them as a vital element in the promotion and maintenance of national and military *élan vital* (roughly translating as energetic momentum), although this view was not universal. In 1911 *Ministre de la Guerre* Adolphe Messimy, a former infantry officer, presciently pointed out that such 'blind stupid attachment to the most visible of colours will have cruel consequences'. Such practicality had no place in the argument however. The *Echo de Paris* newspaper denounced drab camouflage uniforms as a Masonic plot and in 1913 *Ministre de la Guerre* Eugène Etienne opined 'Abolish red trousers? Never! Red trousers are France!' The fact that the garment had only been adopted in 1829 to support the French madder dye industry was conveniently overlooked amid the rhetoric. In the event further tests were conducted and a drab pale blue-grey uniform popularly known as *bleu horizon* (horizon blue) was adopted before the outbreak of hostilities, although it did not go into production until August 1914 and was not on general issue until the middle of the following year.[29] As a result the French army went to war in 1914 wearing the same uniform of dark blue greatcoat and red trousers the *Armée du Rhin* had worn forty-four years earlier.

The harking back to the glories of the First Empire had an even more deleterious impact on the army's doctrine. A key factor in the French defeat at Prussian hands in 1870 was a lack of drive by senior commanders like Bazaine and MacMahon, but by the early 1900s a school of thought had emerged in the French officer corps that extrapolated this failure to apply to the entire army, building upon the offensively focussed 1904 *Règlement Tactique* (tactical regulations). This school of thought saw the cure for this perceived failure to be offensive action as the solution to every eventuality at the tactical, operational and strategic levels by imbuing all ranks with boldness and impetuosity, fuelled by a semi-mystical reliance on *élan vital*. The inventor and primary exponent of this philosophy, which was dubbed *attaque* or *offensive à outrance* (attack to excess), was the officer heading the *Grand Quartier Général's Troisième Bureau, Colonel* Loyzeau de Grandmaison. While acknowledging the likely futility of launching attacks over open ground, de Grandmaison propagated his theories in a manner that suggested the opposite and insisted that the key to battlefield success lay in establishing moral and fire superiority over the enemy: 'The experience of every age shows that in the offensive, safety is gained first by creating this depression in the enemy that renders him incapable of action. There exists no other means but attack, immediate and total ... we must prepare ourselves and others by encouraging with enthusiasm, with exaggeration and in all the infinite details of training everything that bears ... the mark of the offensive spirit. Let us go as far as excess and this will perhaps not be far enough.'[30] In short, it was the duty of commanders at every level to attack the enemy wherever and whenever the opportunity presented itself. Perhaps significantly de Grandmaison had no experience of that which he theorised, being only nine years of age in 1870, but based his thinking on the writings of Napoleonic *Général* Antoine-Henri Jomini and more recently *Colonel* Ardant du Picq. The latter served in the Crimea, Syria and Algeria before being promoted to command the 10ᵉ *Régiment d'Infanterie* and died on 18 August 1870 of wounds sustained two days previously while leading his unit at Mars-la-Tour. His various writings were gathered posthumously into a single volume entitled *Etudes sur les Combat: Combat Antique et Moderne* (Studies in Combat: Combat Ancient & Modern) which was part published in 1880 and in its entirety in 1902; de Grandmaison's theorising, which was first published four years later, drew selectively upon du Picq's work.

Be that as it may, *attaque à outrance* was received enthusiastically by a large segment of the French officer corps including a number who would figure prominently in the First World War, such as Joseph-Simon Gallieni, Nöel Éduard de Castelnau and future *Maréchal* Ferdinand Foch; the latter enthusiastically, if somewhat optimistically, opined that 'a battle won is a battle in which one will not confess oneself beaten' in a lecture delivered while heading the *École Supérieure de Guerre* at Saint-Cyr.[31] The philosophy appears to have been popular among those with colonial service, presumably because it fitted well with the austere warrior creed necessary for soldiering in the depths of the North African desert or Indo-Chinese jungle. The adherents of *attaque à outrance* did not have things all their own way however, as some had drawn less flamboyant and more rationally grounded conclusions on how to carry out offensive action from the events of 1870. During his tenure as head of Saint-Cyr between 1892 and 1896 *Colonel* Henri Bonnal developed a less impetuous scaled up Napoleonic approach to offensive action, for example. Sometimes referred to as vanguard doctrine, this advocated guaranteeing flank security with detachments up to *bataillon* size while pushing corps-sized advance guards a day's march ahead of the main body. The advance guards were to engage and pin the enemy, allowing the following main body to deploy without interference to overwhelm and destroy the preoccupied enemy using the aggressive tactics laid out in the French *Règlement sur le Service des Armées en Campagne* (Army Field Service Regulations) published in 1904.[32]

The philosophy of *attaque à outrance* also came in for criticism from a number of other quarters. *Général* Charles Lanrezac, a committed exponent of vanguard doctrine, lectured trenchantly against Foch's perspective while serving on the staff at Saint-Cyr from 1905, not least by presciently pointing out the potential problem *attaque à outrance* created for command and control, 'If every subordinate corps commander has the right to ram home an attack on the first opponent he sees, the commander in chief is incapable of exercising any form of direction.'[33] *Lieutenant-Colonel* Pierre Ruffey, who served as assistant professor of artillery tactics at Saint-Cyr from 1887 to 1893 and then headed the course from 1897 to 1901, complained about his arm's lack of modern heavy guns, an omission rooted in the fact that close-range support for attacking units was the only task artillery that was required to perform within the *attaque à outrance* philosophy, and the *Soixante-Quinze* was perfectly configured for that task. Interestingly, then chief of staff *Général* Auguste Dubail was to object to *Général* Victor Constant Michel's 1911 scheme for reconfiguring the army on the grounds that the proposed increase in infantry was not matched by a parallel expansion of supporting artillery and called for provision of an additional 216 assorted artillery pieces, including heavy guns.[34] Conversely, advocates of *attaque à outrance* reportedly considered the 75 mm gun to be 'God the Father, God the Son, and God the Holy Ghost', drawing the comment from future *Général* Maxim Weygand that 'one would have liked to have seen it surrounded by a few saints'.[35] *Colonel* Philippe Pétain, then commanding the 33ᵉ *Régiment d'Infanterie* based at Arras, was both scathing and succinct in his response to the semi-mystical outpourings of de Grandmaison and his acolytes: '*le feu tue*' (firepower kills).

The struggle for the French army's institutional soul between the proponents of *attaque à outrance* and vanguard doctrine came to a head just three years before the outbreak of the Great War. On 10 January 1911 *Général* Michel, a member of the vanguard group, was appointed vice president of the *Conseil Supérieur de la Guerre* and thus in line to head the army in the event of war. Michel was convinced that the Germans would commence hostilities with their reserves fully integrated into their field army from the outset and he was also convinced that any German attack would come through Belgium rather than through the Ardennes or against Lorraine. The former would place the French at a serious numerical disadvantage given that French war planning was predicated on the standing army bearing the operational brunt while the reserves mobilised, and the latter would nullify the huge expenditure incurred in fortifying France's eastern frontier. The then-current French mobilisation scheme was *Plan XVI* of March 1909, which followed the offensive/defensive combination first included in *Plan X* of 1889 and paid some heed to the possibility of a German attack through Belgium by deploying reserve troops to cover the Belgian frontier.[36] However, this was insufficient in Michel's view, and he set about reorganising the French reserves for use from the outset of any future hostilities. However, this task was complicated by the Two Year Law of 1905 which had expanded the pool of reservists without a concomitant expansion in funding to maintain fitness and continuation training, and restored French mobilisation planning to a wholly defensive posture. This did not go down well. De Grandmaison's *Troisième Bureau* vehemently but mistakenly insisted that the Germans would not deploy their reserves from the outset of hostilities, in part due to assuming the poor state of their own reservists was universal. Michel also attracted a good deal of personal antagonism from many of his fellow officers for being a republican, a political rather than an army appointee and thus allegedly being easily manipulated by politicians, and also for being pro or anti-Dreyfus or a Boulangist, depending on the critic.[37]

Michel nonetheless spent seven months preparing the ground for his ideas while serving as vice president of the *Conseil Supérieur de la Guerre*, possibly assisted by the fact that there were four separate *Ministres de la Guerre* over that period. This ceased on 27 June 1911 with the appointment of the fifth, former infantry officer and Saint-Cyr graduate Adolphe Messimy. Michel presented his scheme for a major reorganisation of the army's structure and staff leadership intended to increase immediately available trained manpower to 1.3 million men to Messimy and the *Conseil Supérieur de la Guerre* on 19 July 1911 along with *Plan XVI Variant Nr.1*. This argued for a total reversal of previous strategy by standing *le Groupe de la Meuse* and *le Groupe Vosges* on the defensive, while concentrating half a million men around Lille in *le Groupe Nord* in readiness for an immediate counter-attack into Belgium, oriented on Antwerp, Brussels and Namur. However, Messimy was of a conservative bent himself and was more concerned with immediate combat readiness in the midst of the Second Moroccan Crisis, and consequently inclined to heed operational advice from the *Troisième Bureau*. Perhaps more importantly, Messimy had been persuaded by a number of senior officers and members of the *Conseil Supérieur de la Guerre,* including Dubail and Joseph Gallieni, that Michel was incompetent and a 'national danger'.[38]

The *Ministre* and *Conseil* therefore rejected the scheme; Michel resigned on 21 July 1911 and was subsequently appointed Military Governor of Paris. Messimy then took the opportunity to engage in some reorganising of his own by amalgamating the *Grand Quartier Général* and *Conseil Supérieur de la Guerre*, abolishing the post of vice president to the latter and making the *Grand Quartier Général* chief of staff the head of the army in peace time and commander-in-chief in times of war; this had the presumably not unintended consequence of reinforcing the authority of the *Troisième Bureau* and by extension the influence of de Grandmaison.[39] The new appointment was offered to *Général* Gallieni, who ruled himself out because he thought selecting a Colonial officer might not sit well with the metropolitan army, because of his fragile health and because at age sixty-four he was only two years or so from retirement. Messimy's second choice, sixty-three year old *Général* Paul-Marie Pau, also declined the post on the grounds of age and because he disagreed with civilian politicians being involved in the appointment of senior officers; he was also compromised by his devout Catholicism and involvement in the *affaire des fiches*. The appointment thus went to Messimy's third choice, *Général de Division* Joseph Jacques Cesaire Joffre, a fifty-nine year old Colonial engineer with extensive and varied experience gained in Formosa, Indochina, Sudan and Madagascar.[40]

Joffre's appointment on 28 July 1911 marked the triumph of the proponents of *attaque à outrance* and the new *Grand Quartier Général* chief of staff immediately set about weaving that philosophy into every aspect of the French army. The *Règlement sur le Service des Armées en Campagne* (Service Regulations for the Army on Campaign) were rewritten and expanded into two documents in 1913. The volume dealing with operational formations at army group, army and corps level appeared in October prefaced with the blunt statement that 'The French army, returning to its traditions, accepts no law in the conduct of operations other than the offensive'. It was followed in December by the tactical level volume for division, brigade and regiment-sized units which also circumscribed the focus and amount of support the artillery was tasked to provide for the infantry in a similarly blunt and rigid vein: 'The artillery does not prepare attacks; it supports them.'[41] At the top of the army officers deemed lacking in *élan vital* and/ or insufficiently committed to the philosophy were purged. For example, Michel was removed from his post as Military Governor of Paris on Messimy's order when France mobilised on 28 August 1914 and never held another military command, and Joffre continued the practise ruthlessly after the outbreak of war in 1914 to the extent it gained its own verb, to *limogé*, due to his penchant for despatching the purged to a backwater HQ at Limoges in south-west France.[42]

Joffre also swiftly turned his attention to Michel's *Plan XVI Variant Nr.1*. A modified *Variant Nr 2* appeared on 6 September 1911, followed by the presentation of a new proposal to the *Conseil Supérieur de la Guerre* on 18 April 1913 and finally a full-blown *Plan XVII* published on 7 February 1914, although all the connected documentation was not complete until 1 May that year. The former involved rejigging deployment plans to cover more of (but not the entire) length of the Belgian border, in part by redeploying units from the Italian frontier and from the second line and reserve, as well as altering the deployment frontage of the 5ᵉ and 6ᵉ *Armées* to cover the border with Luxembourg and the Belgian Ardennes between Mézières and Verdun. The subsequent *Plan XVII* reversed Michel's plan and indeed past precedent by dispensing with the defensive aspect; as the preamble put it, 'The intention of the commander-in-chief is to deliver, with all forces assembled, an attack against the German armies.' Despite this unambiguous statement of intent, *Plan XVII* was not actually a detailed blueprint for offensive action but a deployment scheme intended to permit attacks into Alsace-Lorraine and/or the Belgian Ardennes as the situation required.[43] The latter was included as Joffre shared Michel's conviction that any future German attack was likely to come through neutral Belgian territory, to the extent he tried to obtain permission for a pre-emptive attack into Belgium from *Premier Ministre* Joseph Caillaux on 9 January 1912 and again from his successor *Premier Ministre* Raymond Poincaré on 21 February 1912. The attempt was unsuccessful because neither politician, nor the bulk of the *Conseil Supérieur de la Défense Nationale*, was willing to countenance violating Belgian neutrality as such a move would alienate British support for France and possibly push the Belgians to side with the Germans.[44]

At the bottom of the army, newly conscripted recruits were indoctrinated with the philosophy of *attaque à outrance* from the moment they reported for service. Tactical training focussed upon advancing on divisional frontages of between 1,500 and 2,500 metres to within striking distance of the enemy, who would then be suppressed by small-arms fire and possibly a short but intensive bombardment from supporting *Soixante-Quinze* field guns. The infantry would then close to within 50 metres of the enemy before performing a bayonet charge to overwhelm or rout them, led by regimental officers and accompanied by bugles and drums.[45] By 1913 any coyness regarding the focus of *attaque à outrance* had also evaporated as illustrated by a greeting address for new recruits to the 33ᵉ *Régiment d'Infanterie* by then *Lieutenant* Charles de Gaulle:

> Everywhere, always, one should have a single idea: to advance. As soon as the fighting begins everybody in the French Army, the general in command, the officers and the troops have only one thing in their heads – advancing, advancing to the attack, reaching the Germans, and running them through or making them run away.[46]

Closing with *la Rosalie*, as the issue bayonet was nicknamed, was considered the ultimate military virtue and recruits were obliged to memorise a catechism extolling that virtue: 'From the moment of action every soldier must ardently desire the assault by bayonet as the supreme means of imposing his will upon the enemy and gaining victory.'[47] The training of junior officers and NCOs was restricted to preparing for and carrying out the bayonet charge, with the latter being authorised to use physical force on any of their soldiers demonstrating a lack of enthusiasm. As far as the French army was concerned the key to triumph was therefore simply a matter of *élan* and *cran* (guts), predicated on unquestioning obedience to orders, a principle that was not restricted to launching attacks immediately when an enemy force was located. Every inch of French territory was to be 'defended to the death, and, if lost, regained by an immediate counter-attack, however inopportune'.[48] The counter-attacks were to continue until the territory was retaken or there was no one left to continue and this philosophy of *attaque à outrance* and immediate counter-attack in place of a more flexible and measured approach was to cost the French army dearly from August 1914.

The pendulum of prevailing orthodoxy that had swung to the

defensive end of the curve in the years immediately following the Franco-Prussian War thus slowly swung back in favour of the offensive in the forty years between the framing and implementation of Séré de Rivières' defensive scheme and the outbreak of the First World War. By 1914 there was no place in French military thinking for the likes of the *camp retranché de Verdun* created at such huge expense. Their only purpose was to provide shelter for manoeuvre units to regroup and reorganise behind before returning to the attack; the forts themselves were to be denuded of their garrisons and any guns that could be removed without major deconstruction. In a textbook case of fighting the next war with methods designed to win the last, the French army went to war in 1914 with an operational philosophy tailored to solve the problems of 1870. The casualty toll upon both sides at Mars-la-Tour, Gravelotte and the other major engagements of 1870 showed that raw courage had its limits in the face of firepower. By 1914 the advent of bolt-action magazine rifles, machine guns and quick-firing artillery had increased the lethality of the battlefield manifold and *attaque à outrance* and *Plan XVII* were set to provide an equally updated method of feeding manpower into the maw.

3

THE BELFORT GAP AND *PLAN XVII*: SETTING THE SCENE, AUGUST 1914 – FEBRUARY 1915

The French army did not have to wait long for the opportunity to test the efficacy of its military doctrine and fixed fortifications. The catalyst for the test was the assassination of the heir to the Austro-Hungarian throne, Archduke Franz Ferdinand and his wife Duchess Sophie, in Sarajevo on 28 June 1914 at the hands of Slav separatists backed unofficially by elements of the Serbian military. Eager to force a reckoning with its troublesome neighbour, and having sought and received assurances of German support on 5 July, the Austro-Hungarians issued a forty-eight hour ultimatum to the Serbs on 23 July deliberately framed to be unacceptable. Thereafter the alliance system that had divided Europe between the Triple Alliance and the Triple Entente came into play and drew in the other European powers in what has been likened to a group of roped-together mountaineers being pulled from a cliff face one by one after losing their grip. On 25 July Austria-Hungary mobilised its forces facing Serbia and declared war three days later. Russia, taking up the cudgels in defence of their fellow Slavs, responded by ordering partial mobilisation on 29 July, which was expanded to full mobilisation the following day. This in turn prompted full Austro-Hungarian mobilisation on 31 July 1914 followed the next day by the French, who were bound by alliance from the early 1890s to support Russia in the event of a conflict with Germany. The key player in all this was Germany, for while the other powers could pause after mobilisation for diplomacy to do its work, Germany was tied into a scheme to offset her geographic vulnerability that involved fighting a delaying action against Russia, while seeking a swift decision in the mould of 1870 against France. Therefore for Germany, mobilisation equalled war and, guided by a system that placed military expediency above diplomacy or international law, Germany mobilised and declared war on Russia on 1 August, invaded Luxembourg and demanded that the Belgian government permit German troops free passage through Belgian territory the following day, before declaring war on France and invading Belgium on 3 August. This action promptly appealed to Britain to guarantee her neutrality according to a treaty dating back to 1839, and Britain duly declared war on Germany on 4 August. Almost the whole of Europe was thus at war just thirty-five days after the assassination in Sarajevo.

The French response to the incident was two-pronged, consisting of urging the Austro-Hungarians to show restraint while ensuring French forces would be ready to launch operations simultaneously with their Russian ally. To that end, *Président* Raymond Poincaré and *Premier Ministre* René Viviani visited St Petersburg for week-long talks with Tsar Nicholas II and his government and military commencing on 16 July; a subsequent visit to Stockholm was terminated after four days on 27 July following news that Austria-Hungary had begun mobilisation. Back in Paris preparations for war were firmly in the hands of *attaque à outrance* advocate and former infantry officer Adolphe Messimy, who had been reappointed to the post of *Ministre de la Guerre* by Viviani on 13 June 1914. Attendees at a high-ranking meeting to discuss the Austro-Hungarian ultimatum to Serbia in the evening of 24 July noted Messimy's eagerness at the prospect of hostilities, which was also transmitted to *Général* Joffre at a meeting later the same evening. On being informed that the French army would be ready to fight if necessary, Messimy exclaimed 'Bravo!' while enthusiastically pumping Joffre's hand.

Despite his eagerness Messimy initially restricted himself to enacting a series of precautionary measures with the approval of the *Conseil des Ministres*. On 25 July Messimy recalled all serving general officers to their posts and requested a report on the combat readiness of units stationed in Africa from *Grand Quartier Général* (GQG). The following day he recalled all officers from leave, cancelled all scheduled troop movements and initiated preparations for rapid mobilisation on the basis of reports of German military activity from French agents in Alsace and Lorraine. Thereafter, however, Messimy's activities became more proactive. On 27 July the French commander in North Africa was warned to prepare for the despatch of the bulk of his force for service in metropolitan France and, following badgering from Joffre, the Russians were pressed to abide by a prior agreement to attack into East Prussia in the event of hostilities, while the Austro-Hungarian declaration of war on Serbia on 28 July saw all French military personnel on pass or leave recalled to their units immediately. Messimy's eagerness for war had its limits however, as Joffre discovered when he requested permission to deploy covering forces on the German border; the request was denied and the decision was passed on to Poincaré and Viviani on their return from Sweden, who confirmed the refusal. The overt reason for keeping French troops a minimum of 10 kilometres back from the border was to avoid compromising the ongoing diplomatic effort, but the underlying rationale was intended to avoid providing the

Germans with an excuse for offensive action and to maintain the impression that France had done everything possible to avert war, in order to retain the support of the international community and French public opinion; as Poincare put it to Viviani in a meeting that day, 'It is better to have war declared on us.' In the event this was overtaken by the German declaration of war on Russia on 1 August and Joffre's resultant urging for immediate mobilisation in order to avoid gifting the Germans an advantage. A hastily convened meeting of the *Conseil des Ministres* gave Messimy permission to sign an order at 15:30 authorising general mobilisation to commence the following day, Sunday 2 August 1914.[1]

Messimy's mobilisation order was to expand the strength of the French metropolitan army from 884,000 men to between 2.2 and 2.6 million men, with a further 408,000 men being called up to serve in administrative and public service capacities.[2] These numbers were realised by recalling twenty-seven separate year classes in three increments over a fourteen-day period. A total of 621,000 reservists were to be absorbed by the forty-five divisions assigned to the five field armies spaced along France's eastern border by 10 August. The 1er *Armée*, commanded by *Général* Auguste Dubail, was deployed east of Epinal forward of the *Trouée de Charmes*, with *Général* Édouard de Castelnau's 2e *Armée* just to the north-west in the area of Nancy. *Général* Pierre Ruffey's 3e *Armée* was concentrated north of Verdun near Longwy on the Luxembourg border, backed by *Général* Fernand de Langle de Cary's 4e *Armée* in the area of Sedan, with *Général* Charles Lanrezac's 5e *Armée* covering the Belgian border near Mézières; an independent *Armée d'Alsace* (Army of Alsace) commanded by *Général* Paul Pau was formed later and was located at the southern extremity of the French line near Belfort. Another 655,000 men were to fill out twenty-five reserve divisions by 13 August while a further 184,000 were to form twelve territorial divisions, and

units earmarked for the defence of Paris were to be called up by
15 August; a further million men were retained at their regimental
depots. In contrast to the confusion and incompetence of 1870 and
in a shining testament to Joffre's planning, the 1914 mobilisation
process ran like clockwork. French planners had expected a 13 per
cent mobilisation shortfall but only 1.5 per cent failed to report,
equivalent to approximately 1,600 men. Of these, many were
Bretons who did not speak French and were thus unable to read
their mobilisation papers, some were mentally unfit for service
and some were vagrants.[3] The mobilised men were transported to
railheads in 4,278 trains moving along fourteen separate railway
lines, each carrying around fifty-six separate trains per day, of
which only a score were late. From the railheads the men moved to
their units or concentration areas on foot, marching 16 to 20 miles
a day and spending their nights bivouacked by the road.[4]

As we have seen, *Plan XVII* was not a detailed plan of attack
but a deployment scheme intended to permit attacks into Alsace-
Lorraine and/or the Belgian Ardennes as the situation required.[5]
Moreover, it was dependent on French mobilisation being
completed without interference. To that end Joffre, who had set
up his *Grand Quartier Général* at Vitry-le-François on the River
Marne 50 miles south-west of Verdun, ordered Dubail's 1er *Armée*
to launch a spoiling attack into southern Alsace with the intent of
unbalancing German mobilisation and channelling any German
riposte into the *Trouée de Belfort* (Belfort Gap). Responsibility for
this was devolved to *Général* Louis Bonneau's 7e *Corps*, reinforced
with *Général* Louis Aubier's 8e *Division de Cavalerie*, and was
intended to advance on Mulhouse, 16 miles east of the border,
from the north and south-west in order to secure a foothold on
the west bank of the River Rhine. The advance into southern
Alsace began on 7 August, just five days after mobilisation, and
the first troops across the frontier enthusiastically tore up the
German marker posts and sent them to be laid on the Paris grave

of Paul Déroulêde, an extreme French nationalist and founder of the *Ligue des Patriotes*. The southern column then went on to fight a six-hour battle for Altkirch on the Rhine, 10 miles south of Mulhouse, which was secured after the regulation bayonet charge at a cost of a hundred casualties; the second column, advancing on Mulhouse from the north-west, secured the town of Thann after quelling minor resistance. Even though he had yet to secure his primary objective, Bonneau promptly despatched a telegram to Messimy in Paris proclaiming his victory in glowing terms, to Joffre's irritation.[6]

In the event the spoiling attack secured Mulhouse the following day without a fight but things then began to go awry. Although Joffre had insisted that the area was undefended, elements of *Generaloberst* Josias von Heeringen's 7. *Armee* were stationed in the thick woods nearby and the French were driven out of the city by a German counter-attack on 9 August. Bonneau, worried by a lack of reinforcements and reports of large German forces moving to cut him off, retired to the safety of Belfort after a stiff fight with German troops advancing from Mulhouse on 10 August. He and *Général* Aubier were promptly relieved of their commands by Joffre, who was merciless in removing commanders who failed to perform to expectations, although he was not as harsh as Messimy, who advocated executing officers deemed to have exhibited 'weakness or pusillanimity'. In the first five weeks of the war Joffre relieved two *Armée* commanders, ten *Corps* and thirty-eight *Division* commanders, all of whom were despatched to kick their heels in Limoges in south-western France; the remote location was selected to prevent Paris becoming overpopulated with disgruntled senior officers.[7]

The main French attack into Alsace began on 15 August after four days of intensive preparation and with regimental bands in the van. It was a three-pronged affair with Dubail's 1er *Armée* in the centre oriented north-east on Sarrebourg, 20 miles or so inside Lorraine, de Castelnau's 2ᵉ *Armée* on the left also oriented north-east from its concentration area around Nancy toward Morhange, while on the right Pau's newly formed *Armée d'Alsace* was to retake Mulhouse. Once again things went well initially. Within two days de Castelnau's men were closing on Morhange, Sarrebourg was secured on 18 August and Mulhouse the following day after a sharp battle that included a cavalry charge by the French 19ᵉ *Dragons* to secure the nearby village of Brunstatt and saw the first French general officer killed in action, a *Général* Plessier from the 159ᵉ *Régiment d'Infanterie*. Casualties were relatively heavy on both sides; the 97ᵉ *Régiment d'Infanterie* suffered 614 killed and 441 wounded, while *Generalkommando* 16, which was responsible for defending the area under *General der Infanterie* Hans Gaede, suffered a total of 2,300 killed or taken prisoner and lost twenty-four assorted artillery pieces.[8] The French window of success, in what became known as the Battles of Alsace and Lorraine, only lasted for five days however, in part because Dubail and de Castelnau became separated by the difficult terrain. A series of well-executed German counter-attacks then drove them out of Alsace and pushed deep into French territory, occupying Saint-Dié and Lunéville on 23 August, threatening Nancy and prompting Pau to abandon Mulhouse for the final time on 27 August.

While all this was going on Joffre launched *Plan XVII*'s main offensive on 21 August, a two-pronged advance upon Metz and Neufchâteau in the Belgian Ardennes by *Général* Pierre Ruffey's 3ᵉ *Armée* and *Général* Fernand de Langle de Cary's 4ᵉ *Armée* respectively, sparking a series of costly clashes collectively dubbed the Battle of the Ardennes.[9] Although the Germans were not expecting to fight in the area as it formed the pivot between their operational fronts, they nonetheless had many more troops in the area than French reconnaissance had indicated. As a result the French army's window of success was significantly shorter than it had been in Alsace, with French advance being stymied within forty-eight hours. Ruffey's force attacked dug-in German troops in heavy rain and fog without the benefit of artillery support near Longwy and was rebuffed with heavy losses, while 4ᵉ *Armée* force was stopped in the area of Rossignol and Neufchâteau with a similar result. The 3ᵉ *Division d'Infanterie Coloniale* had 10,272 of its 16,000 combat strength killed, wounded or missing by nightfall on 23 August, for example; 228 of the dead were officers and included division commander *Général* Léon Raffenel and two of his brigade commanders.[10] Joffre ordered both *Armées* to resume the advance on 23 August but circumstances dictated otherwise. Ruffey reported himself unable to comply at 09:25 as his units were still disorganised from the previous day's fighting, and a German counter-attack in the afternoon that pushed his centre 5ᵉ *Corps* back 5 miles put paid to the idea altogether and prompted a general withdrawal to maintain the integrity of the line. To the north Langle de Cary's 17ᵉ *Corps* was also obliged to pull back after elements of the 33ᵉ *Division d'Infanterie* broke during the night of 22/23 August after a day's unopposed pounding from German artillery. The remainder of 4ᵉ *Armée* withdrew to the River Meuse on 24 August carrying their wounded in whatever transport could be found, covered by *Général* Paul Leblois' 2ᵉ *Division d'Infanterie Coloniale* under 'une pluie de schrapnel' (a rain of shrapnel) from German artillery controlled via flares from spotter planes.[11] By 25 August both formations were back in their starting positions and were subsequently pushed further back by continuing German pressure. The 3ᵉ *Armée* retreated into the protection of Verdun's fixed defences, while 4ᵉ *Armée* withdrew west to Sedan; Ruffey was *limogé* on 30 August and replaced by *Général* Maurice Sarrail while Langle de Cary continued in command, presumably because his formation was swiftly embroiled in the Battle of the Marne.[12]

The first month of fighting in Alsace, Lorraine and the Ardennes, collectively labelled the Battle of the Frontiers, cost the French army a total of 260,000 casualties, 140,000 of which were sustained between 21–25 August; the overall total included 75,000 dead, 27,000 of whom were killed on 22 August alone.[13] The dead also included 4,778 officers, equivalent to a tenth of the army's entire officer corps.[14] Responsibility for this enormous scale of loss is routinely laid at the door of *attaque à outrance*; as Alistair Horne put it:

> Then the enemy was located. The trumpeters sounded the call … the [French] infantrymen in their red trousers and, thick blue overcoats, carrying heavy packs and long, unwieldy bayonets, broke into the double behind their white-gloved officers. Many sang the *Marsellaise*. In the August heat, sometimes the heavily encumbered French attacked from a distance of nearly half a mile from the enemy … The French stubble-fields became transformed into gay carpets of red and blue. Splendid cuirassiers in glittering breastplates of another age hurled their horses hopelessly at the machine guns that were slaughtering the infantry.[15]

The flaws in such tactics were noted at the time. On 23 August *Général* Ruffey issued an order specifically blaming such impromptu and unsupported bayonet charges for the failure of the attacks by 3ᵉ *Armée* the previous day for example, and instructed his three corps commanders to desist from attacking without artillery preparation in the future.[16] Similarly, *Lieutenant* Charles de Gaulle, hitherto an advocate of *attaque à outrance*, later commented that 'Tactically the realisation of the German firepower made nonsense of the current military doctrines'.[17]

However, while the reckless aggression of *attaque à outrance* was not helpful in minimising casualties, neither was it the primary reason for the scale of French loss, the real reason for which was inadvertently touched upon by de Gaulle. As the casualty roll at Mars-la-Tour and Gravelotte demonstrated, by 1870 contemporary weaponry had rendered movement on the open battlefield hazardous in the extreme, and by 1914 technological advance had increased this lethality manifold. The real killer in the Battle of the Frontiers was therefore not so much *attaque à outrance* but a combination of modern quick-firing field artillery, magazine-fed rifles and machine guns and it cut both ways, as is clear from the casualty rates incurred by German units as they pursued the French army westward. Some units from *Generaloberst* Josias von Heeringen's 7. *Armee* suffered as many casualties in August 1914 while pursuing Dubail's 1er *Armée* across Alsace and into Lorraine as their forebears had lost in the whole of the Franco-Prussian War. *Reserve Infanterie Regiment* 15 suffered a total of 408 casualties in a single engagement at Diesbach, *Infanterie Regiment* 105 lost 97 dead, 322 wounded and 17 missing at Badonviller and the *Kaiser Ulanen Regiment* lost 158 men and 149 horses in another single engagement at Lagarde, for example.[18] The August fighting in Alsace cost von Heeringen's formation a total of 32,054 casualties including 10,328 dead, approximately a third of its mobilised strength. Its running mate, *Generaloberst* Crown Prince Rupprecht of Bavaria's 6. *Armee*, lost 11,476 dead and 23,122 wounded, sick or missing across the same period in Lorraine, equivalent to a fully mobilised *Korps*. In all 60 per cent of the German infantry deployed in Alsace and Lorraine became casualties, with a death toll of 15 per cent.[19] The experience of suffering these losses was also similar. An eyewitness from *Reserve Infanterie Regiment* 5 referred to fighting through 'felled trees, barricades made with branches, barbed wire entanglements and trip wires' while under constant rifle fire and to the deadly effect of French machine gun fire that prompted a panicked rout while crossing the River Robinot fifty miles east of Épinal.[20] In practical terms there was thus little difference between the French and German experience in the Battle of the Frontiers, *attaque à outrance* not withstanding.

In addition to testing the efficacy of French military doctrine, the fighting in Lorraine also provided a sobering test of the integrity of French fixed fortifications, specifically Fort Manonviller, 6 miles from the German border and 10 miles east of Lunéville. The fort engaged German troops on a number of occasions in the first ten days of the war, including assisting elements of the 6e *Division de Cavalerie* holding crossings over the River Vezouze 3 miles to the south-east on 9 August, and providing artillery support for the 2e *Bataillon de Chasseurs à Pied* from the 2e *Division de Cavalerie* holding the Forêt de Parroy to the north two days later.[21] The French offensive into Alsace then pushed the action east until 21 August when elements of the 1er and 2e *Armées* were observed retiring westward and the following day German troops were spotted bypassing the fort to the north and south. Landline telegraph contact with Lunéville was lost at 13:00 and the telegraph and telephone connections to Marainviller, where the fort's garrison was responsible for demolishing the bridge carrying the Nancy–Strasbourg railway line over the River Vezouze, were severed at 18:30. By 23 August the general French withdrawal west and south had left Fort Manonviller high and dry and the point was underlined by a German reconnaissance aircraft circling to photograph the fort at 18:00; German troops moved up to encircle the fort the following day.[22]

Although the 820-strong garrison of Fort Manonviller had no way of knowing it, German preparations to reduce their haven were already afoot by this point. Appreciating the strategic significance of the fort's location, dominating the road and railway linking Nancy and Strasbourg, the *Oberste Heeresleitung* (Supreme Army Command) instructed *Generaloberst* Crown Prince Rupprecht's 6. *Armee* to eliminate the fort, which delegated the task to its senior engineer commander, *Generalleutnant* Karl Ritter von Brug. To achieve his mission, von Brug was allotted an infantry brigade, two regiments of engineers and two artillery regiments augmented with a variety of heavy howitzers in 150 mm, 210 mm, 305 mm and 420 mm calibres. There were up to eight Škoda M11 305 mm pieces on loan from the Austro-Hungarian army and two 420 mm weapons, code-named the *Kurz Marine Kanone Batterie 3* as a security measure, built by Krupp and nicknamed *Dicke Bertha* (big or heavy Bertha) after their dumpy truncated barrels. Mounted on a two-wheeled field carriage, they had a range of almost 8 miles, weighed 43 tons, fired projectiles weighing up to 420 lb and were towed by specially built Daimler Benz tractors. The weapons appear to have detrained at Avricourt, 8 miles north-east of the fort, and were emplaced nearby.[23]

The German bombardment of Fort Manonviller commenced at 09:30 French time on Tuesday 25 August, controlled via an observation balloon and initially utilising the 210 mm and 305 mm calibre weapons. *Kurz Marine Kanone Batterie 3* did not arrive on the scene of the action until 14:00 that afternoon followed by the detachment equipped with 210 mm *Mörser 10s* at 18:00 and neither detachment appears to have been ready to join the bombardment until the following day.[24] The shelling, which continued until dark and possibly later, jammed one of the fort's two Mougin retractable turrets, put the bakery and kitchen out of commission by destroying the chimney vents, damaged the optical signalling station and at 14:30 severed the underground signal cable running east to Toul, leaving the fort reliant on its loft of pigeons for external communications. More importantly, the fort's ventilation system did not function as intended and fumes, smoke and dust began to permeate throughout the fort, some drawn in from outside through vents located low down in the fort's defensive ditch. Fire from the 210 mm and 420 mm pieces caused more damage when the bombardment was resumed the next day. The second Mougin turret was put out of action in the early morning, the western twin 155 mm Galopin turret was damaged by 420 mm fire, which then switched to the second turret of that type to the north-east and a 305 mm shell distorted the mounting of the south-eastern 57 mm Bussière turret sufficiently to prevent it from rotating; a second direct hit then damaged the counterweight housing and prevented the turret from fully retracting. One of the counterscarp casemates built into the outer walls of the moat was also badly damaged, along with the railings and barbed wire apron protecting the scarp.

According to a German eyewitness, by the late afternoon the fort 'looked like a hill spouting fire'.[25] The pattern continued on 27 August with *Kurz Marine Kanone Batterie* 3 continuing to deliberately target the second Galopin turret until it was irreparably jammed by a chunk of broken concrete. By the early afternoon fumes and dust had rendered areas of the fort's interior uninhabitable and after consulting his subordinates the fort commander hoisted the white flag at 15:30 on 27 August 1914. The garrison was evacuated the following day, although the French did not become aware that the fort had surrendered until 29 August following aerial reconnaissance of the site.[26] According to French sources the garrison was afforded full military honours by von Brug, but Herwig refers to this being countermanded by *Generaloberst* Crown Prince Rupprecht on the grounds that French troops had deliberately targeted German medical personnel during the fighting at Lunéville.[27]

The bombardment had been spread over fifty-four hours, during which German guns of all calibres had fired approximately 17,000 assorted shells. Of this total, 5,868 were fired by the assembled heavy howitzers including 157 rounds from the two 420 mm pieces and 134 rounds from the loaned Austro-Hungarian 305 mm weapons.[28] One German artillery officer, who inspected the scene of the action after the French surrender, expressed shock at the 'unbelievable devastation' wrought by the shelling and likened Manonviller to a 'rooted-up molehill'.[29] The French garrison lost four dead, two of them killed while patrolling in the open, thirty wounded and between 120 and 150 cases of poisoning from the accumulated fumes, although all later recovered.[30] The failure of the fort's ventilation system to function as intended was the key factor in Manonviller's rapid fall, exacerbated by the unprecedented psychological impact of the constant pounding from the German guns, which the garrison were poorly prepared to withstand. However, beneath the surface devastation the physical fabric of the fort was largely undamaged. At least two of the fort's gun turrets, a Galopin 155 mm and a 57 mm Bussière, remained operational with plenty of ready ammunition to hand and more importantly, although one of the counterscarp galleries was badly damaged and some masonry gave way in the barracks, the fort's concrete carapace remained intact. This fact remained unknown to the wider French army however as, after inspecting and photographing the battered fort for propaganda purposes, the Germans spent seventeen days systematically demolishing it, detonating the individual turret magazines and setting demolition charges in the counterscarp galleries and other smaller features, presumably to deny the French any future use of the fort and possibly to conceal the ineffectiveness of their heavy howitzers, according to a French source. The main magazine, containing sixty tons of assorted ordnance, was detonated as the Germans withdrew on Sunday 13 September and the blast obliterated the concrete carapace. The French thus recaptured a shattered ruin when they reoccupied the surrounding area the following day, and they understandably assumed that the German bombardment had wrought much of the destruction. The truth was not revealed until members of the garrison returned from captivity some time later and in the meantime the *Grand Quartier Général* had drawn erroneous and far-reaching conclusions about the resilience and utility of their other permanent fortifications.[31]

Joffre and *Grand Quartier Général* were working on the assumption that their opponent's operational focus was also fixed primarily upon the Alsace-Lorraine border. The German trespass through neutral Luxembourg and the Belgian Ardennes was therefore interpreted as a piece of tactical expediency to outflank the northern end of the Séré de Rivières line in the same way Joffre himself had strenuously advocated a pre-emptive attack through Belgian territory in 1912.[32] This was not the case however, and the premeditated German violation of neutral Belgian territory went much further than Joffre and his colleagues imagined. German operations were based on the work of *Feldmarschall* Alfred Graf von Schlieffen, who had served on the *Große Generralstab* (Greater General Staff) from 1884 and as its head from 1891. Appointed by *Kaiser* Wilhelm II as the latter abandoned Bismarck's carefully crafted diplomatic measures designed to maintain French isolation, Schlieffen spent his entire tenure as head of the *Große Generralstab* working on plans to counter French resurgence and a two-front war following the French 1892 *Entente* with Russia. The fruits of this labour were revealed in December 1905 in a three-part memorandum; *Aufmarsch* (attack march or onslaught) I focussed upon attacking France in isolation; *Aufmarsch* II focussed on war with France and Russia simultaneously, beginning with an invasion of German territory by the former; and *Aufmarsch Ost* (East) I, was a variation designed to counter a Russian invasion. A fourth variation, code-named *Aufmarsch Ost* II, which focussed on a war against Russia in isolation, was added after Schlieffen's retirement in 1906 by his successor as head of the *Große Generralstab*, *Generaloberst* Helmuth von Moltke.

Apart from *Aufmarsch* I, which went into extreme and meticulous detail despite the truism that no plan survives first contact with the enemy, the various *Aufmarsch* iterations were deployment schemes rather than formal plans of attack.[33] The absence of the latter has led to academic claims that an overarching Schlieffen Plan, as popularly envisaged, did not actually exist and that the memorandum was merely a hypothetical intellectual exercise, or that it was an unfinished rough draft of a hypothetical plan that Moltke misread as the real thing.[34] On the other hand, elements of the scheme implemented in 1914 were war-gamed from 1907 at Moltke's request by the head of the Bavarian *Generralstab*, *Generalmajor* Karl von Fasbender, and *Oberst* Wilhelm Müller-Loebnitz from the *Große Generralstab* participated in military exercises held to field test elements of Schlieffen's Plan. Müller-Loebnitz had also been involved in numerous detailed discussions of the Plan with Schlieffen in person from 1905, and contemporary comment and accounts from highly placed individuals including Moltke's successor as head of the *Große Generralstab*, *Generalmajor* Erich von Falkenhayn, *Generaloberst* Prince Rupprecht of Bavaria and the head of the *Große Generralstab* railway section, *Oberstleutnant* Wilhelm Groener, also clearly referred to the existence of a plan.[35]

Be that as it may, Moltke took the *Heer* into a two-front war in August 1914 using a variation of Schlieffen's *Aufmarsch* II. The process involved seven distinct steps: Stage One 'State of Security' merely alerted the entire *Heer* to intelligence on emerging threats; Stage Two 'Political Tension' saw commanders placed on alert; Stage Three 'Imminent Threat of War' cancelled all leave, summoned reserve staffs to duty, called up the first-line reservists for eleven of the *Heer*'s twenty-five *korps*, enacted legislation designed to quell possible civilian unrest and officially announced the developing situation to the general public. Stage Four 'War Mobilisation' directed a total of twenty-seven brigades to move to pre-arranged locations on Germany's borders, including a 30,000 strong force that was tasked to move immediately to the Belgian border in readiness to attack the fortified city of Liège. All active units, the remaining first-line reserves and second line reserve *Landsturm* and *Landwehr* units were to join their assigned commands and civilians were to be evacuated from the vulnerable area along the East Prussian border. Stage Five, the 'Military Travel Plan', was the most complex phase, involving moving approximately three million men, 600,000 horses and all their weapons, equipment, rations and fodder to precise destinations across the length and breadth of Germany according to a strict timetable scheduled virtually to the minute. Stage Six, dubbed 'Concentration', involved detraining the mobilised multitude as close as possible to their destinations in the border areas and marching them formation by formation into their jump-off positions in readiness for Stage Seven, the 'Attack March' into enemy territory.[36]

The deployment of the *Feldheer* (field army) was divided between Germany's eastern and western borders. Deployment on the former relied upon an assumption of tardy Russian mobilisation, and responsibility for the defence of East Prussia was allotted to the *Ostheer* (east army) made up of around a tenth of the available German force, primarily the 149,000-strong 8. *Armee* commanded by sixty-six-year-old *Generaloberst* Maximilian von Prittwitz. The remainder were assigned to the *Westheer* (west army), numbering 1,485,000 men divided into seventy divisions grouped into twenty-five *korps*, which was despatched west in requisitioned railway rolling stock totalling 65,000 passenger carriages and 800,000 freight cars drawn by 30,000 steam locomotives, according to the minutely detailed Military Travel Plan. The plan saw approximately 11,000 trains of fifty-four cars each shuttling troops westward at a rate of 560 trains per day for thirteen days; in the period 2–8 August 2,150 trains crossed Cologne's Hohenzollern Bridge at ten minute intervals.[37] As we have seen, 345,000 of this host were grouped into the 6. and 7. *Armeen* and directed to the Franco-German border to form the left wing of the German effort in the west, tasked to block any French attack into German territory and then fix the French forces in the area and prevent them being redeployed elsewhere. The centre of the German line consisted of *Generaloberst* Grand Duke Albrecht of Württemberg's 4. *Armee* and *Generaloberst*

Crown Prince Wilhelm's 5. *Armee*, 180,000 and 200,000 strong respectively, which were tasked to push west into Luxembourg and the Ardennes.

The remaining 760,000 men formed the main striking force of the German attack in the west. Dubbed the *Schwenkungsflügel* (pivot wing), this force was divided into three armies. In the north *Generaloberst* Alexander von Kluck's 320,000-strong 1. *Armee* was to strike west into Belgium through a 6-mile gap between the fortified city of Liège and the Dutch border toward Antwerp and Brussels and on over the French border to Lille. In the centre the 260,000 men of *Generaloberst* Karl von Bülow's 2. *Armee* was tasked to eliminate Liège and advance west through the 12-mile gap between there and the River Meuse toward Namur, Gembloux and Mons. The proximity of the Dutch border and the layout of the German road and railway network also created choke points inside Germany, notably at Aachen where six complete *korps* from 1. and 2. *Armeen*, each taking up approximately 200 miles of road, had to pass through the city to reach their pre-battle concentration areas. To ease their passage the entire city was placed under martial law with military police manning every major road junction, 600,000 individual rations were stockpiled in the city in advance and both *Armeen* temporarily left their heavy equipment and supplies in Düsseldorf, 50 miles to the north-east. Even then it took five full days for all six *korps* to pass through the city ready to cross the River Meuse into Belgian territory on Tuesday 18 August.[38] The third, southern prong of the *Schwenkungsflügel* was *Generaloberst* Max von Hausen's 180,000-strong 3. *Armee*, which was to push through the French Ardennes and into France south of the fortress city of Maubeuge. All three *Armeen* were to push deeper into France before wheeling south, with 1. *Armee* passing east of Paris, before curving back to strike the French forces deployed on the Franco-German border in the rear and trap them against 6. and 7. *Armeen* advancing west through Alsace and Lorraine. The encircled French forces in the field could then be destroyed in a final, climactic *Schlacht der Vernichtung* (battle of annihilation).[39]

The detail of the Schlieffen Plan thus illustrates how very wide of the mark Joffre's appreciation of German intentions actually was, although this was due at least in part to the poor quality of French military intelligence. Just two months before the outbreak of war the *Deuxième Bureau* was insisting that the Germans would not deploy reserve formations alongside their active units, that their operational focus would be on the area between Verdun and Saint Dié and any trespass into Belgium would be limited and confined to the area south of the River Meuse. As one source put it, the *Deuxième Bureau* 'prophesied the war that it wished to see, in the process fortifying Joffre's own preconceptions'; the result was that French deployments under *Plan XVII* played almost literally into German hands.[40] The detail of the Schlieffen Plan also explains the speed and violence of the German reaction to the attacks by the 3e and 4e *Armées* toward Longwy and Neufchâteau in the Belgian Ardennes on 21 August; that area was the hinge upon which the northern *Schwenkungsflügel* was to pivot and Ruffey and Langle de Cary had thus inadvertently touched their opponents in a highly sensitive spot. That said, it is fair to question whether the Schlieffen Plan was a viable proposition as envisaged by its creator and von Moltke, given that it was predicated upon the men making up the *Schwenkungsflügel* marching and fighting their way anywhere up to 600 miles through French territory before fighting and winning a final climactic battle, all within forty days of mobilisation.[41] This would have been a tall order by any standard, and the more so for a force relying upon muscle power rather than mechanised transport.

In the event, circumstances conspired to prevent matters reaching the point of the climactic battle. In the east the Russians moved against East Prussia on 17 August, far faster that German planning had assumed and put *Generalleutnant* Hermann von François' I. *Korps* to flight at Gumbinnen three days later, prompting a somewhat shell-shocked von Prittwitz to appeal for reinforcements and suggest withdrawal behind the River Vistula, which effectively equated to abandoning East Prussia. Von Moltke responded by directing some units en route for Belgium to the east and dismissing von Prittwitz on 23 August in favour of *Generalleutnant* Paul von Hindenburg who pushed the Russians back out of German territory via the Battles of Tannenberg and the Masurian Lakes.[42]

In addition, the carefully timetabled German advance into Belgium did not unfold according to schedule either. After declaring war on Russia and ordering mobilisation on 1 August 1914, the Germans delivered an ultimatum to the Belgian government on 2 August, demanding permission to transit German forces across Belgian territory. Unsurprisingly, the ultimatum was rejected by the Belgians the following day. The German demand was somewhat disingenuous given that their inflexible mobilisation plan involved despatching *General der Infanterie* Otto von Emmich and the *Armee der Maas* (Army of the Meuse) to the Belgian border in readiness for an immediate attack upon the fortress city of Liège; von Emmich's force consisted of five infantry brigades and three cavalry divisions numbering 33,000 men along with 124 assorted artillery pieces. The initial attack on the city on 4 August coincided with the German declaration of war on Belgium and was repulsed, not least due to the unexpected presence of a 30,000-strong reinforced Belgian infantry division deployed among the city's fixed defences. A second attack commencing on the night of 6/7 August, supported by bombing from a Zeppelin LZ6 that killed nine civilians, secured the town, its citadel and vital bridges across the River Meuse; this prompted the Governor of Liège, *Général* Gérard Mathieu Léman, to release the reinforced infantry division to avoid encirclement and destruction. It then took a deliberate, eight-day siege operation commanded by *Generaloberst* Karl von Einem to reduce the twelve forts girdling the city using *Kurz Marine Kanone Batterie* 3's 420 mm howitzers and the borrowed Škoda 305 mm pieces that were later deployed against Fort Manonviller. By 15 August only five forts remained. Fort de Boncelles surrendered at 07:30 that day, followed by Fort de Lantin just after midday, while Fort de Loncin was totally destroyed at 17:20 when a 420 mm round pierced the fort's carapace and detonated a magazine containing 24,000 lbs of powder. The resulting blast devastated the fort, popping some of the fort's massive turrets clean out of their mountings and killing 250 men. *Général* Léman survived but was either captured in the ruins or shortly after leaving them, depending on the source. Loncin's spectacular demise unnerved the garrisons of the last two works, forts de Hollogne and de Flémalle, which surrendered the following day at 07:30 and 09:30 respectively. *Generaloberst* von Bülow's 2. *Armee* was therefore unable to begin moving through the Liège gap until 16 August and initially only by road, as the Belgians had blocked the Nasproué tunnel on the Aachen–Liège railway line by the simple expedient of crashing seventeen locomotives into it. The fight for Liège had taken twelve days and cost the Belgians 20,000 men. German casualties are unclear, although an unofficial Belgian report claimed 10,000 dead from the initial German attack against Fort de Evegnée east of the city and another source refers to German casualties totalling 5,300 by 8 August. Perhaps more importantly, the battle delayed the Schlieffen timetable by at least two days and possibly more.[43]

The Germans were obliged to repeat the process against the nine forts surrounding Namur, 40 miles upstream on the Meuse west of Liège, between 18 and 23 August, after which the *Schwenkungsflügel* began its sweep through Belgium and northern France as ordered by von Moltke on 17 August, pushing *Général* Charles Lanrezac's 5e *Armée* and Field Marshal Sir John French's newly arrived, seven-division strong British Expeditionary Force (BEF) before it. However, a combination of interference with von

Kluck's 1. *Armee* by von Bülow, who had been placed in overall charge of the *Schwenkungsflügel* on 18 August as a command rationalisation measure, and a change of focus by von Moltke redirected the German advance to the east of Paris rather than enveloping the French capital simultaneously from east and west. This presented an open German flank to *Général* Michel-Joseph Maunoury's 6ᵉ *Armée*, formed on 23 August in the area of Amiens by combining the *Armée de Lorraine* and elements of the *Armée d'Alsace* totalling nine infantry and two cavalry divisions; the new formation was shuttled to the front in 163 trains between 27 August and 2 September at an average of thirty-two trains every twenty-four hours.[44] The garrison of the *camp retranché de Paris* also despatched elements to assist Maunoury including *Général* Edgard de Trentinian's 7ᵉ *Division d'Infanterie*. The bulk of the latter travelled by rail or road but, concerned that railway problems might block the reinforcements, the Military Governor of Paris, *Général* Joseph-Simon Gallieni, commandeered 1,200 of the capital's Renault taxi cabs and used 500 of them to shuttle the 103ᵉ and 104ᵉ *Régiments d'Infanterie* the 30 miles to their concentration area near Nanteuil-lès-Meaux. Thus was born the enduring legend of the 'Taxis of the Marne', although the execution was somewhat less efficient and decisive than is popularly imagined; 'with dimmed lights and few maps, the taxis veered off the dark roads, ran into one another, missed road signs, and endured countless flat tires.' The use of a single route also caused severe congestion between outgoing and returning vehicles, and some infantrymen were thus obliged to debus and march the final stretch.[45] Nonetheless, by 6 September the British and French armies had mustered forty-one divisions to the German's twenty-four-and-a-half, and the *Schwenkungsflügel* was fought to a standstill in the Battle of the Marne along a 160-mile line stretching east from Paris between 6 and 9 September 1914, with the *camp retranché de Verdun* serving as the secure eastern anchor of the Entente line.[46] The subsequent German withdrawal prompted the so-called 'Race to the Sea', a series of outflanking moves that continued north until the Belgian coast and mutual exhaustion brought operations to an end, with the Germans astutely holding on to the most defensible terrain.

By the end of 1914 German casualties totalled approximately 800,000, including 118,000 officers, of which 116,000 had been killed; this was two-and-a-half times the death toll for the whole of the Franco-Prussian War.[47] On the Entente side the British Expeditionary Force had suffered a total of 89,964 casualties, including 3,627 officers by 30 November, more than the total initial establishment for its seven divisions.[48] French casualty records for the period are incomplete but included 265,000 dead by the end of the year, while the total casualty figure stood at 385,000 by 10 September 1914. According to one source, by the end of the year the total of wounded, missing and captured totalled in the region of 600,000.[49] Despite losses of such magnitude some French troops continued the fight after they could reasonably have been expected to desist. After being cut off in Lorraine in August a 300-strong party under a *Capitaine* de Colbert waged a guerrilla campaign against the Germans that lasted until the last survivors were captured or killed in December 1914, for example.[50] The fighting front of the first five months of mobile operations thus stabilised into a continuous line running from the Swiss border to the English Channel, along which the Germans had selected the most advantageous terrain features. They occupied the small folds that pass for high ground to the east of Ypres, the Messines Ridge, the mining spoil heaps and steep ridges of the Artois running south toward Arras, and the rolling chalk crests straddling the River Somme. They burrowed into the *Chemin des Dames* (Ladies Way) ridge overlooking the River Aisne, fortified crests in the Champagne, hilltops in the Argonne and Meuse Heights and mountaintops in the Vosges region, where the French staked a claim to a small corner of Germany. Thus securely ensconced the Germans were content to generally sit back and let the British and French armies come to them through the second year of the war.

The *Entente* powers were not so passive. The French launched their first major offensive against the German interlopers occupying the rolling chalk uplands of the Champagne region east of Reims on 16 February 1915; it petered out on 18 March after an advance of 3 kilometres that cost 40,000 casualties. Attention then shifted north to Picardy and the Artois. The British lost over 11,000 men at Neuve-Chapelle in March 1915, another 11,000 at Aubers Ridge in May and 61,000, including over 7,000 dead, at Loos in September, for minimal territorial gain. French operations on the British right flank in the Artois cost them over 16,000 dead, nearly 80,000 wounded and a further 20,000 missing, principally while trying to push the Germans off the commanding heights above the village of Vimy. The final French attack in the Artois coincided with a renewed effort in Champagne, beginning on 25 September 1915. The latter started well, piercing the German first line and taking 14,000 prisoners, but the French were unable to maintain their momentum through a German defence zone up to 5 kilometres deep. The Champagne offensive was called off on 6 October, that in the Artois five days later, for a combined cost of 30,000 dead and 160,000 wounded and missing; this increased the total of French casualties by the end of 1915 to 1.2 million, including 350,000 killed or missing.[51] The remains of 40,058 dead from the three separate Battles of the Artois are interred in the *Nécropole Nationale* atop the Notre Dame de Lorette ridge west of Vimy, the largest French military cemetery in the world.

The exception to all this was Verdun, where the most defensible terrain was already occupied by French fortifications. There the front line bulged north and east into German held territory on the east bank of the Meuse, before swinging south toward the foothills of the Vosges. Fire from the outlying forts east of the Meuse prevented the Germans from outflanking *Général* Maurice Sarrail's 3ᵉ *Armée* as it retired from its abortive advance toward Metz and reoriented north to face the German advance into the Argonne. The Germans treated the works close to Verdun with respect but launched a concerted effort to cut the town off in September 1914. This came close to success, and not merely because the German advances south through the Argonne and west on the Meuse Heights came within 7 miles of linking up on 10 September.[52] Joffre, considering the city doomed and keenly aware of how the French field armies had bottled themselves up at Metz and Sedan in 1870, ordered Verdun abandoned. Sarrail, the man on the spot, did not share Joffre's opinion and chose to ignore the order. In so doing he arguably saved the French from losing the war, for it would have been more difficult to halt the *Schwenkungsflügel* along the line of the Marne without the eastern lynchpin provided by the *camp retranché de Verdun*, and there would also have been little to stop a concerted push by Crown Prince Wilhelm's 5. *Armee* sweeping across the River Meuse toward Paris.[53]

The German effort to outflank Verdun from the south began on Tuesday 8 September 1914 with an attack by 5. *Armee* on Fort Troyon, on the east bank of the Meuse 15 miles south of Verdun. The attack was carried out by *Infanterie Division* 10 from *General der Infanterie* Hermann von Strantz's 5. *Korps*, reinforced with artillery, including four Austro-Hungarian Škoda 305 mm howitzers. The attackers were driven back by a French counterattack on 13 September, by which time the fort had been hit by 3,000 artillery shells, 200 of them from the 305 mm pieces, which had killed four men and wounded forty-one, knocked out six of the fort's twelve 90 mm guns, destroyed a magazine of artillery ammunition and badly damaged the barracks. The bombardment was resumed on 23 September after a renewed German attack obliged the supporting French troops to withdraw, and the fort was rendered untenable the following day after two 305 mm shells pierced the main powder magazine and interred eighteen men; it remained in French hands however and von Strantz's men were thus prevented from crossing the River Meuse as intended.[54] The 6. *Armee* enjoyed better success with an operation by *General der Kavallerie* Ludwig Freiherr von Gebsattel's 3. Bavarian *Korps* against Fort Camp des Romains, 10 miles south of Fort Troyon near Saint-Mihiel on Wednesday 23 September. The attack was carried out by *Generalmajor* Edward Lang's Bavarian *Infanterie Brigade* 11 supported by a dozen 150 mm and 280 mm guns which commenced an intensive bombardment of the fort at 08:25 French time on 23 September. Within thirty-six hours the bombardment, which delivered up to fifteen shells per minute at its height, had severed the fort's telephone and optical signalling links, knocked out some of its gun positions, destroyed the bakery and infirmary, severely damaged the barracks and weakened the structure of the counterscarp casemates covering the dry moat to the extent that troops refused to man them. A German infantry assault at 04:30 on 25 September penetrated the fort before the defenders were aware of their presence, sparking a three-hour fight before the garrison surrendered at 08:00, having lost a total of forty-eight dead and 130 wounded.[55] The Germans then crossed the River Meuse and established a foothold on the west bank around the village of Chauvoncourt, forming what became known as the Saint-Mihiel salient.

In crossing the Meuse at Chauvoncourt, von Gebsattel's men also cut the mainline railway running into Verdun from the south. The city was served by two other railway lines. The twin-line running west to Paris via Châlons-en-Champagne was within sight of German artillery observers located on the Butte de Vauquois feature 5 miles to the north where it looped around Aubréville, 15 miles west of Verdun. *Général* Maurice Sarrail's 3ᵉ *Armée* failed to drive the Germans off the feature at the end of October 1914 in an effort to reopen the line.[56] Verdun's third major rail link, the mainline running north along the west bank of the Meuse, was also cut by German shelling that destroyed the last train on the line 5 miles north of the city, where the line curved out to the west around a loop in the Meuse near Vacherauville. The *camp retranché de Verdun* and the cathedral city at its centre were thus left reliant upon the 30-mile long narrow gauge military railway and parallel road running south-west to Bar-le-Duc as its sole line of communication.[57] This rather tenuous link was to become more vital than its builders could ever have imagined.

4

MINE WARFARE AT THE SHOULDERS: FRAMING THE BATTLEFIELD AND THE EVOLUTION OF OPERATION GERICHT, FEBRUARY 1915 – FEBRUARY 1916

When a combination of exhaustion and the onset of winter brought the fighting to a halt at the end of 1914, the Western Front had stabilised along a 400-mile line running across Belgium and northern France. Beginning on the Channel coast just east of Nieuport, the line ran south to the River Oise, just east of Compiegne, before veering east past Soissons and Reims to the River Meuse and then south-east to Saint-Mihiel and on past Nancy and Lunéville, before running south past Saint-Dié and Belfort to the Swiss border. The sole major irregularity in the line was formed by the *Camp Retranché de Verdun*, which thrust north and east into German occupied France astride the River Meuse.

The bulge had been formed by the German attacks of September 1914, which wisely held back from Verdun's formidable defences, and the shoulders of the resulting salient were a major focus when operations were resumed in the area in 1915. The southern shoulder was formed by the Les Eparges ridge, 15 miles south-east of Verdun, which provided a commanding view over the French lines toward the River Meuse; the Germans dubbed the feature *die Combres-Höhe* (the Combres Heights) after the closest village on their side of the line. Tadpole-shaped, around a mile in length and a thousand feet high, the ridge climbs eastward from *Pointe A* near the village of Les Eparges to an intermediate peak roughly midway along its length dubbed *Pointe C* and then rises to the peak dubbed *Pointe X*, where the ridge drops away almost vertically to the Woëvre Plain. The feature was secured by elements of 5. *Armee* on 21 September 1914 likely from *General der Infanterie* Hermann von Strantz's 5. *Korps*, given that it was subsequently garrisoned by *Infanterie Divisionen* 9 and *Reserve Infanterie Division* 33. The occupiers immediately set about transforming the feature into a veritable fortress, turning *Pointe C* into a strongpoint protected by five successive defence lines spaced along the length of the lower half of the ridge, although *Général* Maurice Sarrail's 3ᵉ *Armée* succeeded in establishing a presence on the north-western slope through a series of limited attacks that ended on 16 October 1914.

Between November 1914 and January 1915 the French consolidated their proximity to the Eparges ridge, securing the villages of Les Eparges and Saint-Remy-la-Calonne, just over a mile to the south. In January 1915 *Général* Joffre and *Grand Quartier Général* decided to eliminate the German foothold on the west bank of the River Meuse near Saint-Mihiel by simultaneously attacking into the shoulders of the salient near Fresnes-en-Woëvre and Trésauvaux to the north and Regniéville and Ailly to the south. As it totally dominated the northern attack sector and gave uninterrupted views to the south, the Les Eparges ridge had to be taken before the main offensive could go ahead, and the task was allotted to *Général* Marie-Jean Paulinier's 12ᵉ *Division d'Infanterie*. As the strength of the German defences boded ill for a conventional assault, the French also decided to tunnel under the ridge and place explosive charges under the enemy positions on the north-western slope, called *der Finger* by the German defenders, in perhaps the first example of the mine warfare that was to become increasingly prevalent on the Western Front. Four tunnels were thus pushed into the ridge, oriented using information gleaned from German prisoners of war presumably taken in trench raids. The French attack began at 14:00 on 17 February 1915 with the detonation of four mines under the German front line, followed by an intensive hour-long artillery barrage. The 106ᵉ and 132ᵉ *Régiments d'Infanterie* then seized the 100-foot deep craters created by the mines and pushed on into the German trench network, securing *Pointe A* and the western end of the feature, but they were still short of *Pointe C* by nightfall, sparking three days of back and forth fighting. A German counter-attack by elements of *Infanterie Division* 9 and *Reserve Infanterie Division* 33 at 08:00 the following day after an all-night bombardment pushed the French back to their start line, prompting another attack by the 106ᵉ and 132ᵉ *Régiments d'Infanterie* at 15:00 that regained the lost ground and held onto it in the face of German counter-attacks through 19 February. By this point the 106ᵉ *Régiment d'Infanterie* had lost 300 killed, 1,000 wounded and 300 missing, but another attack, reinforced with elements from the 67ᵉ *Régiment d'Infanterie*, came close to *Pointe X* before being forced back with heavy losses by German reinforcements, likely from *Infanterie Division* 10. The French managed to retain their hold on *Pointe A* and the lower end of the ridge west of *Pointe C*, however.

Général Frédéric-Georges Herr, the commander of 6ᵉ *Corps*, ordered a resumption of the attack at 16:00 on 17 March by 132ᵉ *Régiment d'Infanterie* supported by elements of the 54ᵉ *Régiment d'Infanterie* after a forty-five-minute bombardment from a hundred guns. The attack was largely rebuffed, in part by the triggering of German counter-mines containing 20 to 30 tons of explosive apiece and thus failed to secure *Pointe C* as envisaged, although it did capture several hundred yards of the German trench system and the left flank of the attack pushed to within a hundred yards of *Pointe X*. A renewed effort on 27 March was also rebuffed with heavy French losses. The 12ᵉ *Division d'Infanterie*'s third attempt to conquer the ridge began on 5 April, in conjunction with a general attack on the Saint-Mihiel salient by three French corps and a cavalry division devised by *Général* Auguste Dubail, commander of the *Groupement des Armées de l'Est* (Group of Armies in the East). The attack began in wet and muddy conditions at 16:00 after an intense thirty-minute barrage, and while the 106ᵉ *Régiment d'Infanterie* succeeded in seizing *Pointe C* the 132ᵉ *Régiment d'Infanterie*'s attack on *Pointe X* was beaten back by intense German machine gun and artillery fire. In addition, all the attackers experienced difficulty keeping weapons functioning in the cloying mud and the attack again sparked several days of back and forth fighting. Another assault on *Pointe X* on 6 April by the 67ᵉ *Régiment d'Infanterie* supported by elements of the 132ᵉ *Régiment d'Infanterie* was again stopped cold and a German counter-attack then drove the French back to their original start line. A French artillery barrage stabilised the situation from 15:00 and a further French effort in the late afternoon recaptured the strongpoint atop *Pointe C*, but a German counter-attack the following day drove the survivors of the 106ᵉ and 132ᵉ *Régiments d'Infanterie* back again. On 8 April the 12ᵉ *Division d'Infanterie* was reinforced with the 8ᵉ *Régiment d'Infanterie* in preparation for another concerted effort on 9 April that saw the 106ᵉ *Régiment d'Infanterie* and a light infantry unit, the 25ᵉ *Bataillon de Chasseurs à Pied*, finally secure *Pointe C*. A simultaneous attack by the 8ᵉ and 166ᵉ *Régiments d'Infanterie* on *Pointe X* was halted short of the objective however, and the Germans maintained their hold on *Pointe X* and the southern side of the feature. The overall French offensive against the Saint-Mihiel salient failed and the units involved paid a heavy price for their gains on the Les Eparges ridge. By 10 April the 25e *Bataillon de Chasseurs à Pied* had lost 474 men, and a casualty count by the 67e *Régiment d'Infanterie* two days later recorded 1,029 killed, wounded and missing; overall the fight to secure the crest of the ridge cost the French 12,000 casualties.[1] The French held onto their gains in the face of heavy German counter-attacks from *Infanterie Divisionen* 9 and 10 and *Reserve Infanterie Division* 33 between 24 and 28 April. Both sides then reverted to mine warfare, with forty-six French and thirty-two German mines being blown on a frontage of just 800 yards by April 1917. *Pointe X* remained in German hands until September 1918, by which time the topography of the ridge had been permanently altered by scores of huge craters along the crest and slopes.

Events unfolded in a similar fashion over roughly the same time frame at the Butte de Vauquois, an elongated and isolated 295-metre high feature that formed the western shoulder of the Verdun salient, 15 miles west of the city. German troops from Crown Prince Wilhelm's 5. *Armee* occupied the village of Vauquois atop the feature on 3 September during the advance to the Marne, and the 168 inhabitants were evacuated on the night of 3/4 September; the German troops appear to have abandoned it again after the Battle of the Marne. The deserted hilltop was then occupied by the 82e *Régiment d'Infanterie* from *Général* Émile Martin's 9e *Division d'Infanterie* on 15 September. For their part, 4. and 5. *Armeen* were looking to stabilise their line in the Argonne by keeping up the pressure on *Général* Maurice Sarrail's beleaguered 3e *Armée* and the value of the Butte as an observation platform had not gone unnoticed, not least due to the panoramic view it offered over the French lines, and particularly the Verdun to Paris railway line 5 miles to the south. *Infanterie Division* 33 from

General der Infanterie Bruno von Mudra's 15. *Korps* thus attacked and drove the French off the hill on 24 September in a fight that cost the French 50 dead and 150 wounded. Defence of the hill was then handed to *General der Infanterie* Max von Fabeck's 13. *Korps*, and *Infanterie Divisionen* 26 and 27 set about fortifying the hill with customary Teutonic efficiency. The French attempted to regain the butte on 28 October 1914 with an attack by the 46ᵉ and 89ᵉ *Régiments d'Infanterie*, from *Général* Henri Gouraud's 10ᵉ *Division d'Infanterie*, but only managed to establish a lodgement on the lower slope of the butte in the face of devastating artillery and machine gun fire.

There matters remained for three months until *Général* Sarrail decided to attack the butte in an effort to wrest the initiative from the Germans, on the grounds that it offered the least wooded and broken terrain in the area. The attack was a two-pronged affair, with the 31ᵉ *Régiment d'Infanterie* attacking Vauquois while the 44ᵉ *Régiment d'Infanterie Coloniale* put in a supporting attack on the village of Boureuilles, just over a mile west of the butte. Originally scheduled to begin on 15 February, the attack was delayed for two days due to bad weather and began with a three-hour artillery bombardment and the detonation of mines under the German positions. The assault on Boureuilles failed but the 31ᵉ *Régiment d'Infanterie* entered Vauquois before being obliged to withdraw due to a lack of reinforcement and intense German shelling. A second attack by the 46ᵉ and 89ᵉ *Régiments d'Infanterie* on 27 February also reached the village, only to be driven back and it took a third attempt on 1 March involving all three *Régiments* to reach and hold on to the crest of the butte. The fighting between 28 February and 4 March cost the 10ᵉ *Division d'Infanterie* 3,000 dead and missing, and ended with the front lines occupying the ruined buildings lining the village's central main street, which ran the length of the crest. With fighting above ground stalemated, both sides turned to mine warfare to drive their opponents off the hilltop. Recognising the suitability of the butte's strata for mining, the Germans had deployed *Pionier Bataillon* 30 to the hill on 7 January 1915 while the French detonated their first charge on 3 February 1915. Thereafter the size and depth of the mines escalated to the extent that the Butte de Vauquois became 'the most heavily-mined spot on the earth's surface'.[2] In March 1915 the average charge was in the 500 to 1,500-kilogram range and 5 to 15 metres deep; within a year charges had grown to an average of 15 tons buried at depths of up to 40 metres and by the end some workings were up to 100 metres below the surface.

The mining war began in earnest on 3 March 1916 with a 4.7 ton German mine detonated under the eastern end of the hill that killed eleven French soldiers; the French responded on 25 March with a 12-ton charge that killed thirty and totally demolished Vauquois church, which the Germans had transformed into a strongpoint. The largest mine, containing 60 tons of explosive, was detonated by the Germans on 14 May 1916. The explosion destroyed a section of the French first and second lines, killed 108 French soldiers from the 46ᵉ *Régiment d'Infanterie* and an attached engineer unit and blew out the whole western end of the hill, creating a crater 250 feet wide and 60 feet deep. In the end over 500 separate charges were detonated in the Butte de Vauquois, some intended to destroy positions on the surface and some smaller camouflet charges designed to collapse enemy tunnels and mine workings. The hill became honeycombed with 17 kilometres of tunnels on three levels that incorporated chambers to house barracks, stores, infirmaries, electrical generators and compressors to channel air to the deepest tunnels. On 24 February 1917 a German mine destroyed the village well and the last surviving chestnut tree, the last visible signs of human habitation on the hilltop, which by this point had been reduced to a string of huge, interlinked craters up to 80 metres wide and 10 to 20 metres deep; the frontline trenches ran along the rims of the craters, in places incorporating the foundations of vanished buildings. Both sides were planning to finish things once and for all by virtually levelling the butte using up to 160 tons of explosives, but French excavations were hamstrung by a shortage of labour and the war ended just before the German works were completed. The final two charges exploded on the Butte de Vauquois were a French mine in March 1918 and a German camouflet on 9 April 1918. Between February 1915 and April 1918 the French had detonated 320 separate charges and the Germans an additional 199, consuming over a thousand tons of explosives in total. The shattered remnants of the feature were liberated without a fight by troops from the US 35th Infantry Division on 26 September 1918, almost exactly four years after the vanished village of Vauquois had been occupied by elements of Crown Prince Wilhelm's 5. *Armee*.

While all this was going on at the periphery, Verdun itself remained an island of relative calm and consequently gained a reputation as a rare quiet sector of the front. As *Sergent* Étienne Gilson put it, the line there was 'a very tranquil and peaceful place' where the combatants exchanged occasional rifle shots to stave off the boredom.[3] In February 1915 the city was bombed by German aircraft which doubtless assisted in the ongoing reduction of the town's civilian population, which had dropped from 15,000 to 3,000 by the beginning of 1916.[4] Out on the defensive ring surrounding the city Fort Douaumont had been hit by 138 rounds from 150 mm guns on 8 October 1914 with no effect, and in mid-February 1916 the Germans tried again with *Kurz Marine Kanone Batterie* 3's 420 mm guns. On 15 and 17 February Douaumont was struck by a total of fifty 380 mm and 420 mm shells which collapsed the eastern end of the fort's external barracks into the central courtyard, blew off part of the inscription over the main entrance and damaged the bakery, the gallery linking the twin 75mm turret and put the retracting mechanism of the 155 mm Galopin turret out of commission for several days.

The resultant huge plume of dust and smoke, in conjunction with a lack of return fire, persuaded German observers into assuming they had inflicted lethal damage upon the fort, whereas the impact was largely superficial. However, the lack of return fire was due to the fact that the German guns were firing from outwith the 7.2 kilometre range of the fort's single 155 mm gun; at this point the front line also lay beyond the range of the fort's guns. The German gunners then turned their attention to Fort Vaux, dropping twelve 420 mm rounds onto the fort on 18 February but with little effect.[5]

However, Douaumont and Vaux's resilience under shellfire availed them little against a more insidious threat. As we have seen, there was little room in the *attaque à outrance* doctrine for fixed defences; the army's operational manuals decreed that the only legitimate purpose for fortresses and fixed defences was to allow manpower to be freed up for the attack elsewhere.[6] In Joffre and the *Grand Quartier Général*'s view the fact that Douaumont and Vaux had shrugged off hits from the largest guns the enemy could muster, or that the Belgian defences at Liège had inflicted a critical nine-day delay on the German advance, counted for little. For them the crucial point was that the forts at Liège had fallen, and their obsolescence was confirmed by the erroneous conclusions drawn from the fall of Fort Manonviller on 23 August 1914 after the fumes created by 1,500 German shells of up to 420 mm calibre rendered it untenable.[7] The forts were therefore dismissed as dangerous shell traps, the use of which risked a rerun of the fate of Metz and Sedan in 1870–71, and the doctrinal antipathy was paralleled by a more practical imperative. After a year of fighting the war was making serious inroads into French reserves of manpower and materiel, and especially artillery. The various *camp retranchés* including Verdun were thus seen as a quick and easy source of reinforcement, guns and ammunition, not least because after the failed French offensives in Artois and the Champagne Joffre was gathering resources for a renewed effort on the Somme in 1916.[8] At the beginning of August 1915 *Grand Quartier Général* therefore ordered all forts on the eastern borders to be demobilised and prepared for demolition in the event of capture, and the process of reassigning their assets was eased by relieving the *camps retranché* of their independent status, rechristening them *Régions Fortifée* and making them subordinate to their local field army commanders. The *camp retranché de Verdun* thus became the *Région Fortifée de Verdun* and its commander since May 1912, *Général* Michel Coutanceau, soon fell foul of the new edict. The change of status subordinated Coutanceau to *Général* Auguste Dubail's *Groupement des Armées de l'Est* and when Coutanceau questioned the wisdom of the demobilisation decree in August 1915 Dubail promptly demoted him to commanding the line north of Verdun, and sacked him altogether in January 1916. Coutanceau was replaced by *Général* Frédéric-Georges Herr who had commanded the effort to capture the Les Eparges ridge, and Dubail left him in no doubt that the artillery-stripping policy was not open for discussion. He also expressly forbade Herr from fighting for Verdun or becoming invested there, ordering him to prepare defences on the west bank of the Meuse for use if the city had to be abandoned, although the latter task was hamstrung by a shortage of labour due to units being hived off to other sections of the front, notably the fighting in the Champagne.[9]

In the event the *Région Fortifée de Verdun* proved to be a fruitful source of men and materiel. Fort Douaumont's wartime garrison numbered by nine officers and 811 other ranks for example; by February 1916 this had been reduced to fifty-eight overage territorial soldiers commanded by *Adjutant* Chenot, and the process was repeated at the other defensive works girdling Verdun. All artillery pieces that could be easily dismantled, such as the *Canon de 75 Modèle 1897* field guns mounted in the flanking *Casemates de Bourges* attached to the larger forts and *ouvrages*, were removed. The only guns left in Fort Douaumont were the single 155 mm and two 75 mm pieces built inextricably into its retractable Galopin and R05 turrets for example. In many instances the Hotchkiss machine guns were removed from their retractable GF4 turrets, and Verdun's conventional artillery parks were also plundered of their substantial holdings of older 95 mm, 120 mm and 155 mm field guns. By the end of October 1915 sufficient guns to equip forty-three heavy batteries and eleven batteries of field guns had been stripped from the *Région Fortifée de Verdun* along with 128,000 rounds of ammunition. The *Grand Quartier Général* then began preparations to permanently eradicate the defensive installations that had done so much to restore French national pride after the debacle of 1870–71 at such vast cost to the public purse. Teams of engineers were set to laying demolition charges in the denuded forts, *ouvrages* and other works to allow them to be destroyed if there were any danger of them falling into German hands, a mammoth task that was completed by January 1916. At Fort Vaux the engineers cached their explosives at the bottom of the shaft supporting the Fort's 75 mm R05 turret as a central location while they created chambers to house the demolition charges at key points around the fort. A substantial charge was left in place beneath the turret, which was to have unforeseen repercussions when the fort came under sustained attack in February and March 1916.[10] This severe weakening of Verdun's fixed defences was exacerbated by the growth of complacency among the French troops manning the front line over the same period. The German approach in 1914 had prompted the construction of a belt of trenches linking and protecting the forts and *ouvrages* up to 3 miles deep in places. By June 1915 this urgency had evaporated however, and troops exhausted from the fighting elsewhere on the front were being posted to the Verdun sector to rest. Such troops were understandably reluctant to expend their energy in digging or needlessly provoking their opponents, and the quiet sector attitude morphed into a live-and-let-live mentality on both sides of the line. French participant accounts refer to a comfortable routine developing for example, and at least one French officer was obliged to issue a stern warning to his men about the perils of communicating or even fraternising with the enemy.[11]

All this might not have mattered had the German formations facing Verdun remained quiescent but that was not to be the case, although the *Westheer* (western army) had been through its own trials and tribulations. *Generaloberst* Helmuth von Moltke suffered a breakdown on 12 September 1914 following the failure of the Schlieffen Plan on the Marne and was removed from his position as head of the *Oberste Heeresleitung* (Supreme Army Command) two days later, although this was not officially announced until 6 November to avoid handing the *Entente* a propaganda coup. Thirty-three high ranking officers were also replaced over the same period including *Generaloberst* Max von Hausen and *Generaloberst* Josias von Heeringen, commanders of 3. *Armee* and 7. *Armee* respectively amid a veritable orgy of recriminations and blame attribution that effectively stultified any meaningful operational analysis of what had actually gone wrong.[12] Moltke was replaced by *Generalmajor* Erich von Falkenhayn on 14 September; the newcomer was already serving as *Kriegsminister* (Minister of War) from 8 July 1913 and initially continued in both posts, believing this would lead to a more efficient prosecution of the war. One of Falkenhayn's first acts was to relocate the *Oberste Heeresleitung* from Luxembourg to Charleville-Mézières, just over 60 miles north of Verdun, in order to be closer to the various *Armee* headquarters under his command.[13] He also immediately became responsible for the stabilisation of the line on the River Aisne, the outflanking campaign running north popularly dubbed the Race to the Sea, overcoming Antwerp and most of the remainder of Belgium, and the final attempt to salvage victory from the Schlieffen Plan on the River Yser and Ypres in Belgium, and at Armentières and La Bassée just over the Franco-Belgian border between September and November 1914. This provided an early test of Falkenhayn's organisational abilities as it not only involved redeploying Grand Duke Albrecht of Württemberg's 4. *Armee* from the Ardennes to northern Belgium and Crown Prince Rupprecht of Bavaria's 6. *Armee* from Lorraine to the Artois, but also involved moving 280 separate trains along a single double-track line running north from Metz. The subsequent fighting cost the 4. and 6. *Armeen* a total of 80,000 casualties before mutual exhaustion brought the fighting to a halt.[14]

The failure of the Schlieffen Plan and the subsequent effort in Flanders to deliver a swift and decisive victory cost Germany 800,000 casualties including 116,000 dead, and persuaded Falkenhayn that Germany could not win the war in the west with the resources available. On 18 November he therefore approached Chancellor Theobald von Bethmann-Hollweg and suggested making peace with one of the *Entente* powers, preferably Russia, to ultimately allow a refocusing of effort upon Britain, which he considered to be Germany's most implacable foe.[15] The result of this new strategy was a severe bout of Machiavellian infighting in the upper echelons of the German command, orchestrated by *Major* Hans von Haeften, an intelligence officer serving at *Generalleutnant* Paul von Hindenburg's *Oberbefehlshaber Ost* (Commander in Chief East) headquarters while also serving as von Moltke's personal adjutant. The rift involved von Hindenburg indulging his personal animosity toward Falkenhayn while seeking to garner more resources for the fight against Russia, von Moltke seeking to regain leadership of the *Oberste Heeresleitung* by unseating Falkenhayn and von Bethmann-Hollweg seeking to make all round political capital from the situation by also seeking Falkenhayn's removal. In the end it took two personal interventions from the *Kaiser*, the second on 20 January 1915, to quell the disorder which ended with von Haeften narrowly escaping a court martial, *Oberbefehlshaber Ost* receiving the additional reinforcement *Korps* it had been seeking and von Hindenburg receiving permission to resume the offensive in the east. Von Falkenhayn remained in post as head of the *Oberste Heeresleitung*, although he was obliged to hand over the post of Prussian *Kriegsminister* to his deputy, *Generalleutnant* Adolf Wild von Hohenborn.[16]

Falkenhayn thus oversaw the end of the *Bewegungskrieg* (war of movement) period in the west and the transition to *Stellungskrieg* (position warfare) as the *Westheer* stood on the defensive on the Western Front through 1915 while Hindenburg's *Ostheer* stabilised the Eastern Front. In the process the *Ostheer* inflicted eye-watering losses upon the Russians, notably at the Battle of Gorlice-Tarnów in May 1915 which cost the Russian army over a million men; 151,000 dead, 683,000 wounded and 895,000 taken prisoner.[17] Remaining on the defensive in the west was by no means a softer option however, for it meant standing firm against repeated *Entente* attempts to break through the German line and push them out of French territory. The French were first off the mark in February 1915 with a resumption of the previous December's attack in the Champagne by *Général* Fernand de Langle de Cary's 4ᵉ *Armée* that continued until 17 March; the intensity and unremitting nature of the French artillery fire during the battle introduced the Germans to the concept of *Trommelfeur* (drum fire).[18] Next Field Marshal Sir John French's British Expeditionary Force attacked at Neuve-Chapelle between 10 and 12 March followed by a series of engagements in the Ypres Salient over the month between 22 April and 25 May; the latter overlapped a series of attacks by *Général* Victor d'Urbal's 10ᵉ *Armée* toward Neuville-Saint-Vaast and Souchez in the Artois just west of Vimy Ridge that began on 9 May and lasted for five weeks. In the event the French attacks gained a minimal amount of ground as did the British at Neuve-Chapelle, while at Ypres German counter-attacks that included the first use of poison gas overran a significant portion of British-held territory and pushed the perimeter of the Salient to within 2 miles of Ypres proper. The successful repelling of these *Entente* attacks persuaded Falkenhayn that German strategy in the west was fundamentally sound, albeit with some reorganisation to standardise defensive systems to free up troops for future offensive action, and update artillery techniques and deployment doctrine to counter French artillery tactics.[19]

The failure of the Anglo-French attacks in the first half of 1915 also persuaded Falkenhayn that there would be no further attacks in the west in 1915, and that the French were ready to embark upon peace talks, an opinion he relayed to Bethmann-Hollweg on 30 June. His senior subordinates were less optimistic however. Crown Princes Wilhelm and Rupprecht expressed disquiet over the *Westheer*'s ability to weather further attacks, not least because Falkenhayn had despatched much of the *Westheer*'s reserves to the Eastern Front leaving only four *Infanterie* divisions and independent brigades to cover the whole front. More pertinently *Generaloberst* Karl von Einem, who had replaced von Hausen as commander of 3. *Armee*, reported increasingly clear signs of an imminent French offensive in the Champagne from at least the beginning of August. Despite this Falkenhayn continued to insist that no French attack was imminent even after the French artillery bombardment began visiting *Trommelfeur* upon 3. *Armee* on 22 September, although he did take the precaution of reinforcing von Einem's formation with *Infanterie Division* 5 earmarked for the Balkans and twenty-three additional heavy artillery batteries between 22 and 24 September.[20] In fact the *Entente* launched a coordinated effort on 25 September with renewed French offensives in the Artois and Champagne and a British attack at Loos that included a reciprocal, if not particularly effective, use of poison gas. The attacks, collectively labelled the *Herbstschlacht* (autumn battle) by the Germans, again achieved little in the Artois and Loos, with the latter pushing the German line back just over a mile along a 4-mile front at a cost of 60,392 casualties and leading to Sir John French being replaced as head of the British Expeditionary Force.[21]

However, it was the French attack in what became known as the Second Battle of the Champagne that gave the Germans most serious pause for thought. The three-day preparatory bombardment pitted up to thirty-five French artillery batteries against each German division along a 20-mile stretch of the 3. *Armee* front, raining down 3.4 million artillery shells which 'obliterated many German positions, wiped out their garrisons, swept away German wire, destroyed artillery observation posts, and cut rearward communications'. The bombardment also destroyed railway facilities at Challerange and Bazancourt, 6 and 14 miles behind the front line respectively, and French aircraft singled out von Einem's headquarters for attack.[22] The initial phase of the French attack, which began at 09:15 on Sunday 5 September, swiftly overran four sections of the German first line and in two instances pushed ahead as far as the German second line dubbed the *R-Stellung* (R position) where they were only stopped by uncut barbed wire entanglements. Within three hours 3. *Armee* was urgently requesting reinforcements from the neighbouring 5. *Armee*; the situation was complicated further by similar calls from 6. *Armee* facing the Anglo-French attacks in the Artois and at Loos. However, within forty-eight hours the alarm generated by the initial French gains had died away as the attack began to lose momentum, aided by the reinforcing *Infanterie Divisions* 5, 20 and 56 creating an additional defence line behind the *R-Stellung* in the threatened sector, and *Oberste Heeresleitung* drafting in additional artillery units; over the course of the battle gunners assigned to 3. *Armee* fired 400,000 heavy calibre artillery rounds and 1,564,000 rounds of field gun ammunition.[23] After five days the French paused to regroup and reorganise but when the attack was resumed on 6 October, after a two-day bombardment, it made little significant progress apart from securing the Butte de

Tahure feature in the centre of the attack frontage. Joffre therefore reluctantly terminated the operation on 7 October. Overall the Artois and Champagne fighting cost the French 30,386 killed, 110,725 wounded and 50,686 missing; the German casualty count was almost half that at 17,000 officers and 80,000 men.[24]

While the *Herbstschlacht* generated some alarm in the upper echelons of the *Westheer*, Falkenhayn was more sanguine and drew two key lessons from it. First, it reinforced his view that France was reaching the point of exhaustion and that the French army was a 'flawed instrument'. Second, the French failure to secure a clean breakthrough, despite such a huge investment in men and material, persuaded him that while the war would be decided on the Western Front, the prevailing tactical conditions there rendered a decisive breakthrough impossible for either side. While *Stellungskrieg* had proved sufficient to prevent the *Entente* achieving victory, as a passive strategy neither could it provide Germany with the victory she sought. For this Falkenhayn turned to the concept of *Ermattungsstrategie*, literally weariness strategy but usually translated as attrition strategy, formulated by German historian and military thinker Hans Delbrück in the wake of the Franco-Prussian War.[25] With the Eastern Front stabilised and Russia quiescent following their severe drubbing at Gorlice-Tarnów, Falkenhayn considered the conditions ripe to resume the offensive in the west and in November 1915 he therefore set 5. *Armee* to planning three limited and open-ended offensives code-named KAISERSTUHL, SCHWARZWALD and WALDFEST targeted against the Vosges, Belfort and Verdun respectively. Falkenhayn successfully sought permission to proceed at an audience with the *Kaiser* on 3 December, and at the same time clearly indicated that the proposed attacks were not conventional operations intended to simply break through the *Entente* line, but rather to destroy the French army via a process of *Verblutung* (bleeding to death). On 8 December he discussed the matter in detail with his Operations Officer *Oberst* Gerhard Tappen and Prussian *Kriegsminister Generalleutnant* Wild von Hohenborn, and the following day summoned *Generalleutnant* Constantin Schmidt von Knobelsdorf, the 5. *Armee* chief of staff, to Berlin to discuss expanding Operation WALDFEST into a major offensive. Knobelsdorf arrived in Berlin on 14 December and, after detailed discussion the following day, Falkenhayn sidelined the attacks on the Vosges and Belfort in favour of an operation to seize Verdun. Knobelsdorf returned to 5. *Armee* headquarters at Stenay-sur-Meuse, 30 miles north of Verdun, to develop the plan on 16 December.[26]

Falkenhayn presented his plan to the *Kaiser* at a Crown Council at Potsdam on 21 December 1915 as part of a wide-ranging assessment of Germany's strategic situation, which was also deliberately framed to appeal to the *Kaiser*'s preferences and especially his anti-British prejudice. The assessment consequently identified Britain as the major threat to Germany and concluded that the most effective counter to this existential threat would be to remove Britain's 'tool on the Continent' by knocking an allegedly war-weary, depleted and demoralised France out of the war. This was to be achieved by drawing the French into a narrow-front battle it could not refuse without severely damaging national pride, and thus morale. Once engaged the French army was to be destroyed in a battle of attrition, or *Verblutung* to use Falkenhayn's term, with massed artillery being the chief killer. The human cost of this was intended to break France's fragile morale and provoke a collapse of the French government, which Falkenhayn confidently predicted would occur by the summer of 1916. The preferred venue for the operation was Verdun, which offered the narrow frontage required along with a direct threat to Paris and, more importantly for Falkenhayn's purposes, the requisite historical significance. As Falkenhayn put it, Verdun was a location 'for the retention of which the French General Staff would be compelled to throw in every man they have.[27] Overall, this was a two-stage strategy, with the operation against Verdun code-named GERICHT (court of justice) roughly, followed by a mopping-up operation against the remainder of the *Entente* force in France and Belgium who were confidently expected to expend their strength in vain attempts to ease the pressure at Verdun. The ultimate objective was therefore to eliminate France from the war and drive the British off the continent.[28]

The *Kaiser* granted Falkenhayn assent to implement GERICHT at the end of the Potsdam meeting and matters moved swiftly thereafter. Crown Prince Wilhelm and von Knobelsdorf submitted the 5. *Armee*'s detailed plan for the attack on Verdun to the *Oberste Heeresleitung* on 6 January 1916. In line with prior instructions the initial attack was restricted to the east bank of the River Meuse along a 10-mile front that was intended to overrun the ridges and ravines north of the *Région Fortifée de Verdun* proper and capture the northern edge of the French defences along a line running south-east from the *Ouvrage* de Froidterre to Forts Souville and Tavannes, from where German artillery would be able to dominate Verdun itself and the west bank of the Meuse. However, despite the instruction to confine the operation to the east bank of the Meuse, 5. *Armee* also planned for a parallel attack along the west bank of the Meuse, timed to begin almost immediately after that on the east bank. Securing both banks of the Meuse was considered essential to a rapid seizure of Verdun because delay would render the units on the east bank vulnerable to the French artillery deployed on the west side of the *Région Fortifée de Verdun*. Knobelsdorf had stressed the necessity of attacking along both banks in his Berlin discussion with Falkenhayn on 14–15 December 1915 and his opinion was widely shared by others involved in formulating the GERICHT plan and not just at Stenay; *Oberst* Max Bauer, a heavy artillery specialist serving at *Oberste Heeresleitung*, expressed the same view after visiting the 5.

Armee front to monitor preparations at the end of January 1916, for example. Falkenhayn refused to countenance this however, ostensibly on the grounds that attacking on a larger scale ran the risk of repeating the *Entente*'s errors, and more importantly because the *Westheer* lacked sufficient resources to permit it without stretching its reserves too thinly. When the Crown Prince and his staff persisted, Falkenhayn agreed to release the two *Korps* necessary to widen the battle west of the Meuse 'in good time', although subsequent events strongly suggests that initially at least he had no intention of permitting any such expansion. Shortly before the attack commenced, Falkenhayn informed 5. *Armee* that the two *Korps* earmarked for the expansion would remain under *Oberste Heeresleitung* control, one in the 3. *Armee* sector and the other in the overall *Westheer* reserve; in the event the west bank attack did not begin until 6 March, two weeks after the initial attack.[29]

The root of the problem was that Falkenhayn and 5. *Armee* were actually pursuing the same objective for different purposes. The Crown Prince Wilhelm and von Knobelsdorf were seeking to secure Verdun as rapidly and efficiently as possible as their training dictated, while Falkenhayn was looking to draw out the process to carry out his *Verblutung* experiment irrespective of whether Verdun was actually captured. The *Kaiser* was informed at Potsdam that it was immaterial whether Verdun fell or not for example, but Falkenhayn stated elsewhere that a speedy capture of the city or the high ground overlooking it would draw French reserves into his projected artillery killing ground equally well. He also appears to have been confident of a rapid success, given that he told 6. *Armee* chief of staff *Generalleutnant* Hermann von Kuhl and Austro-Hungarian chief of staff *Feldmarschalleutnant* Franz Conrad von Hötzendorf that the follow up offensive to break the *Entente* would be launched very shortly after GERICHT commenced on 12 February, citing a period of fourteen days to von

Hötzendorf.[30] In part this ambiguity was the result of Falkenhayn's near-obsessive penchant for *Geheimhaltung* (secrecy). This extended to his own staff at *Oberste Heeresleitung*, which was left labouring on planning for the attack on Belfort after the decision to abandon it in favour of Verdun had been made. Discussions for GERICHT with 5. *Armee* were conducted face-to-face with nothing committed to paper and access to the planning process tightly restricted to even those of the highest rank; Falkenhayn was telling Bethmann-Hollweg that he had not made up his mind whether to embark on an offensive in the west after approving the 5. *Armee* scheme, for example.[31]

Be that as it may, Falkenhayn approved the 5. *Armee* plan on 6 January 1916, and allotted Crown Prince Wilhelm forty-one infantry divisions and 1,521 additional guns to carry it out.[32] Enamoured with macabre language, Falkenhayn likened GERICHT to a 'gigantic "suction cup" designed simply to "drain" the French lifeblood', and recent research suggests that he did not deliberately conceal his intentions from his subordinates as once thought.[33] In fact the command echelon of 5. *Armee* was aware of and at least tacitly concurred with Falkenhayn's *Verblutung* strategy, although the Crown Prince expressed disquiet at Falkenhayn's repeated reference to bleeding the French army white at the time; von Knobelsdorf did not voice his alleged dissatisfaction until after the war.[34] On the other hand, Falkenhayn does not appear to have overly stressed the reality of his bleeding experiment to 5. *Armee* either, perhaps unsurprisingly given that his strategy boiled down to deliberately trading its soldiers' lives for those of the enemy as a military objective in its own right, for possibly the first time in modern warfare. However, he talked openly elsewhere of achieving a favourable kill ratio of five French lives for every two German and even the title of the operation pointed to its attritional intent, for *Gericht* can also be translated as 'execution place'.[35] The reason for Falkenhayn's circumspection was likely because troops aware of the fact their lives were being sacrificed as part of a deliberate and cold-blooded numbers game were unlikely to apply themselves fully, and maintaining the fiction that GERICHT was merely a conventional attack to capture Verdun was therefore vital to safeguard German morale. Alistair Horne's judgement that Crown Prince Wilhelm was totally and cynically manipulated by Falkenhayn regarding the reality of GERICHT may thus have been a little wide of the mark, but it was nonetheless true with regard to the rank and file of 5. *Armee*.

Be that as it may, German preparations for GERICHT were impressive in both speed and scale. Approximately 140,000 reinforcements for 5. *Armee* began to arrive behind the 8-mile attack frontage running east from the River Meuse from the end of December 1915. Four complete *Korps* were drawn from the *Westheer*'s remaining *Armees* and grouped into a dedicated assault force to spearhead the attack; 3. *Korps* commanded by *General der Infanterie* Ewald von Lochow, *General der Infanterie* Hans von Zwehl's 7. *Reserve Korps*, *General der Infanterie* Berthold von Deimling's 15. *Korps* and 18. *Korps* commanded by *General der Infanterie* Dedo von Schenck. Each formation had also been allotted a reinforcement pool of 2,400 experienced troops and 2,000 recruits fresh from training in addition to their standard two divisions, which lifted the total manpower available to the assault echelon to around 106,000 men. All formations were battle experienced and well rested, having been withdrawn from the front line for recuperation and additional training before being assigned to 5. *Armee*. Their arrival was also spaced out over the month running up to late January 1916 to avoid alerting the French, with 7. *Reserve Korps* arriving first from 24 December.[36] The entire civilian population of numerous villages were evicted to provide accommodation for the newcomers and to remove prying eyes from the concentration areas behind the Meuse Heights. Closer to the front large concrete shelters called *Stollen*, some capable of holding up to a thousand men, were constructed to shelter the assault troops, in part to prevent the French detecting their presence and in part to protect them from the effects of counter-battery fire on packed assault trenches that had proven deadly in previous attacks; the shelters were stealthily constructed at night to hide their existence from the French. In addition, ten new railway lines with two dozen stations were constructed, along with miles of narrow gauge track to carry men, munitions and materiel almost up to the front line. This expansion of the transport infrastructure was necessary due to the sheer volume of materiel involved; one *Korps* alone required a million sandbags, 125,000 hand grenades, 17,000 digging tools and 6,000 wire cutters, for example.[37]

Great though this effort was, it was dwarfed by that for Falkenhayn's chosen bleeding instrument, the artillery. In all, between 1,201 and 1,220 guns were concentrated under 5. *Armee* control by 12 February 1916, the largest concentration of artillery in history to that date.[38] This was achieved by stripping the remainder of the *Westheer* of modern guns, sometimes in exchange for older models or captured Russian pieces.[39] Individual gun positions were reconnoitred by their crews who then dug gun pits, brought up ammunition and then the guns themselves over successive nights, carefully applying camouflage at every stage. In an additional effort to maintain secrecy ranging shots were staggered to make them look like random harassing fire, and in the later stages only guns assumed to be known to the French were used for routine fire tasks. The vast bulk of the guns were in position by 1 February 1916, although the sheer effort of getting them there cost 5. *Armee* 30 per cent of its transport horses, according to *Generalmajor* Herman Beeg, the Crown Prince's senior artillery commander.[40] At the same time 1,300 trains had brought up a stockpile 2.5 million shells, some of them filled with gas, sufficient for six days of intensive fire; this reflected the German preference for prefacing attacks with comparatively short but extremely intense barrages measured in hours, in contrast to the developing British practice of extending bombardment over a period of days. In addition, the GERICHT plan envisaged firing a further 2 million shells over the succeeding twelve days, which would be brought up by dedicated munitions trains at a rate of thirty-three trains per day. To mitigate the wear and tear on the guns, spare parts, barrels and repair equipment were stockpiled at five dedicated workshops close to the front, and arrangements were made to ship pieces requiring more extensive repair back to factories especially configured to turn them around quickly for return to units.[41]

The nine-hour pre-attack barrage for GERICHT was thus to be the heaviest artillery bombardment in history to that date, with 848 guns targeted upon the French front line in the attack sector alone, and was just part of a sophisticated fire plan that reached well behind the front line. The overall aim of the bombardment was clearly laid out in the German artillery orders: 'No line is to remain unbombarded, no possibilities of supply unmolested, nowhere should the enemy feel safe.'[42] Obliterating the French front line trenches was tasked to the 77 mm *Feldkanone* 96, 100 mm *Kanone* 04 and 14, 105 mm *Feldhaubitze* 98/09 field howitzers and 210 mm *Mörser* 10 howitzers; a full battery of the latter was targeted upon every 150 yards of the line, and their fire was thickened by up to 200 *Minenwerfer* (mine launchers) of 75 mm, 170 mm and 250 mm calibre sited in or close to the German front line. Behind this, longer range pieces including the land-adapted naval 150 mm L/40 *Feldkanone* 8 were targeted upon the French support trenches and positions while 150 mm guns concentrated upon wiping out known French artillery positions with a mixture of high explosive and gas shells in addition to stifling any new batteries the French might deploy, and to shell all the roads and tracks linking the French front line to their rear areas.

Finally there was the siege artillery. Thirteen 420 mm Krupp

Dicke Bertha and seventeen Austro-Hungarian Škoda M11 305 mm howitzers were tasked to pound the French forts, along with three 380 mm SK L/45 *Lange Max* (long Max) naval guns, one of which was tasked to drop a steady forty rounds per day into Verdun proper in an effort to interdict traffic over the city's bridges. The remaining two were targeted on the roads and rail lines beyond Verdun and on the west bank of the Meuse. The guns were located approximately 17 miles north-east of Verdun and were manned by the seventy-four-strong *Marine-Sonderkommando* 1 (naval special force) commanded by *Kapitänleutnant* Hans Walther Schulte, which was headquartered at the village of Rouvrois, a mile or so from the gun emplacements. Each weighed over 200 tons with 50-foot long barrels and massive traversable platforms that were rooted in huge concrete emplacements that mimicked the capital ship turrets they originated from and which also closely resembled the installations erected on the Atlantic Wall twenty-five years later. The emplacements incorporated the gun's sophisticated fire control equipment and were linked to adjacent concrete-protected underground ammunition stores by light railway; the latter were necessary as the 380 mm rounds weighed around 1,600 lb apiece. Two of the guns were emplaced in the Bois de Muzeray and Bois de Warphémont and fired their first rounds on 15 February and 1 October 1915 respectively, the former against Fort Douaumont in concert with 420 mm howitzers from *Kurz Marine Kanone Batterie 3*. The third gun was emplaced at Sorel Farm near Spincourt and fired its first round on 21 February 1916.[43]

The Germans went to great lengths to conceal their preparations for GERICHT. French civilians were forcibly removed from the area behind the German lines, and men were employed manufacturing and painting huge amounts of camouflage netting. Additional aircraft and anti-aircraft guns were drafted in to deny French reconnaissance aircraft access to German airspace, which they succeeded in doing almost until the last minute;

once GERICHT was launched they reverted to protecting their own artillery observation balloons. Neither was the German concealment effort restricted to the Verdun area. Internal security was tight. Liaison officers from elsewhere on the front were banned from visiting the 5. *Armee* area and the details of the artillery fire plan were even kept from Falkenhayn's chief artillery officer. Units to the south were encouraged to plan and prepare for an attack on Belfort as a disinformation measure, an illusion reinforced by a well-publicised visit from Crown Prince Wilhelm. Artillery programmes were carried out on other sectors of the front to create the impression of impending attack, and German agents in neutral countries spread rumours that any operations near Verdun were merely a diversion. The German security and disinformation effort was aided and abetted by a combination of happenstance, geography and climate. French intelligence was hobbled by the loss of one of their major spy networks operating behind the German lines just before preparations for GERICHT began. The broken, wooded terrain and foggy winter weather handicapped ground reconnaissance, and as we have seen, the French troops on the spot were less than diligent. Little if any patrolling was carried out as French front line units preferred to rely on the less uncomfortable and dangerous, but also substantially less reliable, listening posts to monitor German activity. All of this exacerbated the general air of complacency that had grown up at Verdun from mid-1915, although many commanders did what they could to counteract it and draw attention to the weakness of Verdun's defences generally. These included *Général* Herr, commander of the *Region Fortifée de Verdun*. Herr constantly badgered *Grand Quartier Général* for reinforcements citing his instruction from the commander of the *Groupement des Armées de l'Est*, *Général* Auguste Dubail, to prepare defences west of Verdun as justification, but to no avail.

Another especially notable boat-rocker was *Lieutenant-Colonel* Émile Driant, the sixty-year-old commander of the 56ᵉ and 59ᵉ

Bataillons de Chasseurs à Pied holding the front line in the Bois de Caures, 8 miles north of Verdun. In July 1915, concerned that he had insufficient men to man the front line or the materiel and equipment to carry out improvements to his positions as ordered, Driant appealed to his immediate superior. When this failed to elicit a satisfactory response he passed his concerns and growing suspicion that the Germans were preparing a major attack in the region to the *Président de la Chambre des Députés* (President of the Chamber of Deputies) in Paris, Paul Deschanel; Driant had been Deputy for Nancy before the war and Deschanel was a personal friend. As Driant put it in a letter written on 22 August 1915:

> We are doing everything, day and night, to make our front inviolable ... but there is one thing about which one can do nothing; *the shortage of hands* ... If our first line is carried ... our second line is inadequate and we are not succeeding in establishing it; *lack of workers* and I add: *lack of barbed wire*.[44]

Deschanel duly passed Driant's concerns on to Joseph-Simon Gallieni, formerly the Military Governor of Paris who had been appointed *Ministre de la Guerre* on 29 October 1915. Gallieni promptly despatched a delegation to Verdun to investigate. When this confirmed Driant's concerns he passed their report to Joffre with a request for an explanation. This did not go down at all well at *Grand Quartier Général*, with an enraged Joffre demanding the source of Gallieni's information via a letter to the *Ministre de la Guerre* that also claimed that communications to the government outside the military chain of command was 'likely to do serious damage to the spirit of military discipline'.[45] Horne is therefore probably correct in his view that had events not intervened, Driant would have been court-martialled by a vengeful Joffre.[46]

Be that as it may, it was impossible to totally conceal preparations for an operation of the magnitude of GERICHT for any length of time, and the signs were becoming increasingly apparent to those concerned enough to notice. On 12 January *Général* Herr's intelligence section reported that German artillery had begun a ranging programme and observers noted the deliberate demolition of church spires behind German lines to deny French gunners their use as ranging markers for counter-battery fire. French reconnaissance aircraft succeeded in penetrating into German airspace on 17 and 26 January to bring back evidence of German gun positions behind the Côte de Romagne directly north of Verdun, but a combination of bad weather, German fighters and artillery fire on the French airfields and lack of application resulted in only a handful of German artillery positions being located by aerial reconnaissance.[47] Rumours of large-scale German troop movements were supported by information from German deserters about large dumps of artillery ammunition including gas shells, and about the *Stollen* constructed just behind the German front line. It was the latter, probably in conjunction with *Ministre de la Guerre* Gallieni's prompting of Joffre, that finally gained *Général* Herr some attention. On 24 January 1916 *Général* Édouard de Castelnau, Joffre's chief of staff, arrived in Verdun. When his inspection revealed the veracity of Gallieni's assessment, de Castelnau rescinded Dubail's order for new defences west of Verdun, ordered Herr to concentrate on strengthening the existing first and second lines east of the Meuse and promised him reinforcements. On 1 February Joffre, presumably on de Castelnau's recommendation, transferred the *Region Fortifée de Verdun* to the more sympathetic control of *Général* Fernand de Langle de Cary's *Groupement des Armées du Central*. After a three-day inspection of Verdun's defences Langle de Cary confirmed de Castelnau's orders, provided additional manpower to work on the neglected defences and made several more visits to monitor progress between 3 and 20 February.[48] The reinforcements promised by de Castelnau also materialised; the 51ᵉ and 72ᵉ *Divisions d'Infanterie Réserve*, formed from reservists from Lille and Lorraine respectively, arrived on 12 February 1916 and the 7ᵉ and 30ᵉ *Corps* arrived shortly afterward.

This was too little too late however, for the French had run out of time. GERICHT had originally been scheduled to begin on 12 February, but was postponed due to gale-force winds that precluded flying observation balloons or aircraft and, more importantly, fog and snow, which effectively blinded German artillery observers. Possibly due to information from German deserters, the French front-line troops stood on full alert through the nights of 11/12 and 12/13 February, which did not go down well when the predicted attack failed to materialise. On the other side of the line the bad weather obliged the German assault troops to spend over a week in their *Stollen*, subsisting on canned rations and frequently in several inches of water as the shelters were only designed for short-term occupation; they also lacked sleeping accommodation, obliging the bulk of the occupants to march as far as 7 miles through the snow and sleet back and forth to their regular billets.[49] By 20 February the wind had died down and clear winter weather returned with occasional flurries of snow. The Germans fired an intense barrage on French front-line positions in the afternoon that stretched as far west as the Butte de Vauquois, possibly to complete their ranging programme; the French responded with an hour-long counter-barrage from 16:00.[50]

The night of Sunday 20 February 1916 was quiet, cold and clear, so much so that the French could hear the German supply trains and the sound of singing from the German trenches.[51] With clear weather forecast for the following day, the order had gone out from *Oberste Heeresleitung* at Charleville-Mézières. Operation GERICHT was to commence on Monday 21 February.

5

WITH *STOLLEN*, *FLAMMENWERFER* AND *ARTILLERIE*: THE FIRST PHASE OF THE BATTLE, 21 FEBRUARY 1916 – 28 FEBRUARY 1916

Unlike the preceding nine days, the early morning of Monday 21 February at Verdun was cold, generally clear and brightly illuminated by a full moon. In the woods north and east of Verdun, in excess of 1,200 German artillery pieces, ranging from 75 mm *Minenwerfer* located in the front line to massive 420 mm howitzers, were sighted on targets in and behind the French lines. As Alistair Horne put it 'there was hardly room for a man to walk between the massed cannon and ammunition dumps'.[1] Each battery of 77 mm field guns had a stock of 3,000 ready rounds cached on the gun positions with a further 3,000 waiting to be brought up; 105 mm howitzers were stocked with 2,000 ready rounds and the

210 mm and 420 mm howitzers with 1,200 ready rounds.[2] The first shots of Operation GERICHT were fired at 04:00 by the three 380 mm naval guns belonging to *Kapitänleutnant* Hans Walther Schulte's *Marine-Sonderkommando* 1 from their emplacements at Sorel Farm, the Bois de Muzeray and the Bois de Warphémont 17 miles north-east of Verdun. The gun's targets included Verdun's railway station and yard and the city's bridges across the River Meuse but a shell from the first salvo landed in the yard of the Bishop's Palace next to the cathedral; this was likely from the newly installed gun emplaced at Sorel Farm, which fired its first round on 21 February.[3] Whether or not, succeeding shots reduced the rail yard to a cratered ruin and set the station building ablaze in short order, thus interrupting the supply of munitions flowing through the city to the front.[4] Other long-range guns sought out French headquarters, road junctions and other installations. Nearer the front Fort Douaumont was hit by the first of sixty-two 420 mm shells that were to pummel the fort in the first four days of the attack.[5]

The main bombardment began between 07:00 and 07:15 French time when permission to open fire was relayed from 5. *Armee* headquarters. Controlled by six observation balloons, all 1,200 guns began firing along the entire perimeter of the Verdun salient from Les Eparges on the east bank of the Meuse to Malancourt on the west, and the barrage was stretched to include around 50 miles of the front as guns from adjacent formations joined in to confuse the French about the precise location of the coming attack. The guns around the salient fired at maximum rate until 08:00, when they dropped back to a more sustainable rate of fire. The resultant concussion was noticeable 100 miles away; *Général* Fénelon François Passaga felt it pulsing through the floor and heard the distant rumble and thump of the guns in his command post in the Vosges, for example.[6] One French participant later described how the whole area behind the German lines seemed 'to be blowing a gale of flame without interruption'.[7] The bombardment was targeted so efficiently that all communications between Verdun and the French front line had been cut within an hour of the bombardment beginning.[8]

The carefully plotted French artillery positions were saturated with high explosive and phosgene gas shells, against which French respirators offered no protection. French counter-fire consequently fell away to almost nothing with the exception of the French guns brought up as part of the last-minute reinforcement initiated by *Général* de Castelnau at the end of January, as German artillery observers had not had time to plot their locations. French long-range guns thus blew up the regimental paymaster of *Infanterie Regiment* 24, complete with his cash box at Billy-sur-Mangiennes near the Bois de Warphémont, and another French salvo straddled 5. *Armee*'s forward HQ at Vittarville just as *Stabschef* (chief of staff) von Knobelsdorf was reporting to Crown Prince Wilhelm. The Crown Prince and his entourage had come forward to be closer to the action, but hastily withdrew to their permanent HQ at Stenay, 15 miles further north. On the other side of the line in the Bois des Caures a *Capitaine* Pujo, possibly an aviation officer on a fact-finding mission for *Général* Ferdinand Foch at the *Groupement des Armées du Nord*, had driven up to observe the German front line accompanied by a staff officer from 30ᵉ *Corps* headquarters. They too departed swiftly when the barrage began to fall, abandoning a planned visit to *Lieutenant-Colonel* Driant in the process. Similarly the beginning of the German shelling almost caught *Général* Étienne André Bapst, commander of the 72ᵉ *Division d'Infanterie Réserve*, who was riding up to inspect front line positions near Brabant, 6 miles north of his headquarters at Bras-sur-Meuse. His early morning ride up the east bank of the Meuse ended 2 miles short of its objective when the curtain of fire descended as he reached Samogneux, coincidentally the headquarters of the 351ᵉ *Régiment d'Infanterie*. After ordering the latter's commander, a *Lieutenant-Colonel* Bernard, to put his units on alert, Bapst returned to his headquarters at Bras 'at a full trot'.[9]

The shelling fell most heavily on the German's chosen attack sector held by *Général* Paul Chrétien's 30e *Corps*, and specifically the 7-mile stretch of front line running east from the River Meuse occupied by *Général* Bapst's 72e *Division d'Infanterie Réserve* and the 51e *Division d'Infanterie Réserve* commanded by a *Général* Boullangé. Each German battery had been assigned a specific section of the front line and the guns worked relentlessly back and forth across it like a giant invisible plough at a rate of up to forty shells per minute, eradicating trenches, collapsing dugouts and shelters, demolishing concrete bunkers and cutting telephone lines. One brigade headquarters from the 51e *Division d'Infanterie Réserve* was obliged to set up a relay of messengers spaced at 300-yard intervals to maintain contact with its sub-units, with all the risks that entailed.[10] A liaison officer named Champeaux from the 164e *Régiment d'Infanterie* attached to the 51e *Division d'Infanterie Réserve* described the resultant carnage in the Bois de Herebois, on the north-east shoulder of the salient:

> The trees are cut down like wisps of straw; some shells come crashing out of the smoke; the dust produced by the upheaval of the earth creates a fog which prevents us from seeing very far ... We have to abandon our shelter and go to ground in a deep crater; we are surrounded by wounded and dying men whom we are totally unable to help.[11]

At around midday the barrage paused, partly to trick the surviving defenders into thinking that the ground attack was beginning and thus draw them out of their cover, and partly to allow the German artillery observers to assess the damage they had inflicted. When the bombardment restarted the smaller calibre field guns and

Minenwerfer continued to pound the surviving stretches of the French front-line, while the 210 mm howitzer batteries lengthened their range to deal with the second line and communication trenches. At 15:00 the tempo of the bombardment increased as the guns resumed their maximum firing rate, rising to a crescendo at 15:40 in preparation for the ground assault; in the Bois des Caures it was later estimated that 80,000 shells had fallen in an area approximately 1,500 by 1,000 yards.[12] The barrage finally lifted from the French front line at 16:00, after nine hours of near-continuous bombardment, and the German assault troops began to pick their way forward through the smoke, churned earth and uprooted trees.

Although it had no way of knowing it, 30ᵉ *Corps* was about to be assaulted along its entire 7-mile frontage by three full German *Korps*. On the eastern end of the line *General der Infanterie* Ewald von Lochow's 3 *Korps* was facing the Bois d'Herebois occupied by the 51ᵉ *Division d'Infanterie Réserve*. In the centre 18 *Korps* commanded by *General der Infanterie* Dedo von Schenck were opposed by *Lieutenant-Colonel* Driant and his composite force from the 56ᵉ and 59ᵉ *Bataillons de Chasseurs à Pied* dug into the Bois des Caures. To the west *General der Infanterie* Hans von Zwehl's 7. *Reserve Korps* were up against the Bois d'Haumont, held by the 165ᵉ *Régiment d'Infanterie* and a *compagnie* from the 324ᵉ *Régiment d'Infanterie*, and the 351ᵉ *Régiment d'Infanterie* deployed across the narrow strip of relatively level ground alongside the Meuse near the village of Brabant. The GERICHT plan did not call for a general advance when the barrage lifted at 16:00 but for relatively small fighting patrols to probe forward and infiltrate into the French line to locate gaps and identify remaining pockets of French resistance; these could then be subjected to further bombardment and dealt with by the main German advance which was to commence at 07:30 the following day. The reason for the twelve hour delay is unclear but may have been intended to allow the French time to deploy their reserves to be chewed up by the renewed German bombardment. Individual troops were equipped with white armbands for identification in the gathering dusk and had removed the spikes from their helmets to prevent them catching in the tangled brush. The patrols were equipped with drums of signal wire to maintain contact with their own lines and some included teams equipped with oxyacetylene cutters to deal with tangles of French barbed wire. The patrols were led by groups of engineers drawn from the divisional *Pionier Bataillonen* and accompanied by sections from the *Garde Reserve Pionier Regiment*, a specialist unit equipped with *Flammenwerfer* (flame throwers). Invented at the turn of the century by Richard Fiedler to meet a German army requirement, the *Flammenwerfer* was adopted for service in 1911 and saw small-scale action in the Argonne and at Hooge in Belgium in 1915. Consisting of a backpack-mounted cylindrical tank, with separate fuel and gas compartments attached to a rubber hose and steel nozzle with an integral ignition device, the *Flammenwerfer* had a crew of two – one to carry the tank and one to wield the nozzle – and a range of around twenty yards with sufficient fuel for two minutes of continuous firing. GERICHT was the first large-scale employment of the *Flammenwerfer* as a dedicated assault weapon.

The *Flammenwerfer* teams rapidly made their presence felt against the units holding the Bois d'Herebois on the right of the French line, a *bataillon* and a half from the 165ᵉ *Régiment d'Infanterie* from the 72ᵉ *Division d'Infanterie* reinforced with elements of 233ᵉ *Régiment d'Infanterie* from the 51ᵉ *Division*. After driving back a dozen French survivors commanded by a *Sergent-Major* Quintin, the German infiltrators came upon an almost intact and fully manned section of the French line commanded by an *Aspirant* (officer cadet) named Berthon; repeated bursts of flame set the wattle revetment of the trench ablaze, badly burned a number of the defenders and put the remainder to flight. The

German patrol then occupied the smouldering trench and set up a machine gun to fire into the backs of their fleeing adversaries. At the western end of the French line the Bois d'Haumont was held by the 362ᵉ *Régiment d'Infanterie,* a battalion from 324ᵉ *Régiment d'Infanterie* and half a battalion from the 165ᵉ *Régiment d'Infanterie* commanded by *Lieutenant-Colonel* Bonviolle. The latter was holding the eastern end of the wood and was especially hard hit, with trenches levelled, weapons and ammunition buried or unusable and some *compagnies* reduced to a handful of men. More seriously, a half-mile stretch of the front line was held by the survivors from just two platoons, who were exhausted from digging their comrades out from buried trenches and collapsed dugouts. Infiltrators from *General der Infanterie* Hans von Zwehl's 7. *Reserve Korps* overran the entire French front line in short order; the *Flammenwerfer* again proved to be a potent weapon, with one team taking an overawed French officer and thirty-six men prisoner in a single incident. This would have been creditable progress on its own but von Zwehl had unilaterally decided to despatch the first wave of his main assault hard on the heels of his fighting patrols rather than leaving them in their *Stollen* until the following day. His men therefore surged forward through the Bois d'Haumont before Bonviolle could organise a coherent response, isolating and eliminating pockets of French resistance like an incoming *feldgrau* tide. The entire wood was secured after five hours of fighting, with the French survivors withdrawing south to regroup at Haumont village. On learning of the success of 7. *Reserve Korps'* ploy von Knobelsdorf ordered 3. and 18. *Korps* to push forward in the same manner, but the message took too long to reach the former and the latter had run into problems of its own.[13]

The 18. *Korps'* push into the centre of the French line in the Bois des Caures was carried out by elements of *Infanterie Division* 13, *Infanterie Division* 25 and *Reserve Infanterie Division* 13. Rather than a continuous trench, Driant had instead opted to deploy his

Chasseurs in clusters of dugouts on the front line, which ran just inside the northern edge of the wood. Each cluster was manned by a company with 7e *Compagnie* on the left, 9e *Compagnie* in the centre and slightly further north and 10e *Compagnie* on the right commanded by *Capitaine* Séguin, *Lieutenant* Robin and *Capitaine* Vigneron respectively. Behind the front line positions a line of strongpoints had been constructed, with a cluster protecting the right flank, code-named S1 to S4, with S7, S8 and S9 spaced out along and behind the front line running east to west; the left flank was protected by *Abris* (shelter) 17, a larger strongpoint dominating the front line in the west of the Bois des Caures and the open ground to the left toward the Bois d'Haumont. Further back another series of larger concrete bunkers formed Driant's main line of resistance. R1 stood guard over the right rear of the position, deeper in the woods facing south-east toward the neighbouring Bois de Champneuville, R2 occupied by *Adjutant* Carré stood in the centre close to Driant's *Poste de Commandement* (command post) while R3, occupied by *Lieutenant* Simon's 8e *Compagnie* acting as reserve, stood a little further north protecting the south-western aspect of the wood.[14] Driant himself had left the house he rented near Samogneux before dawn for his headquarters at La Ferme de Mormont, riding from there at 06:00 for the Bois des Caures accompanied by his groom; he was at *Lieutenant* Simon's location at R3 by 06:45 supervising the construction of a tunnel shelter shortly before the German bombardment commenced. The shelling worked its way steadily and methodically across a short step back from the French front line, repeating the pattern four times in fifteen-minute increments before shifting and repeating the process across the next step. The initial salvos on the cluster of dugouts occupied by 9e *Compagnie* drove two old soldiers grinding coffee into forty-six year old *Caporal* Marc Stéphane's dugout, which was promptly collapsed by heavy 210 mm shells, as was the nearby 4-metre-deep aid post, although the four medics within dug their way out shaken but unharmed. Further back, one end of the R2 bunker was collapsed by a direct hit, seriously wounding almost a dozen men including a *Lieutenant* Petitcullot, who subsequently succumbed to his injuries, and at S3 *Lieutenant* Simon's unit suffered a number of casualties when a direct hit demolished a 90 mm gun and detonated its store of ready ammunition.[15]

A number of 9ᵉ *Compagnie* had taken shelter in strongpoint S7 and when the barrage lifted to fall on French positions behind the Bois des Caures, Robin had his men stand to, but it was already too late. A German patrol from *Leibgarde Infanterie Regiment* 115, moving close behind the barrage, had infiltrated unseen into the French positions on the left and attacked Robin's party from a communication trench to their rear. Robin was wounded in the foot in the ensuing close-quarter fight in which one *Chasseur* was killed and several more wounded, but Robin managed to retire in good order to S6 before being outflanked and obliged to withdraw again. By this point 9ᵉ *Compagnie* had been reduced to around eighty men and *Caporal* Stéphane was despatched to R2 in search of reinforcements and instructions from *Lieutenant-Colonel* Driant. On the left flank one of *Capitaine* Séguin's two machine gun teams, commanded by a *Caporal* Pot, was taken by surprise by elements of *Infanterie Regiment* 87 while baling out their gun pit and retreated hastily to S9. That strongpoint was manned by a detachment commanded by a nervy *Sergent-Major* Dandauw and the arrival of Pot's team coincided with the approach of German troops in the gathering dusk. Dandauw initially mistook the German troops for friendly stretcher-bearers due to their white recognition armbands but then panicked and ordered a retreat down a communication trench leading to R2 where they were halted by Driant in person. On the French left the situation on the 7ᵉ *Compagnie* front was saved temporarily by Séguin's other machine gun team, commanded by a *Sergent* Léger, occupying *Abris* 17 assisted by a *Sergent* Legrand and six *Chasseurs* with only two working rifles in a nearby trench; Léger fired off all his ammunition and exhausted the *Abri*'s supply of forty grenades before being wounded and rendered unconscious. Only *Caporal* Hutin survived, also wounded, from Legrand's party. *Capitaine* Séguin rallied approximately fifty men along the line linking strongpoints S8 and S9 and held out until a combination of darkness and snow obliged the attackers to pull back.[16]

Driant was informed that the German ground attack had begun by a runner with the immortal words "Voilà les Boches!" He immediately seized a rifle and sallied forth to rally his men with the equally immortal words "We're here, it's our position, and we're not moving from it." Driant single-handedly prevented *Sergent-Major* Dandauw's precipitate retreat from S9 from degenerating into a fully-fledged rout, shrewdly directing Dandauw and his men into a nearby shelter to recover their nerve in preparation to retake their lost position after first light, and gave *Caporal* Stéphane the unfortunate news that no support was likely to be forthcoming and that there were no reinforcements to despatch to *Lieutenant* Robin. In the meantime Robin had organised a counter-attack at 20:00 as demanded by French doctrine that recaptured strongpoint S6 and pushed on to recover a section of 9ᵉ *Compagnie*'s original front line. The attack took the Germans by surprise; assisted by the darkness and more snow, Robin's men captured a number of prisoners, likely from *Leibgarde Infanterie Regiment* 115, who had settled down in the wrecked French front-line shelters to sleep. The prisoners also revealed the unsettling fact that the fighting thus far had only been a patrol action and that the main attack was scheduled to begin at midday the following day. This was likely the reason for Robin's oft-quoted question 'What am I to do against this with my eighty men?' to Driant when the latter visited 9ᵉ *Compagnie* around midnight. The reply was equally unsettling: 'My poor Robin, the order is to stay where we are' and Driant relayed the information to *Général* Bapst's headquarters at

Bras-sur-Meuse in a situation report that ended by assuring Bapst that 'We shall hold against the Boche although their bombardment is infernal'.[17]

Renewed snow and the onset of darkness gradually brought the confused fighting to a halt along the attack frontage. The degree and doggedness of the French resistance came as an unwelcome surprise to the German patrols, which had been assured that nothing would survive their bombardment. Over and above French resilience and stubbornness the barrage had not been as effective in thickly wooded sectors despite its unprecedented weight and duration. The fighting had cost the relatively small German force 600 casualties by midnight on 21 February, Driant's force had lost approximately the same number, and losses in the Bois d'Haumont were likely at least as high if not heavier given the circumstances of the French ejection from their positions.[18] Progress was also uneven; von Zwehl's men had overrun the Bois d'Haumont in its entirety and pushed the French line back for almost a mile, while von Lochow's 3. *Korps* had made more modest gains in the Bois d'Herebois, but in the Bois des Caures the French had driven out some of the *Leibgarde* patrols to the extent of recapturing their original front line in places. The main problem for the Germans was that their tactic of halting the barrage for the night in order to despatch fighting patrols to infiltrate and locate remaining areas of resistance simply failed to work as envisaged; ironically the German's greatest success occurred where von Zwehl elected to ignore the tactic. Even with the attached *Flammenwerfer* teams the patrols lacked the strength to overcome anything but the weakest and most demoralised French opposition and the infiltration mission was hampered even further by a combination of the tangled conditions created by the shelling and the onset of darkness. It is unclear whether the hiatus idea originated from Crown Prince Wilhelm and von Knobelsdorf at 5. *Armee* headquarters or from Falkenhayn at *Oberste Heeresleitung*, but it has all the hallmarks of the latter's *Verblutung* strategy, given that the overnight pause would permit the French to bring up and deploy reserve units ready to be annihilated by the renewed German bombardment.

Be that as it may, on the French left *Lieutenant-Colonel* Bonviolle spent the night rallying the survivors of his detachment from 165ᵉ *Régiment d'Infanterie* and from the 324ᵉ and 362ᵉ *Régiments d'Infanterie* for a counter-attack to retake the Bois d'Haumont. A local attack was ready by 05:00 on Tuesday 22 February but was delayed by the arrival of a runner from *Général* Bapst at 72ᵉ *Division* headquarters informing Bonviolle that reinforcements were en route and ordering an attack against the whole wood at 06:00; the message had been issued at 23:00 the previous night and had thus taken over five hours to cover approximately 5 miles. Bapst then postponed the attack again until 08:30 via a shaky field telephone connection to Bonviolle's headquarters in Haumont village as he waited in vain for the arrival of the 365ᵉ *Régiment d'Infanterie*, which *Général* Chrétien at 30ᵉ *Corps* had transferred to Bapst's command at 22:35. The reinforcements left their billets near Fort Belleville at 02:35 but at 06:30 were ordered to instead take position on a new defensive line established south of the Bois de Caures along the line Samogneux-Côte 344–La Ferme de Mormont.¹⁹ By that point it was already too late for *Colonel* Bonviolle's counter-attack. The German bombardment began again at around 07:00 in its full fury, controlled in part by observers brought up during the night, and von Zwehl elected to repeat his previous day's trick of launching his infantry forward immediately behind the barrage.

Colonel Bonviolle spotted the *feldgrau* mass of *Reserve Infanterie Division* 13 moving out from the Bois d'Haumont from his *Poste de Commandement* in Haumont and immediately cancelled the attack but the word did not reach his depleted 21ᵉ *Compagnie* led by a *Lieutenant* Derome, who led a futile but incredibly courageous charge directly into the rolling wall of German shellfire and the division of German infantry moving up behind it; there were only fifty survivors, a badly wounded Derome among them. Von Zwehl also set *Reserve Infanterie Division* 14 loose along the relatively flat strip of land running alongside the Meuse. A detachment from 44ᵉ *Régiment Réserve Territoriale*, made up of overage and low medical category men, was ejected from the Bois de Consenvoye in short order by *Reserve Jäger Regiment* 5, with one entire French company fleeing back to Samogneux in panic. The remainder of the German formation then rolled over and virtually wiped out a *bataillon* from 351ᵉ *Régiment d'Infanterie* as it tried to plug the widening gap. While this was going on, *Reserve Division* 13 was fighting house-to-house into Haumont in the face of stubborn French resistance, using targeted artillery fire, including that from two 420 mm pieces, to reduce specific locations; a single hit from a 420 mm shell demolished one concrete machine gun post and buried the eighty men within, for example. By 15:00 the French defenders had been reduced to less than 500 effectives and the village was surrounded on three sides; *Colonel* Bonviolle and his headquarters group barely escaped when their cellar *Poste de Commandement* was attacked by a *Flammenwerfer* team. At 16:00 Bonviolle was finally obliged to abandon the village and led the sixty-five survivors to safety. Haumont thus became the first village to fall into German hands during GERICHT, and von Zwehl's 7. *Reserve Korps* had pushed around 2 miles from its jump-off positions, outflanking the French line to the east and threatening Samogneux.[20]

In the neighbouring Bois des Caures *Lieutenant-Colonel* Driant's little band of *Chasseurs* spent the night trying to shore up their shattered defences, but their efforts were inhibited by the darkness and exhaustion and the results were swiftly rent asunder when the German bombardment recommenced at 07:00. The 18. *Korps* had been reprimanded by von Knobelsdorf for its tardy performance the previous day, and *General* von Schenck had concentrated both his divisions in readiness for when the barrage lifted at midday, with *Infanterie Division* 25 ranged against *Lieutenant* Robin's eighty survivors from 9ᵉ *Compagnie* holding the northern tip of the wood, while *Infanterie Division* 21 renewed the attack on *Capitaine* Séguin's depleted 7ᵉ *Compagnie* on the west face. In addition, *Reserve Division* 13, from von Zwehl's neighbouring 7. *Reserve Korps*, attacked from out of the Bois d'Haumont to outflank the Bois des Caures from the west, while *Infanterie Division* 5, from *General* von Lochow's 3 *Korps*, advanced out of the Bois de Ville to do the same from the east. Driant's *Chasseurs* contested every inch of ground, resorting to rifle butts and even stones when the supply of ammunition and hand grenades gave out and in so doing inflicted over 440 casualties on the German first wave.[21] This was the heaviest loss on the whole attack frontage, but the sheer weight of numbers meant the unequal fight could have only one end. *Lieutenant* Robin's party were occupying strongpoint S2, presumably for shelter from the shelling, and the advancing Germans were virtually on top of the bunker before those inside became aware of the threat. According to *Caporal* Stéphane the nearest *Chasseurs* demurred when Robin ordered them to open fire and the young officer then broke down in tears asking what he was supposed to do; the situation was resolved by a German officer calling for surrender in perfect French and all in the strongpoint were captured.[22] Stéphane later trenchantly criticised Robin for lacking 'the guts ... to take responsibility for the outcome of a situation so desperate that it could issue only in senseless death or humiliating surrender' but this seems somewhat harsh.[23] Given that Robin was only twenty-three years of age and consequently lacked independent command experience, it could be equally argued that his performance was exemplary in standing firm in the face of two days of the most intense artillery bombardment in history to that date, as well as carrying out a successful counter-attack on his own initiative. Every man has a breaking point and the evidence shows that Robin travelled a creditably long way down that road before giving way.

Over on the west side of the Bois des Caures, *Capitaine* Séguin's fifty survivors from 7ᵉ *Compagnie* were whittled down to a mere ten with just half a dozen serviceable rifles. The end came when the attackers deployed a *Minenwerfer*, or possibly a 77 mm field gun, at point-blank range. Séguin, already wounded in the foot, reportedly lost his right arm to a shell, and his little band was overwhelmed as his *Sergent-Major* attempted to apply a bootlace as a tourniquet; he was later congratulated on his gallantry by an officer from *Infanterie Regiment* 87.[24] The German tide closed inexorably on Colonel Driant's *Poste de Commandement* near the R2 bunker. While *Lieutenant* Simon's 8ᵉ *Compagnie* managed to hold *Infanterie Regiment* 87 at bay in the west, R1 was overrun by *Infanterie Brigade* 10's advance from the Bois de Ville which swept on to attack R2 from the south-east at around 13:00. As the other pockets of resistance were extinguished, Driant's location attracted more and more attackers who eventually infiltrated between R2 and R3 and attacked the latter in regimental strength, overrunning it and obliging *Lieutenant* Simon to fall back to the area of the regimental aid post. Driant was in the thick of it, rifle in hand, encouraging and exhorting his ever-shrinking band of *Chasseurs* to beat off repeated attacks from three sides in up to battalion strength.

The tipping point came at some point between 14:00 and 16:30 when *Hauptmann* Helmuth Wienskowski from *Feldartillerie Regiment* 61 managed to have two of his 77 mm field guns manhandled up through the debris to bring R2 under direct fire. By this point Driant's force had been reduced to around eighty men and with no effective counter to the field guns, Driant held a brief conference with his surviving officers that decided to attempt a break out south-east to Beaumont, which was still held by a heavily pressed 208ᵉ *Régiment d'Infanterie*. The surviving *Chasseurs* in the vicinity of R2 were therefore divided into three groups to be led by Driant, *Capitaine* Vincent and *Major* Renouard. Driant burned his papers, punctured the regimental rum barrel, and then led his group south via the regimental aid post where *Lieutenant* Simon and the survivors of his 8ᵉ *Compagnie* were still holding out. The latter appear to have acted as a rearguard for the breakout and Simon led them out to Beaumont later only for them to be berated for cowardice by a *bataillon* commander from the 208ᵉ *Régiment*.[25] In the event, Driant barely made it out of the Bois des Caures. He was killed applying a field dressing to a wounded *Chasseur* Papin, gifting the Battle of Verdun its first icon; *Major* Renouard was also killed and *Capitaine* Vincent was wounded twice. In all only a *Capitaine* Hamel, *Lieutenant* Simon and 118 men survived to reach Beaumont from the 1,200 who had manned the Bois des Caures a mere forty-eight hours earlier, although the figure subsequently rose to around 500 as stragglers and wounded were accounted for.[26]

The Germans had thus eliminated or driven out the French defenders of the Bois des Caures by nightfall on 22 February but fighting was still going on to the east. The survivors of 165ᵉ and 233ᵉ *Régiments d'Infanterie* had clung onto their tenancy of the Bois d'Herebois in the face of *Infanterie Division* 6's renewed attack, assisted by the first effective French artillery barrage of the battle, but by the end of the day the Germans had overrun the entire French front line as far south as Brabant and Beaumont. The former was almost cut off by 7. *Reserve Korps* pushing south from Haumont to Samogneux and fell at midday on 23 February, while the latter fell the same day when von Zwehl's men broke through the French second line. The latter then pressed on to encircle Samogneux at 01:00 on 24 February and secured it two hours later; the process was eased by a French artillery bombardment that mistakenly landed on the defenders from the 324ᵉ and 351ᵉ *Régiments d'Infanterie*.[27]

By midnight on 24 February the Germans had overrun the French first and second line trenches and pushed on to a line running east from the Côte de Talou overlooking the Meuse, over the Côte du Poivre and on to the village of Louvemont, almost 4 miles from the original French front line.[28] Falkenhayn's attrition strategy was also working well. *Général* Chrétien's 30ᵉ *Corps*, which had borne the brunt of the initial German assault, had been virtually destroyed. The 72ᵉ *Division d'Infanterie Réserve* had lost 9,828 men killed, wounded and missing and it also lost its commander as *Général* Bapst was relieved of his command on 23 February for withdrawing from Brabant; he thus became the first *limogé* of the Battle of Verdun.[29] Similarly, the 51ᵉ *Division d'Infanterie Réserve* lost a total of 6,396 men in just four days of fighting, with the Germans taking 10,000 prisoners, sixty-five artillery pieces and seventy-five machine guns.[30] Perhaps more importantly, the fighting was drawing in French reinforcements and Falkenhayn's insistence on a measured step-by-step advance was allowing them time to arrive. *Général* Deshayes de Bonneval's largely North African 37ᵉ *Division d'Infanterie* was thrown into the battle piecemeal from 24 February and within thirty-six hours had lost 4,700 men.[31] *Général* Maurice Balfourier's 20ᵉ *Corps* was rushed into the line from Vézelise, 70 miles south of Verdun near Nancy, to buttress the failing 30ᵉ *Corps*. Balfourier's two leading brigades arrived at Verdun in the early hours of 25 February after a gruelling forced march from Bar-le-Duc but without machine guns and with only limited ammunition. Despite this and the protests of the brigade commanders, Chrétien pushed both formations straight into the line without food or rest.[32]

The seemingly inexorable German advance was also starting to adversely affect French morale. A combination of the hellish bombardment, freezing conditions and being parcelled out to unfamiliar commanders caused many of the 37ᵉ *Division d'Infanterie*'s North African soldiers to abandon their posts, in one instance allowing the advancing Germans to capture a number of French heavy guns and four batteries of 75 mm field guns in the Ravin de la Vauche, at the eastern end of the French line near Bezonvaux. Two 240 mm guns, one at Vaux and the other at Cumières west of the Meuse, were also destroyed and abandoned for no clear reason by their panicky crews.[33] Although it was due to the German bombardment, the paucity of French counter-fire raised suspicions among the infantry that their artillery was being withdrawn and they were being abandoned to their fate. Perhaps most damaging of all was the treatment of the wounded, as French medical provision, which was barely adequate at best, began to collapse under the pressure.[34] Pierre-Alexis Meunier, an ambulance driver in the opening stages of the battle, reported hundreds of badly wounded men being obliged to lie exposed to constant German shellfire on the frozen ground at the clearing station at Bras as there were insufficient ambulances to evacuate more than a handful at a time. The 4-mile journey back to Verdun could take up to twelve hours as the shelling rendered the roads increasingly unusable by motor ambulances and panicked what horse-drawn transport was available. For those lucky enough to reach Verdun it all too frequently became a case of out of the frying pan and into the fire, as conditions at the base hospitals in and around the city were only marginally better than those closer to the front, and the transport problem was equally acute. The German 380 mm naval guns had cut the railway line to Châlons-en-Champagne and there were again only a handful of motor ambulances to carry casualties further afield; consequently it could take up to ten hours for a vehicle to complete a 20-mile journey.[35]

After four days of intense fighting the German tide was lapping at Fort Douaumont, which projected north from the main line of defence atop a 390-metre plateau with clear fields of fire to the north and east. Douaumont ought to have presented a formidable and possibly impregnable obstacle to the German advance but, as we have seen, by February 1916 the fort had been stripped of all armament apart from the single 155 mm and two 75 mm guns built inextricably into its retractable Galopin and R05 turrets and its garrison been reduced to a mere fifty-eight overage *Territoriale* soldiers, commanded by *Adjutant* Chenot and a lone sapper sergeant. Having finally cleared the Bois d'Herebois, von Lochow's 3. *Korps* had pushed on to occupy the Bois de la Vauche, less than a mile north of Fort Douaumont on 24 February. The fort lay to the direct front of *Generalleutnant* Georg Wichura's *Infanterie Division* 5, specifically *Grenadier Regiment* 12 on the extreme left of the division frontage where it butted up to *Infanterie Regiment* 24 from *Generalleutnant* Richard Herhudt von Rhoden's *Infanterie Division* 6; the latter had been reinforced with elements of *Infanterie Regiment* 20 from the *Korps*' reserve, presumably to replace losses incurred in clearing the Bois d'Herebois.

The French line facing 3. *Korps* was manned by a mishmash of units, some of them depleted by previous fighting, including the 208ᵉ *Régiment d'Infanterie* from the 51ᵉ *Division* and the 95ᵉ *Régiment d'Infanterie Territoriale*, reinforced with the 2ᵉ *Bataillon de Chasseurs à Pied* and 9ᵉ *Régiment de Zouaves* from *Général* Balfourier's still arriving 20ᵉ *Corps*. The presence of the 95ᵉ *Régiment* and elements from other *Territoriale* units in 3. *Korps*' path was due to the threat the German advance presented to the north-eastern sector of the Verdun salient overlooking the Woëvre Plain where the defences were weak and incomplete. *Général* Fernand de Langle de Cary was concerned that the *Territoriale* units deployed there might panic and compromise the French hold on the east bank of the Meuse, a fear prompted at least in part by *Général* Herr, commander of the *Region Fortifée de Verdun*.[36] Langle de Cary therefore ordered a withdrawal from the Woëvre Plain onto the Meuse Heights at 19:00 on 24 February on his personal responsibility to avoid compromising Joffre in such a potentially controversial move, although the latter confirmed the order when it was referred to *Grand Quartier Général* with the proviso that 'You must hold, facing to the north, the front between the Meuse and the Woëvre with every means at your disposal'.[37] The withdrawal was complete by 22:30 on 25 February but in the meantime Langle de Cary and Herr had gone further despite Joffre's proviso, the former prohibiting the despatch of further troops to the east bank of the Meuse and the latter ordering the defensive works on that side of the river to stand-by to detonate their pre-placed demolition charges, and the evacuation of support units and heavy equipment to the west bank.[38]

The 3. *Korps'* plan for 25 February was for a general advance to the next stage in the step-by-step advance under the by now usual hurricane bombardment, which was scheduled to begin at 08:00. The objective was a line running along the southern edge of the Bois de Hassoule around 750 yards short of Fort Douaumont, which the Germans assumed had been rendered inoperable by their artillery fire. In the event, *Infanterie Regiment* 24 ended up advancing alone when the barrage lifted because runners bearing the advance order failed to reach the other units involved. The elements of the 208e *Régiment d'Infanterie* and the 2e *Bataillon de Chasseurs à Pied* holding the French front line were swiftly swept aside with the loss of two hundred prisoners and *Infanterie Regiment* 24 was on its objective a mere twenty-five minutes after leaving its start line. Precisely why is unclear but, despite its orders to stop short of Fort Douaumont, *Infanterie Regiment* 24 was then drawn piecemeal toward it and one of the world's most modern and sophisticated fortifications fell without a fight in the late afternoon of 25 February. Credit at the time went to *Hauptmann* Hans-Joachim Haupt and *Oberleutnant* Cordt von Brandis, who were awarded the *Pour le Mérite*, Germany's highest gallantry award, by the *Kaiser* in person. However, the first officer involved appears to have been a somewhat less photogenic *Leutnant* Eugen Radtke, and arguably the real conqueror of Fort

Douaumont was a stolid *Pionier Unteroffizier* named Felix Otto Kunze who did the deed in a manner more suited to a comic opera than a military operation, beginning at around 15:30 when he was either blown into the moat by the blast from a shell burst or simply found a way to climb down into it, depending on the account. Armed only with a pistol, Kunze was deserted by his nine-strong *Pionier* section after climbing into one of the unmanned counterscarp casemates set in the outer wall of the moat. Undeterred, he penetrated into the fort and arrested the crew of the fort's 155 mm Galopin turret who promptly escaped down a side corridor, and then locked up another group undergoing a lecture who also escaped while Kunze treated himself to a meal in a deserted mess. By that time Radtke had arrived with his platoon, closely followed by Haupt and von Brandis. Radtke and Kunze's involvement in the affair was then quietly sidelined in favour of their more photogenic superiors who better fitted the profile of the dashing Prussian officer; the fact that von Brandis took the task of carrying the news back to higher command upon himself also had some bearing on the apportioning of the kudos. Kunze and Radtke's role remained unacknowledged until the publication of the German official history after the war. Radtke then received a signed photograph of the exiled Crown Prince for his trouble, while Kunze, by then a policeman, was rewarded with accelerated promotion to inspector.[39]

In Germany the news of the fall of Fort Douaumont was celebrated with bell-ringing, triumphant newspaper headlines and a special holiday for schoolchildren, and the news was also transmitted to the French troops at the front via propaganda leaflets proclaiming 'Douaumont has fallen. All will soon be over now. Don't let yourselves be killed for nothing.'[40] The loss of the fort struck another serious blow against already shaky French morale which *Grand Quartier Général* tried to minimise by issuing misleading reports that concentrated on the losses inflicted on the

Germans, and then claiming that the fort had been demolished and was no more than a useless ruin in any case. As one French official communiqué put it:

A fierce struggle took place around Fort Douaumont which is an advanced work of the old defences of Verdun. The position carried by the enemy this morning, after several fruitless assaults which involved them in very heavy losses, has since been reached and passed by our troops, all the enemy's endeavours having failed to drive them back.[41]

Grand Quartier Général was unable to prevent the repercussions of the loss at the battlefield level however. Fearing being cut off by the fall of Douaumont, the 37ᵉ *Division d'Infanterie* unilaterally withdrew from its key positions on the Côte de Talou and the Côte du Poivre, north-west of the fort, while the surviving troops from the 51ᵉ *Division d'Infanterie Réserve* refused to leave the Verdun barracks where they had been lodged to reorganise, a precursor of events later in the battle. The flow of deserters seeking shelter in Verdun increased markedly and an officer was arrested while running through the streets of the town crying 'Sauve qui peut!' On seeing the city's Meuse bridges being prepared for demolition many of the remaining civilians began to leave Verdun of their own accord with the rest following when an official evacuation was ordered a few days later.

Henry Bordeaux, who served as a staff officer and became the semi-official historian of the battle, witnessed the departure of one group.

Women carrying babies or dragging along little children whose legs were giving way, wagons piled with mattresses and furniture. People had taken what they could, at random. Two old folk, husband and wife, side by side, were panting horribly and in the cold air their breath hung around them like a halo ... Dogs followed the procession, tails down.[42]

Between 22 February and 7 March 6,000 civilians were carried out of Verdun on military transport that had carried munitions and supplies into the city.[43] In some instances the civilians were obliged to abandon food and wine in their houses, which were then looted by stragglers and deserters sheltering in the abandoned buildings around the city. Neither was this restricted to civilian premises, as a military supply depot near the *Citadelle* was thrown open for passing troops to help themselves.[44] The aftermath of the evacuation and the shelling that had prompted it was graphically described by a British war correspondent who visited Verdun at the beginning of March 1916:

I have just been walking down the main street. Everywhere there is silence except for the crashing of the big shells and the sound of splinters falling on roofs ... It was in the Rue Mazel that I met one of the three civilians of Verdun. He was contemplating the view from his door with a contented smile and looked at me with supreme contempt when I scuttled for cover at a particularly loud explosion. 'You are taking refuge on the wrongside [*sic*] of the road', he remarked mildly. 'The left is the side to escape from the splinters, since that is the side from which the Boches are firing. Anyway it is no use ducking, since by the time you have heard the shell the danger is over.'[45]

Operation GERICHT had thus pushed the French to crisis point within five days. Although *Grand Quartier Général* generally maintained a tight grip on the flow of information from the front it proved impossible to keep the lid on the deteriorating situation at Verdun, and rumours of the impending loss of the city circulating around Paris soon reached the ear of *Premier Ministre* Aristide

Briand, who had replaced Viviani in October 1915. Alarmed that this would deal a catastrophic blow to French national morale, to say nothing of bringing down his government, Briand visited *Grand Quartier Général* at Chantilly in the late evening of 24 February looking for reassurance that everything was being done to retain possession of Verdun and the French lodgement on the east bank of the River Meuse. When staff officers began detailing the alleged advantages of abandoning both, Briand lost his temper and threatened to relieve everyone concerned should Verdun be lost, prompting Joffre to reassure the *Premier Ministre* that French forces would remain on the east bank and defend the city. In fact Joffre was being somewhat disingenuous, as he had already discussed the situation with de Castelnau in some detail immediately after authorising Langle de Cary's withdrawal from the Woëvre positions and had already implemented two measures. First, at 21:15 *Général* Philippe Pétain, commander of 2e *Armée*, was ordered to attend a meeting with Joffre at Chantilly at 08:00 the following morning. Second, de Castelnau was despatched to Verdun just after midnight to assess the situation, equipped with full executive authority to implement whatever measures he deemed necessary, with the caveat that a withdrawal to the west bank of the Meuse was only to be implemented as an absolute last resort.[46] Precisely how sincere Joffre was in this regard remains open to question. Commenting later, Pétain claimed that, to his knowledge, Joffre had never intended to abandon Verdun or the lodgement on the east bank, and Joffre's political enemies were subsequently unable to uncover evidence to the contrary, although this was largely due to his deliberately laconic orders which left no paper trail of his intentions outside their precise instructions. Given that Joffre had built his military career on concealing his true opinions and intentions behind 'his silent imperturbability, his sleepy and non-committal manner and his habit of cloudy utterance' it would be surprising if he had not kept his options open in the circumstances. Joffre may well therefore have been behind Herr and Langle de Cary's seemingly deliberate flouting of his stated intentions in preparing to abandon the east bank of the Meuse, especially given the alacrity with which Herr was to reverse his stance on de Castelnau's orders.[47]

Be that as it may, de Castelnau arrived at Langle de Cary's *Groupement des Armées du Central* headquarters at Avize, 25 miles south of Reims, at 04:00 on Friday 25 February. After a long discussion, de Castelnau demurred from his host's pessimistic assessment that the east bank of the Meuse could not be held, and telephoned *Général* Herr and ordered him to hold the east bank 'no matter what the cost ... [or] ... the consequences would be most grave'.[48] After visiting Herr in person as he relocated his *Region Fortifée de Verdun* headquarters to Dugny-sur-Meuse on the west bank 5 miles south of Verdun, de Castelnau spent several hours visiting a variety of units to gauge the situation. In the process he replaced the badly depleted 30ᵉ *Corps* with *Général* Balfourier's still arriving 20ᵉ *Corps*; *Général* Chrétien's formation was withdrawn over the period 25 February – 9 March to reorganise at Pierrefitte-sur-Aire, 25 miles south of Verdun. By 15:30, ironically around the same time *Unteroffizier* Kunze was commencing his single-handed penetration of Fort Douaumont, de Castelnau contacted Joffre by telephone to report that the east bank could be held. He also recommended that Herr be replaced by Pétain as commander of *Region Fortifée de Verdun* and of all reinforcements posted to the area, with orders to halt the German attack north of Verdun. Herr was to be quietly *limogé* in the wake of *Générals* Bapst, de Bonneval and Chrétien. Joffre approved de Castelnau's recommendation within the hour.[49] With the benefit of hindsight it can be seen that this was the first crucial tipping point in the Battle of Verdun, and indeed a momentous decision in its own right. In deciding that the east bank of the Meuse could be held, de Castelnau and Joffre unwittingly committed the French army to play the role of guinea pig in Falkenhayn's *Verblutung* experiment in deliberate attrition, and thus arguably sentenced hundreds of thousands of French and German soldiers to death. Up to this point it was feasible for the French to cut their losses by abandoning their foothold east of the Meuse, and indeed Verdun itself, in favour of a fighting withdrawal to more defensible terrain in the Argonne. From a solely military perspective this would have been the most logical course of action, but military logic was about to become subsumed in the less straightforward matter of national morale, honour and prestige.

The 2ᵉ *Armée* headquarters was located at Noailles, 40 miles north of Paris, and when Joffre's summons arrived at 21:45 Pétain's staff were confronted with the problem of locating him. It took *aide-de-camp Capitaine* Bernard Serrigny just over five hours to track his commander down to the Hôtel Terminus at the Gare du Nord, where he was spending the night with his mistress, Eugénie Hardon; according to Horne, Serrigny was alerted Pétain's precise location by finding 'the great commander's yellowish boots with the long leggings, which, however, on that evening were agreeably accompanied by some charming little *molière* slippers, utterly feminine' in the corridor outside their room.[50] Pétain appears to have been briefed about his new role during his brief 08:00 meeting with Joffre on Saturday 26 February, given that he despatched his intelligence officer to Verdun before receiving confirmation of his appointment from de Castelnau at around 16:00; he then embarked on the 170-mile journey to Verdun, arriving at Herr's headquarters at Dugny at 19:00. Herr himself was close to a breakdown and his staff seemed unsure of anything apart from the fact that Fort Douaumont had fallen; *Capitaine* Serrigny likened the place to a lunatic asylum.[51]

Rather than take over there, Pétain therefore decided to relocate to the *Mairie* (town hall) at Souilly, 14 miles south-west of Verdun on the road to Bar-le-Duc. En route he ran into de Castelnau at around 23:00, who informed Pétain that he was to assume command of all forces at Verdun with effect from midnight and charged him with defending Verdun on the east bank of the Meuse at all costs. On arrival at Souilly Pétain traced the line to be held on a map, and laid out formation responsibilities and boundaries for his chief of staff, *Colonel* Maurice de Barescut. *Général* George de Bazelaire was to command the half of the *Region Fortifée de Verdun* west of the River Meuse, including the section of front line between Avocourt and the Meuse. On the east bank, *Général* Adolphe Guillaumat and 1er *Corps* was to be responsible for the area running east from the Meuse to Douaumont village and *Général* Balfourier's 20e *Corps* for the sector between Douaumont and the point where the line curved south near Damloup. Pétain then performed his first act in command by telephoning Balfourier and ordering him to hold fast. That the call had the desired effect is clear from Balfourier's response: 'Is that you, my general? That's good! Now everything is going to be alright'; *Général* Bazelaire reportedly reacted in a similar fashion when Pétain called him in turn.[52]

As events were to confirm, de Castelnau had chosen wisely in selecting Pétain to address the crisis at Verdun. His pre-war criticism of the doctrine of *offensive à l'outrance* showed he fully understood the relationship between attrition and firepower at least as well as Falkenhayn and, perhaps more importantly given the tenuous state of French morale, he was also popular with both officers and the rank and file. Despite his aloof and formal manner, Pétain had a reputation for husbanding lives and taking care over the welfare of his soldiers and this popularity was clearly reflected by *Général* Balfourier's reaction to his appointment. At this juncture, however, fate turned a perverse hand. The *Mairie* at Souilly lacked the space for living quarters, and while Serrigny procured access to a nearby solicitor's house for Pétain, his staff were unable to light any fires without the smoke coming back into the building. Pétain was therefore obliged to sleep in a chair huddled under his greatcoat in a freezing dining room and, in addition to the hours-long journey from Noailles in a car without heating, the result was perhaps predictable for a sixty-year-old. By the morning of 26 February Pétain had come down with double pneumonia, an infective illness that all too frequently proved fatal in the days before the invention of penicillin. His staff immediately brought down a wall of secrecy around the Souilly headquarters, swearing the diagnosing physician to secrecy and tightly restricting all access to prevent news of Pétain's illness getting out and impacting on already shaky morale. Pétain himself ran the fight to stabilise the situation from his sickbed for several days, despatching Serrigny and de Barescut repeatedly to the front to act as his eyes and ears. The security measures worked far better than might have been expected, and no hint of Pétain's incapacity leaked out; perhaps typically, Pétain made little of the matter and did not even refer to it in his subsequent account of the battle.[53]

While Pétain was fighting the onset of pneumonia his German opponents were continuing their methodical, step-by-step advance. On the east side of the attack frontage 3. *Korps* moved against the village of Douaumont, less than a mile north-west of the fort. The 95e *Régiment d'Infanterie Territoriale* was virtually wiped out defending the village on 25 February and its replacement, Pétain's old command, the 33e *Régiment d'Infanterie*, then lost a third of its strength within three days when a *bataillon* was virtually wiped out and one *compagnie* reduced to just nineteen men; the losses included *Capitaine* Charles de Gaulle, who was wounded and captured. However, 3. *Korps* did not succeed in totally overrunning Douaumont village either and the fighting took an equally heavy toll on the attackers, with its constituent formations suffering grievous loss as well. One *bataillon* from *Leib Grenadier Regiment* 8 was reduced to 196 men while *Grenadier Regiment* 12 lost thirty-eight officers and 1,151 men; *Infanterie*

Regiment 24 suffered its heaviest casualties of the battle to date, and *Jäger Bataillon* 3 suffered 413 casualties on 27 March alone. This was the first day the German advance failed to take any additional territory, according to the German official history, and *Oberste Heeresleitung* acknowledged that 'the enemy has brought the offensive on the [Meuse] Heights temporarily to a halt'.[54] It took 3. *Korps* until 4 March to finally secure the shattered ruin of Douaumont village, which had been reduced to rubble by German artillery fire, again including the use of 420 mm howitzers to reduce individual buildings and strongpoints.

Events followed a similar pattern in the centre and western end of the attack frontage. In the centre 18. *Korps* was stymied in its attempt to capitalise on the precipitate departure of the 37ᵉ *Division d'Infanterie* from the Côte du Poivre by elements of *Général* Balfourier's 20ᵉ *Corps*; a major factor in this was the deployment of a number of field guns to the *Ouvrage* de Froideterre overlooking the Côte du Poivre, which poured fire into the attackers over open sights. To the west von Zwehl's formerly triumphant 7. *Reserve Korps* suffered equally badly. An attack on the Côte de Talou by *Füsilier Regiment* 37 and *Reserve Jäger Regiment* 5 was stopped cold by French guns massed on the west bank of the Meuse which seemed immune to German counter-fire. On 27 February one of *Reserve Infanterie Division* 13's regiments lost more men to artillery fire while in reserve that it had lost in the initial assault upon the Bois d'Haumont and *Leibgarde Infanterie Regiment* 115 and *Infanterie Regiment* 117 had lost a thousand men apiece. An attempt to break the stalemate before Samogneux by pushing a force over the Meuse ended with virtually all the participants being killed or captured, many after becoming enmeshed in barbed wire entanglements hidden below the surface of the flooded river.[55]

There were two principal reasons for the German loss of momentum. First, the German formations involved had been fighting virtually non-stop for a week and the cost was starting to impinge on their operational effectiveness. By 29 February overall German losses matched French losses at 25,000 men and by 12 March, when 3. *Korps* and 18. *Korps* had to be withdrawn from the line as they were verging on being declared combat ineffective, the latter alone had lost 295 officers and 10,309 men.[56] Second, the German artillery had begun to lose its potency. In part this was due to the German advance pushing up to 6,000 yards from the 21 February start line, which extended the guns closer to the upper end of their range limit; the 77 mm field gun had a maximum range of around 9,000 yards depending on the version, and the 210 mm howitzer around 12,000 yards for example. A meticulous phased plan to move the artillery line forward had been implemented from the night of 23/24 February, which would have been no mean feat in the best of conditions given the sheer physical weights involved; a 210 mm howitzer weighed around 7 tons and a 420 mm piece 42 tons.[57] However, the movement plan became increasingly difficult to implement due to the unanticipated difficulties of moving such weights where the few metalled roads had been destroyed and the already uneven terrain had been comprehensively torn up by shells; the problem was compounded further by a sudden thaw on 28 February that turned the torn-up ground into a morass. This and the lengthening distance from the railheads also interfered with ammunition supply which, in conjunction with growing exhaustion among the gun crews, impacted on rates of fire. The supply situation became so acute at one point that several gun batteries had to be temporarily removed from the line as there was no ammunition for them to fire. In addition, the intensive firing itself was starting to impact on the guns, most spectacularly when one of *Kurz Marine Kanone Batterie* 3's 420 mm howitzers was brought forward to the Bois des Fosses to bring it within range of Fort Souville; the third round from the new location detonated prematurely in the worn out barrel, killing most of the 240-strong crew.[58] The overall result of all this was that German infantry attacks were increasingly being met by unsuppressed French defences and rapid counter-attacks while the French artillery was also becoming increasingly effective; *Generalleutnant* Wilhelm von Lotterer, 3. *Korps'* artillery commander, was killed by a shell splinter on 3 March while visiting *Feldartillerie Regiment* 54's forward observation post in Fort Douaumont, for example.[59]

The other reason for the French resurgence was Pétain who, despite his pneumonia, efficiently and diligently exerted his control over all strands of the battle. One of his first acts was to reverse the policy toward Verdun's forts and other defensive works, which were reinforced with additional guns and infantry with orders to defend them to the death. Between 27 February and 6 March a defence in depth was organised with four distinct defence lines, and, in an effort to reduce casualties from the German *Trommelfeur* barrages, the front line was reorganised into a lightly-held 'advanced line of resistance' up to 500 yards in front of the 'principal line of resistance' which was to be strongly contested and maintained via immediate counter-attack if necessary. At the back the forts in the inner ring of defences, Forts Tavannes, Souville and Belleville were linked together by a network of trenches dubbed the 'Panic Line' by the troops detailed to do the digging, intended as a last-ditch backstop position. In line with his pre-war dictum that firepower killed, Pétain applied himself to expanding the French artillery into a force capable of meeting its German opponent on equal terms. Commanders were instructed to employ their artillery assets in an offensive as well as defensive manner and artillery fire plans were fired daily to boost the morale of the infantry manning the trenches. Pétain also massed large numbers of guns, many of them the accurate and capable de Bange 155 L pieces, on the west bank of the Meuse and on 29 February ordered them to keep the German-held sector of the east bank under constant fire. Many guns were emplaced within or near the forts on the Bois de Bourrus ridge, where the terrain protected them from German counter-fire and from where they could enfilade German troops as they crossed the ravines running down to the River Meuse.[60]

Important as this was, Pétain's most crucial contribution at this point was connected to maintaining the flow of men and materiel into Verdun, a vital concern given that French manpower in the vicinity of Verdun soon totalled around half a million men and 170,000 draught animals, with the latter alone requiring around 2,000 tons of forage per day.[61] As we have seen, the Germans had severed Verdun's mainline rail links to the south and west and the city was thus reliant on two parallel arteries running the 30 miles north-east from Bar-le-Duc. One was a narrow gauge military railway nicknamed the *Meusien* that terminated at Nixéville, 8 miles west of Verdun, and by the end of March 1916 was carrying thirty-two trains per day.[62] The other was an unmetalled minor road which, by a happy accident, had been expanded to seven yards width in 1915, sufficient to allow two-way motor traffic. The route was administered by two engineer officers, a *Major* Richard and *Capitaine* Doumenc, and Pétain lost no time in interviewing them to ascertain what resources were required to keep the road open and ensuring they were forthcoming. The equivalent of a division was thus set to work building a broad gauge railway linking Bar-le-Duc to the existing line at Revigny-sur-Ornain, 11 miles to the north-west while around 10,000 labourers, many from Indo-China and Senegal, were employed in maintaining the surface of the road. The work consumed an estimated 750,000 tons of stone over the ten-month span of the battle, much of it mined in local quarries and shovelled directly under the wheels of moving trucks.

Known at the time simply as *la Route* (the road) and later immortalised by the patriotic writer Maurice Barrès as the *Voie Sacrée* (Sacred Way), the road was divided into six self-contained sections, each with its own repair workshops, mechanics, engineers and labour force. The carriageway was reserved exclusively for motor vehicles, with breakdowns being tipped unceremoniously off the road for repair teams to recover later; horse drawn transport was banned, presumably to protect the unmade road from being ploughed by hooves, and the heavily laden infantrymen were restricted to marching through the fields alongside the road. By the time Pétain took command at Verdun *Major* Richard had presciently assembled a fleet of 3,500 motor trucks by commandeering civilian vehicles across France, no mean feat considering that at the outbreak of war in 1914 the French army could only muster a mere 170 vehicles. Richard also designed the system for deploying the vehicles dubbed *noria*, the French term for an industrial waterwheel. At any given time half the available vehicles would be en route to Verdun loaded with supplies, while the other half headed away loaded with relieved units or the wounded. Between 22 February and 7 March the trucks carried 2,500 tons of supplies and 22,500 tons of ammunition into Verdun and 6,000 evacuated civilians out of the city.[63]

An anonymous French driver, cited in a report in *The Times* on 23 February 1916, graphically described the strain upon the drivers involved:

On arriving ... we did the journey [from Bar-le-Duc to Verdun] twice almost without stopping: that is to say, 48 hours without sleep and almost without eating. I do not know if you can imagine what it means to drive one of these lorries weighing five tons and carrying an equal weight in shells, either during a descent of 12 or 14 per cent and with a lorry just in front and one just behind, or driving during a frosty night, or without lights for short intervals when nearing the front. Can you see a driver alone in his lorry, whose eyes are shutting when a shock wakes him suddenly, who is obliged to sing, to sit very upright, to swear at himself, so as not to sleep, not to throw his lorry into a ravine, not to get it stuck in the mud, not to knock to pieces the one in front? And then the hundreds and hundreds of cars coming in the contrary direction whose lights blind him! If you can imagine all this, be happy that you can spend your nights comfortably in bed.[64]

The system worked, even when the sudden thaw of 28 February turned the road to liquid mud up to eighteen inches deep, although *Major* Richard was obliged to use Pétain's authority to press every available *Territoriale* soldier into service shovelling gravel into the muddy maw. Over the following week 190,000 men flowed north into Verdun, a rate that settled down to a steady weekly flow of 90,000 men and 50,000 tons of materiel; at its peak of activity in June 1916, 12,000 trucks were moving back and forth along the road around the clock, passing any given spot at a rate of one truck every ten to fourteen seconds.[65]

Pétain had thus pulled back the French defence from the brink of collapse despite his double pneumonia, and set up a logistical lifeline to provide that defence with the men and materiel necessary to maintain the fight. This was rapid and prescient work, for the Battle of Verdun was about to expand significantly.

6

LE MORT-HOMME AND *CÔTE* 304: THE BATTLE EXPANDS TO THE WEST BANK OF THE RIVER MEUSE, 6 MARCH 1916 – 29 MAY 1916

In just over a week Operation GERICHT had pushed the French front line back up to 6,000 yards and captured Fort Douaumont, one of the most advanced fortifications in the world. The attack then began to lose momentum in the face of stiffening French resistance and difficulties in keeping the gun line up with the advance and maintaining the unprecedented artillery ammunition expenditure. Neither did progress toward Falkenhayn's *Verblutung* strategy work as expected. By the end of February 1916 German losses were equal with those of their French opponents at around 25,000 men each and by 12 March two of the three German *Korps* that had begun the assault on 21 February had suffered such heavy losses they had to be withdrawn from the line.[1] In addition, a resurgent French artillery arm under the guidance of the new

commander of the *Region Fortifée de Verdun*, *Général* Philippe
Pétain, was extracting an increasing toll on the Germans. This was
especially the case with the guns massed on the west bank of the
River Meuse, which were able to fire largely unhindered into the
exposed flank of the German advance down the opposite bank.

The underlying problem was therefore Falkenhayn's insistence
on attacking down only one bank of the Meuse, a flaw predicted
before the event by a number of high ranking officers, including
Crown Prince Rupprecht, Crown Prince Wilhelm and his chief of
staff *Generalleutnant* Constantin Schmidt von Knobelsdorf from 5.
Armee, and *General der Infanterie* Hans von Zwehl commanding
7. *Reserve Korps*, among others. These criticisms were based on
the findings of German pre-war manoeuvres, which highlighted
the need for a simultaneous advance along both banks of the
Meuse in order to avoid exposing it to fire from the opposite bank,
in this instance the riverside flank created by the German advance
on the east bank to French artillery massed on the west bank.[2]
The flanking fire was making itself felt as early as 27 February to
the extent that *General der Infanterie* Konrad Ernst von Goßler's
6. *Reserve Korps*, which was holding the line west of the Meuse,
launched an unsuccessful *coup-de-main* attack in an effort to
overrun the French artillery positions, presumably on orders from
5. *Armee* headquarters.[3]

In fact, 5. *Armee* headquarters had actually begun requesting
reinforcements to expand the attack to the west bank on 24
February and again by telephone on 26 February, when the
French defence was teetering on the brink of collapse and 5.
Armee possessed only a single regiment in reserve to exploit the
situation. Falkenhayn refused both requests on the grounds that
the advance along the east bank was proceeding satisfactorily,
but did supply around half the replacements necessary to offset
losses there, albeit in small increments.[4] It was not until the attack
effectively stalled on 27 February that Falkenhayn modified his

position, with the failure to secure the Meuse Heights as planned leading him to question the wisdom of continuing with GERICHT against exploring opportunities on other *Armee* fronts, at least according to his own post-war account of events. The upshot was a conference with Crown Prince Wilhelm and von Knobelsdorf at 5. *Armee* headquarters at Stenay on Tuesday 29 February. There, the Crown Prince recommended GERICHT should continue, providing the attack was spread to the west bank to alleviate the pressure on the east bank, that *Oberste Heeresleitung* undertook to provide men and resources to the extent required, and that it should be terminated if German losses exceeded those of the French. For his part, von Knobelsdorf persuaded Falkenhayn that the only impediment to success was the flanking fire from the French guns across the Meuse to the west and Fort Vaux in the east, although the latter was presumably from French guns stationed nearby given that the fort proper boasted only a single 75 mm R05 turret.[5]

Falkenhayn therefore granted permission for an attack on the west bank employing *General* von Goßler's 6. *Reserve Korps*, reinforced with *Infanterie Division* 11, *Reserve Infanterie Division* 22 and twenty-one heavy artillery batteries; the latter reinforcements were immediately released from 10. *Reserve Korps*, which was serving as *Oberste Heeresleitung* reserve at that time.[6] Falkenhayn's acquiescence to 5. *Armee*'s requests suggests his alleged crisis of confidence in GERICHT may have in reality been for later effect, and that his interest in his *Verblutung* experiment at the time remained undiminished. In fact, while a diversion from his initial intent, Falkenhayn's support for expanding the battle to the west bank of the Meuse was entirely in keeping with the bleeding experiment, insofar as the latter could not properly commence until the Meuse Heights were in German hands. This was in part because they were necessary as an artillery platform and to provide sufficient threat to Verdun to draw in the French reserves to be bled, and it is entirely possible that Falkenhayn thus viewed the expansion to the west bank of the Meuse merely as a tangential but necessary expedient toward fulfilling his original aim. Be that as it may, the objective of the west bank assault was three connected sections of high ground around two miles behind the French front line. The 256-metre high Côte de l'Oie (Goose Ridge) ran west from the River Meuse near Regnéville for approximately 3 miles to Cumières before rising to a twin-peaked feature dubbed locally, with sinister prescience, *le Mort-Homme* (the Dead Man) before rising to the slightly higher Côte 304 and then falling away to the village of Avocourt where the Verdun salient gave way to the regular front line running west through the Argonne toward Reims. The *Mort-Homme* provided unrivalled observation in all directions and especially across the valley formed to the south between it and the Bois de Bourrus ridge, where the bulk of the French artillery firing into the German flank on the east bank of the Meuse was stationed. The ground itself was more open and rolling than the broken, heavily forested terrain on the east bank, the only sizeable areas of woodland being the Bois de Corbeaux and Bois de Cumières at the western end of the Côte de l'Oie.

General von Goßler elected for a two-phased attack beginning on 6 March that focussed initially on securing the Côte de l'Oie and *Mort-Homme*; the second phase, scheduled to begin on 9 March, was to secure Côte 304 and Avocourt.[7] In addition the eastern end of the Côte de l'Oie, which projected into a loop in the River Meuse, was to be secured with the assistance of an assault river crossing by *General* von Zwehl's 7. *Reserve Korps*, and a supporting attack against the Fort Vaux sector by *General der Infanterie* Erich von Gündell's 5. *Reserve Korps* was to commence on 7 March. The attack was to be preceded by a bombardment of the same intensity as 21 February, with guns sited on the east bank thickening the fire from 6. *Reserve Korps'* reinforced artillery contingent. With only six days grace, preparations began immediately and while assembling the troops, stores and ammunition for the attack at such relatively short notice was undoubtedly a masterpiece of staff planning and logistics, especially given that the weather reverted to snow storms alternated with heavy rain, this haste also undermined security. French observers noted the German build up while it was in progress, drawing a caustic comment from Pétain that his opponents did not know their business. *Général* George de Bazelaire, commander of 7ᵉ *Corps* and the portion of the *Region Fortifée de Verdun* west of the River Meuse, was thus able to stockpile large quantities of artillery ammunition and reinforce his line with four additional divisions, with a fifth in reserve.

The German preparatory bombardment began at 07:00 French time on Monday 6 March after a night of snow, once again mixing high explosive shells with projectiles containing phosgene gas. Before long de Bazelaire's 7ᵉ *Corps* headquarters was reporting to Pétain that its front line had been badly shattered while the support line, supposedly safely ensconced on reverse slopes, was being ravaged by high trajectory fire from German howitzers that once again effectively severed communications with the front line. The barrage lifted at 10:50 and *General* von Goßler's men advanced southward from their trenches and shelters. Matters went well on the eastern end of the attack frontage alongside the Meuse held by the 67ᵉ *Division d'Infanterie* commanded by *Général* Ernest Jean Aimé, which had only experienced German *Trommelfeur* via second-hand accounts of the fighting on the east bank. *Generalleutnant* Otto Riemann's *Reserve Infanterie Division* 22 quickly overran the French front line, the battered ruins of Forges-sur-Meuse and pushed on toward Regnéville while *Fusilier Regiment* 37 and *Reserve Jäger Regiment* 5 from von Zwehl's *Infanterie Brigade* 77 crossed the Meuse under cover of a snowstorm at Brabant and Champneuville, north and south of the eastern end of the Côte de l'Oie. Von Zwehl, once again exhibiting his flair for the unorthodox, supported the crossing with direct fire from an armoured train driven up almost to the front line until French artillery observers on the Bois de Bourrus ridge spotted the steam plume from the locomotive and obliged it to beat a hasty retreat. Unexpectedly stiff French resistance in Regnéville disjointed the German attack and prevented von Zwehl's men from supporting 6. *Reserve Korps'* effort against *Pointe* 256 atop the Côte de l'Oie, but the latter was taken after repeated costly assaults at 18:00. In a major departure from events on 21 February, the French artillery struck back with extremely effective counter-fire. The effects of this were somewhat nullified in the area close to the Meuse by boggy ground that simply absorbed much of the explosive force but further west it held back the German advance toward the Bois de Corbeaux that linked the Côte de l'Oie and the *Mort-Homme*, where it had been intended to employ the infiltration tactics to outflank the latter feature from the north-east.[8]

The Germans resumed the attack after an even more intense bombardment across the entire sector in the morning of Tuesday 7 March and by the afternoon had secured the whole of the Bois de Corbeaux. The German success was due in part to the gradual collapse of the 67ᵉ *Division d'Infanterie* which was met with customary draconian severity by 7ᵉ *Corps'* headquarters. The commander of the unit that had given up Forges was to face a court martial for failing in his duty and *Général* Aimé was warned that machine guns and artillery would be used against any units attempting to retreat. Despite, or possibly because of, this, 3,000 men from the 67ᵉ *Division* surrendered in the first forty-eight hours of the attack, 1,200 of them from *Lieutenant-Colonel* Mollandin's 211ᵉ *Régiment d'Infanterie* holding the Bois de Corbeaux; Mollandin was wounded and captured conducting a last-ditch defence of the wood which likely saved him from facing a court martial. Possession of the Bois de Corbeaux provided the Germans with a direct route onto the eastern end of the *Mort-Homme* and the task of wresting it from them fell to fifty-year old *Lieutenant-Colonel* Camille Macker and the 92ᵉ *Régiment d'Infanterie* from *Général* Charles Pauffin de Saint-Morel's 26ᵉ *Division d'Infanterie*. When the German attack began Macker and his men were in de Bazelaire's reserve, camped under near constant snow in a wood near Dombasle-en-Argonne, 9 miles west of Verdun and roughly the same distance south of the *Mort-Homme*. On 6 March the 92ᵉ *Régiment* marched in sub-zero temperatures to another wood near Esnes-en-Argonne in the lee of the *Mort-Homme*, where they spent a night with no shelter before moving to a stand-by position near Chattancourt, again with no shelter or field kitchen. It was there that *Lieutenant-Colonel* Macker was ordered to retake the Bois de Corbeaux at 07:00 on 8 March which entailed another sleepless night as the move up to the start line began at 03:00. The speed of the German advance had left no time for digging jump-off trenches, and the *Régiment* was thus obliged to form up for the attack in the open around a thousand yards from the German line on the edge of the Bois de Corbeaux.

The 92ᵉ *Régiment* advanced under continuous German fire led by Macker in person, immaculately shaven and with his magnificent moustache washed and waxed in issue *pinard* wine in lieu of water, armed only with a cane and smoking a cigar. The pace was increased to the double when German machine gun fire began to tear gaps in the French line 200 metres from the wood which, in conjunction with the death of the immediate German commander, unnerved some of the defenders and prompted them to withdraw. At 100 metres Macker ordered a charge, the momentum of which carried the French advance through the Bois de Corbeaux and into the adjacent Bois de Cumières and the objective was cleared at 07:20 after twenty minutes hand-to-hand fighting. Macker then found the time to compose a congratulatory Order of the Day for his men:

Officers, NCOs, Corporals and Soldiers of the 92ᵉ and of the 1ᵉʳ Company of Brigade machine gunners: Today you have, with magnificent élan, executed a superb counter-attack, on a flat ground of more than 800 metres and under a terrible hurricane of fire. The enemy has not been able to hold in the face of your valiant effort. I can only find one thing to say to thank you, and that is that I have lived, thanks to you, the most wonderful hour of my life as a soldier. France has the right to be proud of the 92ᵉ.

However, élan and courage were simply not enough to ward off German superior numbers or their artillery, and the 92ᵉ *Régiment* was slowly but surely forced to give ground as the fighting see-sawed back and forth across the increasingly shattered and churned up forest. *Lieutenant-Colonel* Macker led his now sorely depleted *Régiment* in another attack to clear a small wood adjacent to the Bois de Corbeaux at dawn on Friday 10 March, but at that point his luck ran out and he was killed by a German machine gun while going forward to congratulate one of his *bataillon* commanders, who was also killed. A rapid German riposte then recaptured the entire Bois de Corbeaux after intense fighting that reduced one German *bataillon* to 300 men and the wood remained firmly in German hands thereafter.[9] The near suicidal courage of Colonel Macker and his men and their determination to close with the bayonet provides a textbook example of *attaque à l'outrance* philosophy inculcated in all ranks of the French army in the run up to 1914, but also clearly illustrates the cost. In two days of fighting the 92ᵉ *Régiment d'Infanterie*'s 1ᵉʳ *Bataillon* was reduced to 140 all ranks and the 2ᵉ *Bataillon* to 166, with the latter's losses including 600 wounded.[10]

While all this was going on 5. *Reserve Korps*' attack on the Fort Vaux sector east of the River Meuse was delayed by difficulties with artillery ammunition supply, and did not commence until 8 March. The attack frontage was defended by elements of

Général Amédée Nicolas' 120ᵉ *Division d'Infanterie*, specifically the 408ᵉ *Régiment d'Infanterie* holding the battered ruins of Vaux village a mile or so north of the fort and the 409ᵉ *Régiment d'Infanterie* facing the *Ouvrage* d'Hardaumont a mile beyond that, which had been overrun by *Reserve Infanterie Regiment* 98 and *Infanterie Regiment* 155 from *Reserve Infanterie Division* 10 on 26 February. The sector was far from quiet prior to the attack, with Vaux being constantly shelled from 3 March while the *Ouvrage* d'Hardaumont changed hands three times between 4 and 7 March. The pre-attack bombardment proper commenced at 03:00 on 7 March and in the course of the day the French were driven out of the *Ouvrage* d'Hardaumont, although they managed to hold Vaux village, with the 409ᵉ *Régiment d'Infanterie* beating off twelve separate German attacks in the course of the afternoon of 8 March. A thirteenth attack left the French clinging to one small portion of the village and by 9 March the fighting had rendered both units ineffective; they were withdrawn during the night. The fighting had cost the 408ᵉ *Régiment d'Infanterie* twenty-six officers and 1,009 men killed, wounded and missing, while the 409ᵉ *Régiment d'Infanterie* lost thirty-four officers and 1,479 men.[11] The 5. *Reserve Korps* units involved also suffered badly, and the attack ended in something of a farce. At some point during the confused fighting a rumour reached the commander of *Reserve Infanterie Division* 9, *General der Infanterie* Hans Karl Moritz von Guretzky-Cornitz, that Fort Vaux was undefended as Fort Douaumont had been. Without any attempt to verify the accuracy, or otherwise, of the rumour, von Guretzky-Cornitz, apparently looking to replicate von Brandis' exploitation of the fall of Fort Douaumont, immediately put together a suitably self-aggrandising report for 5. *Armee* headquarters at Stenay, which promptly passed it on up the chain of command without verifying it either. The report was then broadcast across the world as a major triumph and the *Kaiser* awarded von Guretzky-Cornitz the *Pour le Mérite*. Meanwhile the alleged conqueror of Fort Vaux had ordered one of his units to occupy the fort by forming up in column and marching up the glacis. Unfortunately for the German troops involved, the fort was not only fully manned, but the garrison were rather more engaged than *Adjutant* Chenot and his overage *Territoriale* soldiers had been at Douaumont, and the would-be occupiers were driven off with heavy losses. The French troops in Vaux proper also demonstrated admirable application by clinging to their corner of the ruined village until the end of March.[12]

French propagandists seized on the German reverse at Fort Vaux to ease their embarrassment over Douaumont, while to Pétain's chagrin Joffre and the *Grand Quartier Général* began talking enthusiastically of counter-offensives on the assumption that the German attack had run out of steam. This was swiftly proven to be wishful thinking however, as back on the west bank of the Meuse *General* von Goßler's 6. *Reserve Korps* renewed its effort against the *Mort-Homme* on Tuesday 14 March. After a six-hour *Trommelfeur* bombardment, that at its height delivered 120 shells per minute, the attackers finally succeeded in taking the lower, northernmost of the feature's two peaks. In so doing 6. *Reserve Korps* had finally partially secured the primary objective of the west bank attack after a week's costly fighting rather than the two days or so originally envisaged, costing *Reserve Infanterie Divisions* 11, 12 and 22 around 10,000 casualties.[13] As so often during the conflict, possession of the new territory merely brought more problems in its train. German artillery emplaced on the Côte de l'Oie to suppress the French artillery as planned was unable to make any impression on the French guns massed behind the Bois de Bourrus Ridge and, more importantly, came under sustained and increasingly accurate fire from other French batteries located in the lee of Côte 304 to the west. Von Goßler therefore pressed ahead with the second phase of his plan even though the *Mort-Homme* had not been fully secured and tasked *Infanterie Division* 11 to take Côte 304, confusingly supported by *Reserve Infanterie Division* 11. The new assault was aimed at a re-entrant in the Bois d'Avocourt just south of Malancourt and 3 miles west of Côte 304 held by the 111ᵉ, 141ᵉ and 258ᵉ *Régiments d'Infanterie* from *Général* Guyot d'Asnieres de Salins' 29ᵉ *Division d'Infanterie*. This was allegedly the most heavily defended sector in the French line west of the Meuse, fortified with numerous strongpoints and a triple-apron of barbed wire 50 yards wide. Nonetheless, the customary *Stollen* deep shelters had already been constructed in anticipation by *Infanterie Division* 11 along with two mines laid under the French line, in spite of French heavy mortar fire that killed a number of men employed in the construction. In addition, valuable intelligence on the defences had been gleaned from numerous French deserters from the 29ᵉ *Division d'Infanterie* holding the Bois d'Avocourt including details of routes through the barbed wire.[14]

The by now customary *Trommelfeur* bombardment commenced at 07:00 French time on Monday 20 March, thickened with 13,000 rounds from *Minenwerferen* deployed in the German trench lines. The reality of being under such shelling was graphically described by *Sergent* Richard Thoumin, a machine gunner from the 26ᵉ *Régiment d'Infanterie*:

> The pounding was continuous, and terrifying. We had never experienced its like during the whole campaign. The earth around us quaked, and we were lifted and tossed about. Shells of all calibres kept raining on our sector. The trench no longer existed, it had been filled with earth. We were crouching in shell-holes, where the mud thrown up by each new explosion covered us more and more. The air was unbreathable. Our blinded, wounded, crawling and shouting soldiers kept falling on top of us and died while splashing us with their blood. It really was a living hell ... We were deafened,

dizzy, and sick at heart ... our parched throats burned, we were thirsty, and the bombardment seemed endless.[15]

The German ground attack began at 14:30 and, despite the two mines failing to detonate, the Bois d'Avocourt was overrun in its entirety within four hours. The 29ᵉ *Division d'Infanterie*, which was demoralised by serving for a long period in the line without a break, simply collapsed under the assault with an entire brigade of 2,825 men, likely the 57ᵉ *Brigade d'Infanterie*, being captured en masse complete with its commanding officer and the commanders of the 111ᵉ and 258ᵉ *Régiments d'Infanterie*. The 111ᵉ *Régiment* was disbanded in disgrace as a result and the French failure caused widespread dismay; *Président* Poincaré referred to it as 'encore une défaillance' (yet another failure) in his diary.[16] The Germans then committed the error of pausing for twenty-four hours to regroup and reorganise rather than pressing their advantage immediately, although the heavy rain that turned the battlefield into a quagmire also had some bearing. The French made good use of the hiatus to rush in reinforcements and focus their ubiquitous 155 mm guns on the new owners of the Bois d'Avocourt. As a result, when von Goßler's men renewed the attack on 22 March against a French strongpoint on the slopes of Côte 304, dubbed the Termite Hill, it ran into a wall of fire from carefully sited machine guns that stopped the attackers in their tracks and inflicted 2,400 casualties. On 29 March the French launched a counter-attack to retake the Bois d'Avocourt employing the 157ᵉ and 210ᵉ *Régiments d'Infanterie* from *Général* de Vassart's 76ᵉ *Division d'Infanterie*. The attack went in at 04:00, led by the French military writer *Lieutenant-Colonel* Henri Miche de Malleray commanding the 210ᵉ *Régiment*, achieved complete surprise and secured the south-east corner of the wood along with a number of machine guns, *Minenwerferen* and prisoners; the latter included a cow and two pigs. The French gains were held through the day in the face of five German counter-attacks, although *Lieutenant-Colonel* Miche de Malleray was killed by shell splinters at 16:00 while supervising consolidation of the captured ground. Both *Régiments* were relieved the following day by elements of the 11ᵉ *Division d'Infanterie*.[17]

By the end of March 1916 *General* von Goßler's 6 *Reserve Korps* had not secured the *Mort-Homme* or Côte 304 despite incurring 20,000 casualties.[18] Overall the fighting on the west bank of the Meuse between 6 March and 31 March had cost the lives of 81,607 German and 89,000 French soldiers. The lack of forts or other permanent fortifications on or around Côte 304 and the *Mort-Homme* compelled both sides to rely solely on trenches, which were simply erased by the sheer intensity of the artillery barrage. Shellfire ploughed the battlefield into a moonscape of churned mud and shattered trees, burying men and equipment, cutting telephone wires, killing messengers and obliging commanders to rely on pigeons for communication. Rather than a clearly defined trench system, the front line was reduced to small groups of men clinging to clusters of shell craters hastily linked with short saps for communication. *Leutnant* Christian Bordeching gave a graphic description of the conditions from a location in between the *Mort-Homme* and Côte 304 during a ten-day stint in the front line there:

The stench of unburied corpses rises from the ravaged former French trenches. Valuable equipment has been discarded everywhere along the road, weapons, munitions, food supplies, gas masks, barbed wire, grenades and other instruments of war. The last patches of grass are already well behind us and all we can see is a wilderness totally and violently created by explosives. The shell holes merging one into the other testify to the horror of the German artillery fire that preceded our advance and the answering fire of the French guns ... News arrives through relays of runners for no telephone line stays intact for more than an hour, the cables are destroyed as soon as they are laid ... Chancing their arm, some of our pioneers have crept out and dug trenches and set up barbed wire entanglements ... The hill itself was originally partly wooded but by now no more than a few blackened trunks are left visible, and there isn't a green leaf or blade of grass.[19]

On the other side of the line *Caporal* Pierre Teilhard de Chardin was in the same vicinity. A Jesuit theologian and palaeontologist, Teilhard de Chardin was serving as a stretcher-bearer with the 4ᵉ *Régiment Mixte Zouaves et Tirailleurs* from *Général* Jean-Joseph Rouquerol's North African 38ᵉ *Division d'Infanterie* and described the scene from his aid post located between the Bois d'Avocourt and Côte 304:

> From up there, there was a magnificent view stretching from the Argonne to Vaux, but inexpressibly mournful. The ridges that are fought over are completely torn up and as though pock-marked by some disease; between the green and richly wooded banks of the winding Meuse you'd think the hillsides had been ravaged by fire.[20]

The strain was also beginning to tell on both sides. One otherwise healthy French *Lieutenant-Colonel* died suddenly of a heart attack, and German medical officers began to express concern over the mental and physical condition of their troops. There were also signs of morale beginning to slip, with disquieting rumours of German units giving up too easily or even refusing to advance when ordered; one anonymous German letter writer reported 'Of my section, which consisted of nineteen men, only three are left ... Those who got away with a *Heimatschuss* [a 'blighty wound'] say they were lucky'.[21]

Similarly, *Feldwebel* Karl Gartner from *Infanterie Regiment* 243, who was captured near Vaux village on 14 March after straying into a French position while on patrol, reported on 2 March in an unposted diary-style letter to his mother that

> It appears that our losses are more terrible than I understood. I have just met Ludwig Heller, my comrade in the 29th ... [who] ... gives me terrible news of the scenes of carnage which took place in front of Vaux and Douaumont.

Ten days later he went further:

> All I have told you, dear mother, is false. We have been badly informed by our officers. We are just maintaining our positions on the ground we have won after fearful losses and we must give up all hope of taking Verdun. The war will continue for an indefinite period, and in the end there will be neither victors nor vanquished.[22]

Nonetheless, the German attack on the west bank ground remorselessly on, capturing the villages of Malancourt and Haucourt at the north-west foot of Côte 304 on 31 March and 5 April respectively, while Béthincourt, opposite the saddle linking the *Mort-Homme* and Côte 304, was evacuated by the French on 8 April after German attacks left it surrounded on three sides. After a month and two days of some of the most intense fighting of the entire war, the German advance had thus secured the northern end of the *Mort-Homme* and reached the foot of Côte 304, pushing the front line forward by around a mile from the 6 March start line.[23]

By the end of March 1916, and despite Falkenhayn's preferences, Operation GERICHT had thus been extended to both banks of the River Meuse. On the east bank the attack had become stalled before Fort Vaux, with the front line looping south around the German-held Fort Douaumont before running west to the river near Bras-sur-Meuse, while on the west bank just over a month of intense fighting had pushed the front line south just over a mile from the start line, securing one of the *Mort-Homme*'s two peaks and lapping at the foot of Côte 304. On the French side one of Pétain's first acts on assuming command of the *Region Fortifée de Verdun* on 26 February was to guarantee Verdun's supply lifeline along *la Route*, the road and narrow gauge railway running to the city from Bar-le-Duc via the continuous twenty-four hour, seven day a week *noria* system; one observer likened the constant stream of trucks with their dim lights to 'the folds of some gigantic and luminous serpent which never stopped and never ended'.[24] Through March 1916 Pétain extended the *noria* system to encompass all the units posted in and out of the front line at Verdun, presumably influenced in part by events such as the failure of the 67ᵉ *Division d'Infanterie* at the Bois de Corbeaux on 6 March and the 29ᵉ *Division d'Infanterie* at the Bois d'Avocourt on 20 March.

Whatever the immediate prompt, French practice hitherto had mirrored that of their German opponents by leaving units in the line, topping them up with replacement manpower until they became combat ineffective, at which point they would be withdrawn from the line to be rebuilt. This had obvious deleterious implications for the survivor's morale and institutional combat experience and Pétain therefore instituted a system whereby units were rotated out of the front line after eight to ten days, before losses became too heavy and morale and combat effectiveness became degraded. Consequently, forty French divisions had passed through Verdun compared to twenty-six German divisions by 1 May 1916, and as a result the experience of Verdun was seared into a much larger proportion of the French army as a whole. *Sous-Lieutenant* Raymond Jubert of the 151ᵉ *Regiment d'Infanterie* described the marked contrast between those going up to the line and those coming out:

The first crowd are young, their uniforms brand new; their faces and hands are clean; they look as though they were decked out for a celebration, but their aspect is sad, their eyes dream, they are silent like men who have been abandoned to their fate. The second lot are dirty, scruffy; they have black hands and faces; compared with the others they look like outcasts. But their faces are cheerful; they sing; they wouldn't change their situation for anything, yet they have a kind of pity for the men in those fine uniforms whose paths they are crossing.[25]

Humanitarian though it was, the *noria* system also obliged Pétain to constantly badger *Grand Quartier Général* for reinforcements – he requested an additional *corps* on 7 May and another two days later, for example. This brought him into conflict with Joffre, who was trying to maintain a reserve pool of divisions in readiness to counter possible German offensives elsewhere on the front, or for use in attacks such as that planned with the British Expeditionary Force in the Somme region. As Joffre put it, Pétain's constant demands for reinforcement meant that 'the whole French army would have been absorbed in this battle'. Joffre also suspected Pétain of holding on to units in order to build a reserve of his own and his animosity was heightened by Pétain's attempts to prevent raw recruits being posted directly to Verdun, and to impose a policy of rotating units through Verdun only once due to the deleterious impact of serving on the front line there. Although the realities of the situation obliged Joffre to accede in general, he reined things in by capping the size of Pétain's 2e *Armée* to a maximum of twenty-four divisions and began searching for a politically acceptable means of replacing Pétain.[26]

On the other side of the line 5. *Armee* had rationalised its command arrangements by creating separate sub-commands to oversee operations on each bank of the River Meuse. The change was initiated first on the east bank with the creation of *Angriffsgruppe* (attack group) Mudra on 19 March, commanded

Above: 1. Damage inflicted by the German bombardment of Verdun on the Rue Mazel east of the cathedral. *Below left:* 2. The underground citadel had 4 kilometres of passageways and could feed and accommodate 6,000 men. This casemate has been pressed into service as a barrack room. Note the vaulted brick roof, electric lighting and ceramic insulators on the power cable in the upper right. Contemporary accounts suggest that accommodation was much more crowded and the atmosphere much less clear and wholesome, which might explain the rather unnatural stiffness of the 'relaxing' soldiery. *Below right:* 3. Aerial photograph of Fort Douaumont taken in May 1916, three months after it was captured by *Infanterie Regiment* 24 on 25 February.

Left: 4. Fort Douaumont was retaken on 23 October 1916 by North African soldiers after a preparatory bombardment that used a quarter of a million shells. This picture shows men of the *Régiment d'Infanterie Coloniale du Maroc* sheltering in the moat of the fort on the morning of 25 October.

Right: 5. Fort Vaux retaken by the French during the Battle of Verdun.

Below: 6. The view over the barbed wire entanglement from the lines held by *Lieutenant-Colonel* Bonviolle's 165ᵉ *Regiment d'Infanterie* just north of the Bois d'Haumont at the northern edge of the Verdun salient. *General der Infanterie* Hans von Zwehl's 7. *Reserve Korps* attacked from out of the woods and folds in the ground in the background in the late afternoon of 21 February 1916.

7. Contemporary colour poster of soldiers marching beside a river and over a bridge into a shelled Verdun.

8. Shells bursting on the *Mort-Homme* during the fighting in May 1916.

9. French aid post like that occupied by *Caporal* Pierre Teilhard de Chardin, located in a dugout on Côte 304.

10. Fully manned French trench on the *Mort-Homme* after its recapture in August 1917. Note the dugout entrance on the left.

Above: 11. Ghastly mementos of battle at Verdun – a pile of human bones exhumed from a mass burial pit, post war.

Right: 12. *Général* Robert Nivelle, Commander of the French 3ᵉ *Corps*, which arrived at Verdun at the end of March 1916. He was later promoted to command the French 2ᵉ *Armée* when Pétain moved on to take command of Army Group Centre in April 1916.

13. Trench on the *Mort-Homme*. The sparse manning and relatively shallow depth suggests a communication trench on the lower slopes of the hill.

Above: 24. German shock
troops training for an attack.
German stormtroopers were
first used in the Verdun battle.

Left: 25. Verdun's defences,
French guns in Fort Souville,
1916.

Below: 26. German dead
at Dead Man's Hill or
Mort-Homme, the notorious
elevation on the left bank of
the Meuse fought over during
the Battle of Verdun.

Above: 27. A German soldier in no man's land throwing a grenade.

Right: 28. French machine gunners.

Below: 29. The toll of the artillery, German dead in their pulverized trench.

Top: 30. Another recaptured stronghold, French troops in possession of the Haudremont Quarries, 1916.

Middle: 31. Concrete emplacement for one of the three German 380 mm SK L/45 *Lange Max* (long Max) naval gun deployed by *Marine-Sonderkommando* 1 in the Bois de Warphémont north-east of Verdun; the other weapons were located at the nearby Sorel Farm and Bois de Muzeray. Originally designed for heavy warships and with a range of 25 miles, each gun weighed in excess of 200 tons with a barrel length of over 50 feet; the emplacement included fire control equipment and a crane for loading.

Bottom: 32. 380 mm round of the type fired by the *Lange Max* guns from *Marine-Sonderkommando* 1 on display at the Bois de Warphémont emplacement. Rounds like this opened the German bombardment at 04:00 on Monday 21 February 1916, with one of the first landing in the yard of the Bishop's Palace in Verdun Cathedral.

33. Entrance tunnel to one of several underground ammunition storage bunkers on the Bois de Warphémont site, with one of the light railway carriages used for moving the ammunition to the hoist for loading. Each round weighed approximately 1,650 lb, although it is unclear if this includes the propellant charges.

34. Shell craters and the remains of trenches in the western side of the Bois des Caures still clearly evident almost a century after the event; note the corrugated metal used for revetting and as overhead in dugouts.

35. The underground battle entrance to Fort Tavannes, remarkably intact after almost a century.

Above: 36. Built between 1888 and 1894, the *Batterie de Tavannes* is located midway between Fort Tavannes and the southern entrance to the Tavannes railway tunnel. Of masonry construction, the *Batterie* was not included in the concrete-hardening programme initiated from the late 1890s as a response to the 'Torpedo-shell Crisis' of 1885. *Below:* 37. The guardhouse and alternative entrance to the right of the main gateway into Fort Souville. The doorway and windows are a separate ablutions room for the guard; the narrower entrance to the left accesses a narrow passage leading into the fort proper, guarded by an internal firing embrasure.

Above: 38. View down the glacis of Fort Vaux toward the dry moat, up which *Leutnant* Rackow and his men from *Infanterie Regiment* 158 stormed on Friday 2 June 1916. Picture taken near the crater created by the destruction of the retractable 75 mm gun turret; note the footpaths created by visitors around the craters and the mounting for an observation cupola at the left. *Below:* 39. The Douaumont Ossuary, erected near the site of the *Ouvrage de Thiaumont*. Inaugurated on 7 August 1932 by Président Albert Lebrun, the Ossuary houses the unidentified remains of 130,000 men recovered from across the battlefield, fronted by the largest *Cimetière Nationale* in the world containing a further 16,142 graves; this lies beyond the trees left and right of the flagpole.

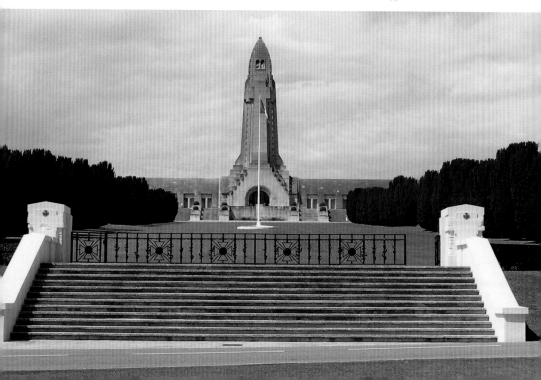

Top: 40. One of the Mardi Gras *Batterie*'s central shelters. Consisting of eight emplacements for field guns atop ammunition storage chambers and two personnel shelters, the *Batterie*'s emplacements are arranged on a north-south axis facing east to cover the Woëvre Plain.

Middle: 41. Hardened sentry position with armoured observation dome located in the centre of the *Batterie* line. Close to the front line, the *Batterie* was extensively shelled during the 1916 battle and acted as a shelter and ammunition dump for troops serving in the area.

Bottom: 42. The main entrance to Fort Souville. Constructed in 1875–77 and hardened with concrete from 1888, the fort marked the high water mark of the German advance on the east bank of the River Meuse in July 1916. Note the firing embrasures flanking the entrance; although not visible, there is also a small moat in front of the entranceway which would have been accessed via a drawbridge. Contemporary photographs suggest there may also have been a narrow gauge railway track leading up to the entrance.

by *General der Infanterie* Bruno von Mudra; this was renamed *Angriffsgruppe Ost* on 4 April at the same time as *General der Artillerie* Max von Gallwitz, an artillery specialist with extensive experience on the Eastern Front and the Balkans, was placed in command of the newly created *Angriffsgruppe West* to oversee operations on the west bank of the Meuse. By the end of March 5. *Armee* had suffered 81,607 casualties for little return but was requesting additional reinforcement to continue the fight. A clarification letter to Falkenhayn dated 29 March justified the request on the grounds that the fighting thus far had rendered the French army at Verdun incapable of offensive action and brought it to the brink of exhaustion, and it was recommended that the attack be resumed on the east bank until the Meuse Heights had been conquered along a line running from Fort Tavannes in the east to Fort Souville, and for the *Mort-Homme* and Côte 304 be secured west of the river to entice the French to expend their trained reserves in counter-attacks. Falkenhayn's insistence on Crown Prince Wilhelm justifying his request for reinforcements has been interpreted as evidence that the head of the *Oberste Heeresleitung* had lost interest in his *Verblutung* experiment and was looking for an excuse to abandon it, but it might merely have been prompted by Falkenhayn's micro-managing tendencies or indeed as contingency planning in case of failure.[27] Be that as it may, 5. *Armee* received the requested reinforcements and Crown Prince Wilhelm launched the first properly coordinated attack along both banks of the Meuse on Sunday 9 April. The assault on the east bank was targeted against the Côte du Poivre ridge to the west of Fort Douaumont, and was presumably intended to extend the line forward in line with earlier gains there and near Fort Vaux to the east. The major effort came on the west bank however and was intended to finally secure Côte 304 and the *Mort-Homme*. Responsibility for securing the latter was given to the 22. *Reserve Korps*, commanded by *General de Kavallerie*

Eugen von Falkenhayn, the older brother of the head of the *Oberste Heeresleitung*.

The preparatory German bombardment, which again commenced at 07:00 French time on Sunday 9 April, was the heaviest since 21 February and consumed seventeen full trainloads of ammunition. At the foot of the *Mort-Homme* the shelling was so severe that the 37ᵉ *Régiment d'Infanterie*, which had just been pulled back to a new position south of the recently evacuated Béthincourt, was obliged to withdraw again to a less exposed location.[28] On the neighbouring Côte 304 *Capitaine* Augustin Cochin from the 146ᵉ *Régiment d'Infanterie* judged the shelling to be the worst ordeal he had ever undergone:

> Like the poor beggars in the Gospel, I pleaded not to die so senselessly, I and my poor *biffins* [rag pickers], who were driven half mad: round-eyed, no longer answering when I spoke to them.[29]

The ground attack began at 13:00 and immediately placed the French under severe pressure. A *bataillon* of the 162ᵉ *Régiment d'Infanterie* holding the Ravin de la Hayette on the north face of the *Mort-Homme* was driven out of its trenches, and the 94ᵉ *Régiment d'Infanterie* from the 42ᵉ *Division*'s second brigade had to fight hard to avoid being pushed out of the village of Cumières at the eastern end of the feature.[30] The momentum of the assault carried the German infantry to the summit of the *Mort-Homme* as marked on German maps, which a cartographical error had rendered 30 metres short of the true summit; the attackers nonetheless secured *Pointe* 295 and the Ravin de Caurettes, driving a 500-yard wide wedge into the French positions. *Sous-Lieutenant* Raymond Jubert and the 151ᵉ *Régiment d'Infanterie* were occupying a reserve position on the southern slopes of the *Mort-Homme* when the German attack began, and an awed Jubert watched the bombardment falling along the entire length of the *Mort-Homme* and on to the crest of Côte 304, with a subsidiary barrage blocking access to the features to prevent reinforcement.[31]

Jubert's unit was selected to drive back the German incursion:

We had just lost the Mort-Homme Ridge, and were ordered to recapture it at once ... Having put down our knapsacks, we took an ample supply of cartridges, as well as additional rations for one day ... Passing the first crest, we descended toward the ravine where ... the deadly explosions and fumes were concentrating in a hellish racket. Another hundred feet and we were in the danger zone ... Beyond the crest, however, there was another crest, and we could still see no enemy trenches ... about five hundred yards to our left, a machine gun suddenly opened fire against us ... other machine guns entered the fray and made our situation most uncomfortable. I heard cries, but began charging ahead ... Our line rushed onward, reached the crest and jumped into the trench which, to our great surprise, was empty – but full of corpses. At nightfall, and for the next thirty hours, we sustained a violent bombardment. By regaining the lost crest, we had restored the momentarily broken continuity of our front line.[32]

The brief German tenancy of *Pointe* 295, which cost one of 22. *Reserve Korps*' divisions 2,200 casualties, was the high point of the 9 April attack, as the French defences on Côte 304 and across the Meuse on the Côte du Poivre held firm against the German assault. The reaction to the outcome on the French side was jubilant, with the normally taciturn Pétain issuing an upbeat Order of the Day on 10 April that ended with a paraphrase from Joan of Arc, while the German attack was still underway:

April 9th was a glorious day for our armies. The furious attacks of the soldiers of the Crown Prince broke down everywhere. The infantry, artillery, sappers and aviators of the 2nd Army vied with each other in valour. Honour to all. No doubt the Germans will attack again. Let all work and watch that yesterday's success be continued. *Courage! On les aura!*" (Courage! We will beat them!)"[33]

Officially the German attack was to continue until 12 April but it began to wind down from 10 April, not least because that day ushered in twelve days of heavy rain that not only again played havoc with troop movement and food and ammunition resupply, but made maintaining trenches and indeed mere existence a major trial in itself; as the German official history noted "Water in the trenches came above the knees. The men had not a dry thread on their bodies; there was not a dugout that could provide dry accommodation. The numbers of sick rose alarmingly".[34] Despite the inclement weather, the French mounted numerous counter-attacks that slowly whittled away the meagre German gains from the 9 April attack. This included retaking the entire length of the *Mort-Homme*'s crest by a number of units including the 251e *Régiment d'Infanterie*, which retook the last summit on 30 April after an intense fight with hand grenades.[35] Although it was not apparent at the time, the April fighting marked another tipping point in the course of the Battle of Verdun. Hitherto Falkenhayn's *Verblutung* experiment had been predicated on the French attacking German defensive positions so they could be destroyed by artillery fire. After the end of April 1916 the method changed and the defensive principle was abandoned in favour of large-scale offensive action against the French defensive positions, with all that entailed for German casualty rates.[36] An even bloodier phase of the battle was thus about to commence.

7

MORE ON BOTH BANKS: REAPPRAISALS AND RENEWED EFFORT, 29 APRIL 1916 – 1 JUNE 1916

The failure of the 9 April attack along both banks of the River Meuse prompted serious differences of opinion within 5. *Armee* headquarters and between its subordinate commanders. By 21 April Crown Prince Wilhelm had come to the conclusion that Operation GERICHT had failed and should be called off forthwith, an opinion shared by the majority of his staff at Stenay and the commander of *Angriffsgruppe Ost, General der Infanterie* von Mudra; the latter had rapidly identified the overarching reality of the fighting at Verdun:

> The attacking infantry is exposed to continuous fire from heavy and field artillery, at times coming from their flanks, at times from their rear. The rearward communications, the rest positions, and even the reserves are similarly exposed to enemy fire of all calibres.

Therefore, the infantry suffers heavy losses daily in their forward positions, and does not suffer any less in the lines of communication and in the rest positions. The bringing forward of supplies and necessary replacements requires an inordinate amount of time and effort.[1]

Mindful of the ever increasing toll the large-scale offensives were inflicting on 5. *Armee*'s constituent formations, von Mudra recommended that future attacks be limited to small scale, local attacks of division size with limited objectives; ironically such tactics accorded perfectly with von Falkenhayn's *Verblutung* strategy.[2]

The notable and crucial exception to this line of thinking was *Generalleutnant* von Knobelsdorf, the Crown Prince's chief of staff, who was convinced that GERICHT was not only viable but the correct course, and that the large-scale attacks were the key to success. This view was unanimously supported in reports gathered from the *Korps* commanders involved in the 9 April attack, partly because the unremitting French artillery fire made their positions barely tenable and partly for reasons of morale; as the commander of 15. *Korps*, *General der Infanterie* Berthold von Deimling, put it, 'Enduring passively the fire of the French heavy artillery and gas rounds, without being able to move forward themselves, places great demands on the moral strength of the infantry.'[3] Furthermore, von Knobelsdorf wielded rather more power than might ordinarily have been expected of a chief of staff because he had been appointed by the *Kaiser* to keep an eye on the inexperienced Crown Prince. Following a heated argument with von Mudra on future action, von Knobelsdorf thus had von Mudra sent from Stenay back to his *Korps* in the Argonne, replacing him as commander of *Angriffsgruppe Ost* with *General der Infanterie* Ewald von Lochow, whose approach was more in line with the French philosophy of *attaque à outrance*. At around the same time von Knobelsdorf also engineered the removal of *Oberstleutnant* von Heymann, the Crown Prince's supportive personal staff officer, who was in the habit of successfully standing up to von Knobelsdorf. The latter then deliberately misrepresented Wilhelm's position to Falkenhayn at a meeting at *Oberste Heeresleitung* at Charleville-Mézières on 20 April, by arguing for a continuation of GERICHT despite agreeing to argue the case for termination on his behalf. In desperation at having his concerns sidelined, the Crown Prince appealed to his father, but the *Kaiser* merely forwarded his son's communication to the appropriate military recipient in line with his long-standing and scrupulously correct practice.[4]

The immediate upshot of all this was a rapid resumption of the offensive on the west bank of the River Meuse, after von Knobelsdorf had persuaded Falkenhayn to grant permission and reinforcements on 20 April. *General der Artillerie* von Gallwitz, commanding *Angriffsgruppe West*, had strongly recommended resuming the attack in his report to von Knobelsdorf and insisted that Côte 304 had to be fully secured before resuming attacks on the *Mort-Homme* because the French artillery deployed in the lee of the former had been instrumental in rebuffing the German assault on the latter. This plan of attack was adopted and von Gallwitz used his expertise to create a fire-plan for the attack on Côte 304 that was intended to simply "… blast the French off the hill" with the heaviest artillery bombardment employed in the battle to date, employing 500 assorted artillery pieces firing for thirty-six hours on a frontage of just a mile. The bombardment commenced at 11:00 on 3 May and French pilots reported the resultant column of smoke, dust and pulverised material rising over 2,000 feet in the air, to the extent that at the end of the battle Côte 304's height had been reduced by several metres.[5] The impact on the French troops unfortunate enough to find themselves on the receiving end was appalling, not least because conditions on the hill had effectively prevented the defenders from constructing the deep shelters necessary to withstand such concentrated shelling. *Soldat* Pierre Rouquet from the 151ᵉ *Régiment d'Infanterie* wrote a graphic account of the experience:

> You couldn't describe the deluge of fire that swept down on us. I was conscious of being in danger of death every second. I had the luck to come through … But I ended up stupefied. I got the impression that my brain was jumping about in my skull because of the guns. I was completely KOd by the severity of the noise.[6]

The 1ᵉʳ *Bataillon, 68ᵉ Régiment d'Infanterie* had moved up to the line on Côte 304 on 29 April and had its positions systematically destroyed by German artillery fire before the pre-attack bombardment increased in intensity from thirty to thirty-five shells falling per minute on each 100 metres of frontage; by nightfall on 3 May the 1ᵉʳ *Bataillon*'s losses for the four days totalled 50 per cent with 250 men killed or wounded, 160 of the former on 3 May alone, and a further 41 missing. The bombardment continued unabated through the night.[7]

The 68ᵉ and 90ᵉ *Régiments d'Infanterie* had been virtually annihilated by the German bombardment on 3 May, and the 268ᵉ and 290ᵉ *Régiments d'Infanterie* were ordered into the line at dawn the following day as reinforcements to meet the expected German ground attack. This began at 16:30 and rapidly penetrated the French line in a number of places, overrunning isolated pockets of French troops and taking many of them prisoner and forcing the remnants of the 90ᵉ *Régiments d'Infanterie* to retreat. A counter-attack by the 268ᵉ and 290ᵉ *Régiments* at dawn on 5 May was stopped cold by a wall of German fire and a further day under constant German bombardment obliged the withdrawal of the 268ᵉ *Régiment* at nightfall on 6 May; two days in the line had cost it 62 dead, 169 wounded and 26 missing. The 290ᵉ *Régiment* held on until 15:30 on 7 May when another major German attack obliged it to retire as well, also to be withdrawn from the line two days later. By 21 May the 290ᵉ *Régiment* had suffered 800 casualties, including 21 officers and 600 men killed, wounded or missing in the five-day period between 4 and 9 May alone. The neighbouring 296ᵉ *Régiment d'Infanterie*, which had gone into the line as reinforcement on 6 May with the 114ᵉ and 125ᵉ *Régiments d'Infanterie*, managed to hold the German advance with a counter-attack that also regained lost territory but it had suffered a thousand casualties by the time it withdrew from the hill on 11 May, many caused by flying clots of blasted sand, earth and other debris rather than German projectiles. The 114ᵉ *Régiment* was totally cut off for a time and its men were obliged to raid the pouches of the dead and wounded for ammunition, with the regimental record referring to its men being drunk on noise, fear and powder fumes and to suffering enormous losses. Two *compagnies* from the 125ᵉ *Régiment* fought to the death after being encircled with only a handful of survivors making their way to the relative safety of the French lines; it too referred to suffering enormous losses.[8]

By 11 May the Germans were finally in possession of Côte 304 in its entirety, at an estimated cost of 10,000 French lives alone; by the end of April the GERICHT toll had risen to 120,000 German and 133,000 French casualties, and the Côte 304 sector remained an active and dangerous place thereafter.[9] On 18 May a fierce German attack at dusk temporarily surrounded the 296ᵉ *Régiment d'Infanterie* and the resultant three days of fighting cost the *Régiment* 143 dead, 408 wounded and 36 missing. Ten days of continuous German shelling between 20 and 30 May cost the 173ᵉ *Régiment d'Infanterie* serious losses on a daily basis, and at one point obliged the survivors to shore up their defences with cadavers.[10] The traffic was not all one way however, as noted by the commander of *Minenwerfer Kompanie* 38 from *Jäger Division* 38:

During the night 20th and 21st [May] we took two light Minenwerfer up to Côte 304. We fired and did a good deal of damage. Grenade after grenade – a great many killed – many terribly injured – blown all over the place ... There is wonderful visibility from Côte 304 and we can see across No Man's Land to Malancourt and Béthincourt. May 22nd. Our trenches were absolutely smashed. 15,000 shells exploded and 4,000 of them were 21cm grenades. Everything in the munition depot, the station line and road was blown to bits ... We had some men wounded – one next to me. They tried to get under cover. Lieutenant Spesshenz had an attack of shell shock. I was just pulling myself together when another shell came over and burst about a yard behind me – a splinter got me in the face. Spesshenz was badly wounded in the right arm.[11]

On the other hand the French artillery could also be a two-edged instrument; the 296e *Régiment d'Infanterie* came under fire from friendly guns several times between 15 and 17 May for example; it is unclear if the fire was simply misdirected or resulted from a degradation in accuracy due to gun-barrel wear caused by incessant firing, which was becoming an increasing problem for both sides.[12]

With Côte 304 securely in German hands, *Angriffsgruppe West* was free to concentrate upon the *Mort-Homme*, where preparations had been continuing apace; after the failure of the 9 April attack von Gallwitz had ordered the digging of a pair of mile-long tunnels to permit troops to move up to the northern foot of the *Mort-Homme* in safety. One was dubbed 'Gallwitz' after its creator; the other, somewhat sycophantically perhaps, was named '*Kronprinz*' (Crown Prince) in honour of his superior at 5. *Armee*.[13] At the eastern end of the feature the 251e, 254e and 267e *Régiments d'Infanterie*, which had moved into the Cumières sector that included the forward edge of the Bois des Caurettes and Bois de Cumières on 19 May, came under heavy German attack the following day as recorded by an unnamed French eyewitness:

At this moment the German curtain fire lengthened ... The Germans attacked in massed formation, by big columns of five or six hundred men, preceded by two waves of sharpshooters. We had only our rifles and our machine guns, because the 75's could not get to work. Fortunately the flank batteries succeeded in catching the Boches on the right.

It is absolutely impossible to convey what losses the Germans must suffer in these attacks. Nothing can give an idea of it. Whole ranks are mowed down, and those that follow them suffer the same fate. Under the storm of machine gun, rifle and 75 fire, the German columns were ploughed into furrows of death. Imagine if you can what it would be like to rake water. Those gaps filled up again at once. That is enough to show with what disdain of human life the German attacks are planned and carried out.[14]

The defenders repulsed the attack at heavy cost but in the early hours of 24 May the survivors of the 254ᵉ *Régiment d'Infanterie* were forced out of the village of Cumières and retired to the positions of the 267ᵉ *Régiment*; a counter-attack by the latter at 06:15 ran into intense German machine gun fire and the village remained firmly in German hands.[15]

Soldat Pierre Rouquet and the 151ᵉ *Régiment d'Infanterie* were also back in the thick of it:

At the end of fifteen days we came back down, seven to eight kilometres from the front ... We had one quiet night's sleep; just one, that's all, then the next day the battalion that had relieved us was wiped out ... There were five or six left out of a whole battalion, no more. We were sent up again with all speed to face another bombardment, one worse than ever. The shells of the 210s were coming over four at a time and we were being buried with every volley. Men were being completely entombed. The others dug them out ... My moment came on the stroke of seven o'clock.

It was my turn to be buried and you must understand I suffered greatly because being unable to move I could do absolutely nothing. I remember saying 'Well, that's it at last!' and I lost consciousness. I was dead. And then I was being disinterred with picks and shovels and they pulled me out, totally exhausted. My captain ... sent me to a first-aid post two kilometres back ... I was evacuated. I gathered I stayed four days in a corner, exhausted, in total shock.[16]

At the western end of the feature the German attack of 20 May pushed the 287ᵉ *Régiment d'Infanterie* out of its positions, losing a large number of prisoners and allowing the Germans to establish a substantial bulge projecting deep into the French line in the process. A counter-attack on 21 May by the 287ᵉ *Régiment*, assisted by the 16ᵉ *Bataillon de Chasseurs à Pied* and the 112ᵉ, 306ᵉ and 332ᵉ *Régiments d'Infanterie* was intended to regain the ground lost the previous day but 'failed to ameliorate the situation'.[17] By the end of May the entire length of the *Mort-Homme* ridge including both peaks was also firmly in the hands of *Angriffsgruppe West*. Despite pre-attack estimates that the Côte de l'Oie, Côte 304 and *Mort-Homme* features would be secured in short order, it had taken eighty-four days, tens if not hundreds of thousands of lives – overall French losses had topped the 185,000 mark by the end of May – and hundreds of thousands if not millions of artillery shells to secure a strip of land 7 miles long and 3 miles deep. With the French artillery on the west bank of the Meuse finally denuded of its protective ridges and observation posts looking across the river, *Angriffsgruppe Ost* was free to resume the attack on the east bank, although von Falkenhayn had given Crown Prince Wilhelm permission to do so a month earlier, on 4 April.

The east bank of the Meuse had not been quiet while 5. *Armee* had been concentrating its energies on the opposite side of the river and, as at Stenay and Charleville-Mézières, not all the French fighting was conducted in the trenches. As we have seen, the relationship between Joffre and Pétain was increasingly strained, with the former becoming frustrated with Pétain's incessant demands for reinforcements and a growing suspicion that he was attempting to build a reserve of divisions that would detract from plans for a summer offensive on the Somme; hence Joffre's capping the size of Pétain's 2ᵉ *Armée* to a maximum of twenty-four divisions while he searched for a politically acceptable means of replacing him. For his part, Pétain was of the view that French efforts should be concentrated at Verdun rather than elsewhere and he was determined to safeguard the battle-worthiness and morale of his units built up by the *noria* replacement system, which by May 1916 had cycled forty of the fifty-two French divisions deployed to Verdun through the heaviest fighting at least once. He was equally determined to avoid having the lives thus husbanded squandered in piecemeal counter-attacks that owed more to doctrinal dogma than tactical necessity or even common sense. This, however, was problematic in an army so deeply imbued with the philosophy of *attaque à outrance*, and the task of keeping a rein on impetuous subordinates increased manifold with the arrival of *Général* Robert Nivelle's 3ᵉ *Corps* on the eastern sector of the *Region Fortifée de Verdun* at the end of March 1916. An artillery *Colonel* in 1914, Nivelle's rise up the promotion ladder had been remarkably swift, not least due to his uncanny ability to charm his military and political seniors and his skill for repackaging old ideas as fresh and original. He was, perhaps predictably, also an enthusiastic proponent of *offensive à outrance*, as was his senior divisional commander *Général* Charles Mangin, a Colonial soldier who had faced the British at Fashoda as a *Lieutenant* in 1898 and commanded the 5ᵉ *Division d'Infanterie* from 31 August 1914, including the capture of Neuville-Saint-Vaast during the Artois offensive in May 1915. Mangin's single-minded diligence and aggression in this regard had earned him the grim nicknames of *le boucher* (the butcher) and *le mangeur des hommes* (the eater of men), although Mangin was not a a stereotypical chateau general – far from it. One of the most technically proficient officers in the French army, Mangin happily shared the discomforts and risks of his men, sleeping in a desert tent whenever possible and on occasion leading attacks in person, rifle in hand. Like many military leaders careless of their own lives however, he was correspondingly careless with the lives of his subordinates.[18]

Pétain's problems with Nivelle began virtually as soon as 3ᵉ *Corps* began to deploy into the area south of German-held Fort Douaumont, dubbed the 'Deadly Quadrilateral', for Nivelle and Mangin started as they intended to go on. The location was problematic because the Germans were using the fort as a giant *Stollen* from which to launch attacks down the ravines running south through the Bois de la Caillette and the la Caillette plateau toward Fleury, opening numerous and potentially serious breaches in the French lines. On 2 April German troops armed with *Flammenwerfer* created a serious breach in the section of the Bois de la Caillette held by the 269ᵉ *Régiment d'Infanterie*, and the first of Mangin's units to arrive at Verdun, the 74ᵉ *Régiment d'Infanterie*, was immediately ordered to attack and retake the lost ground. After an eighteen hour approach march under constant shellfire the 2ᵉ *Bataillon*'s 74ᵉ *Régiment* arrived at Fort Souville after dark on 2 April and moved off again at 02:00 the following morning, reaching its jump-off position on the shattered railway line running south of the Caillette plateau at 04:00.

What happened next depends on the account. According to the 74ᵉ *Régiment* official account the attack went in at 04:30 and after slow and costly progress succeeded in pushing the German interlopers back and sealing the breach, although the Morchée Trench and the Vigoreaux communications trench to the west of Fort Douaumont near Thiaumont Farm remained in German hands.[19] On the other hand *Capitaine* Jean Tocaben from the neighbouring 226ᵉ *Régiment d'Infanterie* claimed that not only did the attack go in without artillery preparation, but that the troops moved in the wrong direction because they had no clear idea of where the enemy actually was; as Tocaben noted, from the German perspective, 'It's certainly a rare piece of luck to see troops coming at you deployed as if they were on manoeuvres, and to shoot them at your leisure, without running the slightest risk.'[20] Whichever, the Germans responded by shelling the newcomers throughout 4 April and launching another attack against Chasseur Trench at 19:00, which was repulsed by a section of machine guns commanded by a *Lieutenant* Boyer, and a French counter-attack thirty minutes later met with a similar lack of success. This set the pattern of constant bombardment, attack and counter-attack that continued thereafter; for its part the 74ᵉ *Régiment* was relieved on 11 April apart from its machine gun *compagnie*, which was attached to the incoming 274ᵉ *Régiment d'Infanterie* for a further three days.[21] Such small-scale attacks became a daily occurrence and confirmed the deadly reputation of the area south of Fort Douaumont while Pétain did his best to rein in Nivelle and his impetuous subordinate, but with limited success.

Nivelle and Mangin had begun as they intended to continue, and the brake on their *attaque à outrance* tendencies was soon removed. Joffre visited Nivelle and the 3ᵉ *Corps'* sector of the front on 10 April and was favourably impressed by the results of Mangin's repeated small-scale attacks. He was so impressed that he relayed a request from Nivelle for more resources to expand the effort to the east and west flanks of Fort Douaumont to Pétain in person, and, when the latter remained obdurate, a means of removing the publically acclaimed saviour of Verdun from his post in a creative and politically prudent manner occurred to Joffre. Pétain was to be promoted out of the way to command the *Groupement des Armées du Central* in the stead of *Général* Fernand de Langle de Cary, who was to be *limogé*, while Nivelle was elevated to command the 2ᵉ *Armée*. As Joffre later charitably explained, his reasoning for the reordering was a 'means of withdrawing General Pétain from the battlefield of Verdun, hoping that by giving him a more distant perspective ... he would take in the general situation with a clearer view ... He was not pleased.'²² Pétain was informed of the change by de Castelnau via a telephone call from Chantilly on 19 April, and moved out of his tiny headquarters in the *Mairie* at Souilly for his new *Groupement* headquarters at Bar-le-Duc on 1 May as Nivelle moved in; Pétain's *aide-de-camp*, *Capitaine* Bernard Serrigny, referred to Nivelle marking his arrival with a typically theatrical flourish by pausing at the top of the *Mairie* steps to announce 'We have the formula!'²³ To add insult to injury Joffre also discontinued the *noria* system shortly afterward, placing Pétain in the invidious position of having to watch from afar as his careful work was undone and the units he had nurtured and husbanded were squandered. The situation on the French side was thus a mirror image of that on the other side of the front line, with the bellicose winning out over the more moderate, while the battle and attendant death toll ran on remorselessly. Interestingly, the idea that the battle had somehow taken on a life of its own and was running beyond human agency or indeed control began to appear among contemporary comment on both sides at around this time.²⁴

Joffre may have discontinued Pétain's *noria* system with regard to the flow of fresh units into Verdun, but the infrastructure remained in place and continued to function. The *Citadelle Souterraine* (underground citadel), a warren of passages and chambers underneath the Vauban citadel, was employed as a shelter, barracks, HQ, cookhouse and supply depot all rolled into one during the battle and acted as a staging post for units moving up to the line along *la Route* from Bar-le-Duc, as described by *Lieutenant* Henri Desagneaux from the 106ᵉ *Régiment d'Infanterie*:

We spend the day in the Citadel waiting. The guns fire ceaselessly. Huge shells (380s-420s) crash down on Verdun causing serious damage. I walk as far as the town: it's in ruins and deserted. One can't stay outside for long as shells are dropping everywhere. The Citadel is a real underground town, with narrow-gauge railway, dormitories, and rooms of every type; it's safe here, but very gloomy.[25]

This was echoed more graphically by *Lieutenant* René Arnaud of the 337e *Régiment d'Infanterie*:

A bridge over a railway line, a road running between mist-laden meadows, zig-zagging alongside the river. Suddenly an enormous dark wall, flights of steps, muffled shouts, and the warm odour of cabbage, mouldy bread and creosol. I went down a long vaulted gallery through which passed tip-up trucks drawn by mules, making a deafening din. Doors opened on to typists' offices, engine rooms, and bakeries smelling of warm bread. Then, in the weak electric light, I passed through hall after hall filled with soldiers, some of them changing their clothes after the march for fear of catching a cold – for great danger did not make them forget the little ones – others eating ravenously from their mess tins and drinking out of their flasks. All these casemates with their tiny windows like portholes and the thick pillars supporting the low ceiling reminded one of the between-decks in a boat full of immigrants.[26]

In all the *Citadelle Souterraine* provided accommodation for 6,000 men among its 4,000 metres of passageways, while its bakery and kitchens produced rations for 28,000 men per day; after the war one of the chambers hosted the ceremony to select one of eight Unknown Warriors for ceremonial entombment at the *Arc de Triomphe* in Paris.[27]

With Pétain's restraining influence removed, Nivelle and Mangin lost no time in expanding their aggressive activities, focussing primarily on Fort Douaumont which overlooked the French lines from atop the la Caillette plateau. By this point the fort's turrets were all out of commission, but the Germans were using it as a shelter and conduit for troops moving between the front line and rear areas at an average of a thousand per night, many of them using new entrances dug into its northern side. Perhaps more importantly, it also provided excellent observation over the French line as noted by *Sous-Lieutenant* Robert Desaubliaux, a machine gun officer with the 126ᵉ *Régiment d'Infanterie*:

> They dominate us from Fort Douaumont; we cannot now take anything without their knowing about it, nor dig any trench without their artillery spotting it and immediately bombarding it.[28]

Both Mangin and his superior Nivelle appear to have been fixated on retaking the fort, and the cachet for personal reputation doubtless played a part in this alongside the need to alleviate the tactical situation in the Deadly Quadrilateral. Mangin made his first attempt to regain the fort on 22 April, possibly employing elements of the 6ᵉ *Division d'Infanterie*, and actually put some men onto the fort superstructure before being driven back. Mangin immediately began agitating for permission to launch a stronger and more carefully planned attack, and increased the pressure after witnessing the aftermath of an accidental explosion inside Fort Douaumont on 8 May. The blast was allegedly caused by soldiers, possibly from a Bavarian Regiment, brewing coffee on a table improvised from boxes of cordite, either by using the explosive filling from a hand grenade for fuel or boosting the flames with alcohol. Whatever the catalyst, a small explosion ignited a store of *Flammenwerfer* canisters stored on the fort's first level which then spread the conflagration down to an ammunition magazine containing sixty rounds of French 155 mm ammunition which promptly detonated. The blasts killed 679 men, including the entire staff of *Grenadier Regiment 12* and injured a further 1,800 to varying degrees; the resulting conflagration ruled out any effort to recover the bodies. The chamber involved was simply sealed off and remains so to this day; a memorial shrine was set up shortly after the event that referred to 1,052 dead rather than the 679 figure cited on the post-war memorial.[29] Some unfortunate survivors who managed to escape from the fort's interior were machine gunned by their own side as they emerged as their soot-blackened faces were mistaken for feared French African troops in the confusion.[30]

Nivelle swiftly granted Mangin permission to renew his effort against Fort Douaumont and while Pétain initially vetoed the idea he was pressured into agreement by Joffre; as a result the attack which followed is sometimes seen as being carried out on his personal initiative, which does not appear to have been the case.[31] Mindful of the likely result of attacking on a narrow frontage, Pétain backed Mangin's initial request for four divisions to carry out the attack on a wide front. This was modified to two divisions with one in reserve when *Grand Quartier Général* refused to provide the necessary reinforcements, and in the end Mangin was obliged to go ahead using just his own *5ᵉ Division d'Infanterie* with *Général* Charles-Victor Lestoquoi's *36ᵉ Division d'Infanterie* in reserve; the stumbling block was Joffre's unwillingness to release units earmarked for his Somme offensive for use in securing 'local objectives'.[32] Nivelle's headquarters issued the orders for the attack, which was the first major French effort at Verdun not undertaken as a direct response to German action, on 13 May. It was scheduled to commence on 22 May, with the units detailed to participate being alerted three days in advance on 19 May. These were the 36ᵉ, 74ᵉ, 129ᵉ and 274ᵉ *Régiments d'Infanterie*, the entire infantry strength of Mangin's *5ᵉ Division d'Infanterie*, which were to go in on a front of just under a mile. The attack also saw the largest concentration of French artillery deployed for a specific operation at Verdun to date, a total of 290 guns including eighty-four 155 mm pieces, 122 Schneider 220 mm howitzers and four brand-new Schneider 370 mm railway guns, which Mangin expected to be a key factor in his coming success.[33] In order to maximise the impact of the preparatory bombardment, and ascertain the best way of attacking Douaumont, Mangin visited Fort Moulainville, but was less than impressed when the fort's commander, *Capitaine* Léon Harispe, respectfully pointed out that the 370 mm howitzers were likely to prove inadequate as Moulainville had withstood ten weeks of regular bombardment by more powerful German 420 mm pieces without suffering significant damage. Mangin was reportedly less than impressed with this news.

The French bombardment began on 17 May and went on for five days, dropping 1000 tons of shells per day on Douaumont. The bombardment obliterated a German signal station established on the fort's glacis, destroyed the surviving observation domes and machine gun turrets and opened a breach in the roof of the west-facing *Casemate de Bourges*. In a rerun of the aftermath of the 8 May explosion, the shell-shocked men wandered the fume and dust-filled corridors of the fort, which rapidly filled with wounded as the barrage took a dreadful toll on the German troops posted in the trenches outside; all was then plunged into blackness when a near-miss brought a section of the roof down on the solitary generator. Once again the traffic was not all one way. Mangin, who had elected to observe proceedings from atop Fort Souville, 2 miles south-west of Douaumont, was almost killed by a shell burst that wounded four of his staff officers. More importantly, just over half an hour before the French attack was due to go in, two solitary ranging shells dropped directly on the French trenches packed with assault troops, a sure warning that the German gunners had the range and were merely waiting for the attackers to show themselves. The five-day barrage had effectively removed any element of surprise but, more seriously, security at Nivelle's headquarters was extremely lax, so much so that 5. *Armee* was fully conversant with the detail of the French plan within two days of the orders being issued on 13 May, and promptly ceased all other operations on the east bank of the Meuse in anticipation.[34]

The French preparatory bombardment rose to maximum rate at 06:00 on Monday 22 May, and at 09:00 French scout aircraft succeeded in downing all six observation balloons controlling the German guns covering the attack sector, using Le Prieur incendiary rockets.[35] The attack commenced at 11:50. On the right the 274ᵉ *Régiment d'Infanterie* was tasked to secure a turret and supporting network of trenches approximately 250 yards north-east of the fort but became pinned down by heavy German fire almost immediately on leaving their trenches, along with a *bataillon* from the 74ᵉ *Régiment d'Infanterie* assigned to the same objective. The latter's 3ᵉ *Bataillon*, commanded by *Major* Paul Lefebvre-Dibon, had better luck, crossing the German trenches relatively intact and reaching its objective with around a score of casualties before setting up a defensive perimeter around a half-demolished concrete store bunker after a bloody hand-to-hand fight; the problem was the bunker was open to German enfilading fire and was full of dismembered German corpses, smashed equipment and debris.[36] On the left side of the attack frontage the 3ᵉ *Bataillon*, 36ᵉ *Régiment d'Infanterie* were tasked to take the Morchée Trench in support of the main assault; the Bishop's Bonnet Trench was swiftly overrun with a bag of 150 German prisoners and a number of others were despatched as they tried to retreat inside the fort. The attackers also suffered grievous losses however, with almost every officer and NCO being killed or badly wounded in the opening stages of the attack.[37] The 2ᵉ *Bataillon*, 129ᵉ *Régiment d'Infanterie*, tasked to envelop the northern aspect of the fort, enjoyed the most success. In a textbook example of *attaque à outrance*, the attackers overran the German trenches and reached the fort in eleven minutes flat, with many German troops simply surrendering without a fight at the French approach. The attackers then pushed on to occupy most of the fort's glacis including the south-western *Casemate de Bourges*, the western portion of the defensive ditch and some southern facing trenches by 12:20, from where they were able to rebuff the first of many German sallies aimed at driving them off from within the fort. A party of sappers from the 3ᵉ *Régiment du Génie* commanded by a *Sergent* Piau penetrated the breach opened in the western *Casemate de Bourges* by the bombardment using hand grenades and reached the fort's central street before a hasty counter-attack by a German *Jäger* unit pushed them back to the peripheral tunnels, where fighting continued for the rest of the day.[38]

From his vantage point atop Fort Souville it appeared to Mangin that Douaumont had been secured, and he lost no time in communicating the erroneous information to Nivelle at Souilly in person, carrying a satchel full of recommendations for awards and promotions for officers involved; from there it was promptly announced to the world.[39] The reality was that the attackers had become bogged down under increasingly heavy German fire. *Major* Lefebvre-Dibon's 3ᵉ *Bataillon*, 74ᵉ *Régiment d'Infanterie* was pinned down by machine gun fire from German positions on the north and south-east corners of the fort and by the late afternoon of 22 May had lost almost half its strength; while messengers were able to maintain contact with regimental headquarters it proved impossible to push reinforcements or additional supplies up to the beleaguered 3ᵉ *Bataillon*. Isolated, under constant German machine gun and artillery fire and saddled with ever increasing numbers of wounded, the survivors nonetheless held their position for two full days. By Wednesday 24 March the *Bataillon* had lost 72 per cent of its strength killed, wounded or missing and had completely exhausted supplies of ammunition, food and water; *Major* Lefebvre-Dibon and the survivors were thus obliged to surrender at 13:30 that day.[40] At the other side of the fort the 2ᵉ

Bataillon, 129ᵉ *Régiment d'Infanterie* began to dig a 200-yard trench forward from the north-eastern aspect of the French salient atop the fort to block German entry and erected a machine gun bunker atop the western *Casemate de Bourges*. The latter dominated the fort's entire superstructure and was instrumental in beating back numerous German forays from within through the day and into the evening, on at least one occasion assisted by misdirected German artillery fire. Some reinforcements did manage to brave the incessant German artillery fire to reach the 129ᵉ *Régiment*; a group from the 36ᵉ *Régiment d'Infanterie*'s 8ᵉ *Compagnie* reached the Fort at 14:30, followed by a *Section* from 5ᵉ *Compagnie*, 34ᵉ *Régiment d'Infanterie* at 23:00 but this turned out to be too little to influence the situation.

The French held on through the night of 22/23 May and repulsed two German attacks against their new trench at 13:00 and 17:00. By the afternoon of 23 May the writing was on the wall however, not least because Mangin's own 5ᵉ *Division* had been used up and he was running out of units from *Général* Lestoquoi's 36ᵉ *Division d'Infanterie* to push into the maw. The 34ᵉ and 49ᵉ *Régiments d'Infanterie* launched near-simultaneous attacks at 07:00 and 07:30 on 23 May that were stopped cold by German artillery, the latter only 200 yards from its jump-off position. The 1ᵉʳ *Bataillon*, 18ᵉ *Régiment d'Infanterie* was decimated in an attack aimed at the entrance to the fort on Mangin's personal order the same day, as was the 218ᵉ *Régiment d'Infanterie* in a relieving attack near Fleury.[41] This all led to Mangin being removed from his command by Nivelle's successor as commander of 3ᵉ *Corps*, *Général* Léonce Lebrun, in the afternoon of 24 May following a heated telephone exchange between the two men. On being ordered to resume the attack Mangin had responded with a terse 'With what?' and when the order was repeated responded angrily 'I don't make second-rate attacks, I don't attack without attacking, really attacking up to the hilt.' He was relieved forthwith.[42] By this point the last elements of the 129ᵉ *Régiment d'Infanterie* had finally been either killed or driven from Fort Douaumont, starting with the improvised machine gun bunker atop the western *Casemate de Bourges*. The Germans had managed to funnel reinforcements into Fort Douaumont via one of their new entrances in the moat at the front of the fort during the night of 23/24 May, including a *Minenwerfer* that was emplaced just 80 yards from the French bunker. As dawn broke on 24 May the *Minenwerfer* fired eight rounds in quick succession and three full infantry *Kompanies* then stormed the shattered French position before the smoke and dust had cleared, bringing the 5ᵉ *Division d'Infanterie*'s tenancy of Douaumont's superstructure to an end; the survivors worked their way back to French lines individually or in small groups in the course of the night.[43] The cost of the abortive attempt to retake the fort was appalling. Three days of fighting cost the 34ᵉ *Régiment d'Infanterie* alone 390 officers and 1,381 men killed, wounded or missing for example. The 5ᵉ *Division d'Infanterie* suffered its heaviest losses of the entire war at 130 officers and 5,507 men, of which 900 had been killed, 2,900 wounded and 1,600 missing; the latter figure included around a thousand men taken prisoner.[44] Ironically, and to his credit given his reservations about the attack, Pétain made no attempt to shift the blame and took full responsibility for the reverse.[45]

The failure of the French effort to retake Fort Douaumont had two significant consequences alongside the lengthening of the list of dead, wounded and missing and the weakening of the front as the destruction of the 5ᵉ *Division d'Infanterie* left a 500-yard wide gap in the French line. On the French side the rebuff was accompanied by disquieting reports of *défaillance* (weakness or breakdown) among the French troops involved, mirroring similar manifestations among their opponents during the earlier fighting for the *Mort-Homme* and Côte 304 across the Meuse. As we have seen, a tacit live-and-let-live system predated the beginning of the battle at Verdun in February 1916, and instances of French troops giving in under German attack became an increasing problem thereafter. Matters came to a head during the fighting for the *Mort-Homme* and Côte 304 on the west bank in March 1916 when 3,000 men from the *67ᵉ Division d'Infanterie* surrendered at Cumières and Corbeaux, and on 20 May when 2,825 men from the *29ᵉ Division d'Infanterie* gave themselves up at Avocourt and Malancourt. Given the drawn-out intensity of the fighting at Verdun, which had cost 23,343 dead, 74,944 wounded and 54,000 missing by the end of May 1916, such failures of morale were unsurprising, and especially on top of the horrendous losses suffered in the 1915 fighting in the Artois and the Champagne. The problem of *défaillance* was to recur with increasing severity as the battle before Verdun ground inexorably on.[46]

On the other side of the line and in conjunction with the seizure of the *Mort-Homme* and Côte 304, the French failure before Douaumont rekindled Falkenhayn's apparently flagging interest in his *Verblutung* experiment in deliberate attrition. The chief of staff of 3. *Armee* visited *Oberste Heeresleitung* at Charleville-Mézières while the French attack on Fort Douaumont was underway, and found the usually taciturn and distant Falkenhayn uncharacteristically animated, 'rubbing his hands with glee', while declaring that the French were behaving in a stupid but accommodating manner. While the fighting on the west bank was underway and despite Crown Prince Wilhelm's wavering, von Knobelsdorf had been busy planning and gathering resources to allow *General* von Lochow's *Angriffsgruppe Ost* to resume the offensive on the east bank of the Meuse. Buoyed up by the French failure at Fort Douaumont, Falkenhayn therefore enthusiastically endorsed von Knobelsdorf's operation, and in so doing initiated an even more intense bout of bloodletting at the original focus of the battle.

8

CLEARING THE WAY FOR THE FINAL PUSH: THE FIGHT FOR FORT VAUX, 1 JUNE 1916 – 8 JUNE 1916

The seizure of the *Mort-Homme* and Côte 304 on the west bank of the River Meuse at the end of May 1916 reinforced *Generalleutnant* von Knobelsdorf, 5. *Armee*'s chief of staff, in his view that Operation GERICHT was both viable and the correct course of action. Despite the wavering of his nominal superior, Crown Prince Wilhelm, he had been assiduously planning and gathering resources to permit *Angriffsgruppe Ost* to resume the offensive on the east bank of the Meuse, and his efforts were endorsed by *Generalmajor* von Falkenhayn and *Oberste Heeresleitung* in the wake of *Angriffsgruppe West*'s success. The new operation, code-named MAY CUP, was scheduled to commence at the beginning of June 1916 and was intended to achieve GERICHT's original objective, that of securing Fort Souville and the Fleury ridge overlooking Verdun from the north-east to act as the jump-off point for the capture of the city. The axis of attack was channelled to the west of Fort Douaumont, running between the fort and the western edge of the Meuse Heights toward Fleury and Fort Souville but there was a crucial stumbling block to be dealt with first. Located 2 miles north-east of Fort Souville, Fort Vaux and the Damloup *Batterie* were ideally placed to fire into the left flank of any German advance on the planned axis; this was especially the case with the Damloup or *Haute* (High) *Batterie*, a hardened artillery position so-called because of its 342-metre elevation which provided a clear line of fire on Fleury and the approaches to Fort Souville. Both works therefore had to be eliminated or at least nullified before the main German attack could proceed, and the mission was allotted to *General der Infanterie* Berthold von Deimling's 15. *Korps*.

Fort Vaux lay midway between Fort Douaumont and Fort Tavannes on the eastern edge of the Meuse Heights, overlooking the village of Damloup and the low-lying Woëvre Plain. Constructed between 1881 and 1884 at a cost of 1.5 million francs, the fort was hardened in 1888 in the wake of the *Crise de l'Obus-torpille* (Torpedo-shell Crisis) and underwent a series of modifications between 1890 and 1912 that raised the price tag to 2.9 million *Francs*; the final phase of modernisation in 1912 involved erecting an apron of barbed wire and metal railings along the outside lip of the ditch and above the counterscarp galleries covering the inside of the ditch.[1] A tapered rectangle in plan 90 metres by 180 metres, Fort Vaux was the smallest fully-fledged fort in the ring around Verdun and was essentially a quarter scale replica of Douaumont, equipped with a single 75 mm turret and girdled with a concrete ditch with machine gun galleries set into the outer faces of the south-western, north-western and north-eastern corners capable of sweeping the ditch with fire and linked by tunnels to the fort interior. In addition, the west and north-western approaches to Fort Vaux were protected by three concrete-reinforced strongpoints located along a line running north-west to south-east in the Bois de Fumin west of the fort to protect the east-facing work from being outflanked and taken from the rear; flanking fire from these strongpoints had proved decisive in rebuffing previous German attacks on the fort proper. The covering positions were called *Retranchement* or R1 through 3, with R1 being closest, only 400 metres west of the fort covering the northern approaches to its glacis. Fort Vaux had been under fire from the heaviest German guns to a more or lesser extent since February 1915 and the fort's sole 75 mm turret had been destroyed when an emergency demolition charge was detonated by a near miss from a 420 mm shell. By the end of February Fort Vaux had been struck by 129 380 mm and 420 mm projectiles and countless smaller calibre shells. The repeated pounding had opened up ominously wide cracks in the fort's reinforced concrete structure, and a direct hit from a 380 mm round had opened up the roof of one of the corridors linking the northern twin counterscarp gallery to the fort proper. The breach was hastily plugged with sandbags.

Conditions within Fort Vaux deteriorated drastically with the commencement of GERICHT, and especially during the intense fighting around the fort in April and May 1916, as testified by a *Caporal* Laurent from the 7/51 *Compagnie du Génie* who was stationed in the fort at that time:

> We lived at Fort Vaux for 15 days, from May 2 to 17 … Eight thousand shells fell every day on the fort and its surroundings on a calm day. We lived in filth, 15-day beard, covered with lice, amid a pungent smell of blood coming from the infirmary, a simple bunker where they piled the wounded and where the dead waited until we could cast them into a pit at night … Everywhere, in the hallways, men were crammed, lying pell-mell into the most diverse positions. The degree of fatigue of all was such that it was enough to sit or lie for just seconds to sleep, sleep like never sleep more.[2]

Conditions for the troops manning the trenches in the vicinity of the fort were not much better, for although the German offensive had petered out at the beginning of March the sector remained active even while French attention was focussed upon Mangin's attempt to recapture Fort Douaumont over the two days beginning 22 May. In the early hours of 21 May the 124ᵉ *Régiment d'Infanterie* launched an attack to capture Sarajevo Trench north-west of the fort and held onto their gains in the face of strong German counter-attacks through the following day for example, while the 142ᵉ *Régiment d'Infanterie* spent the period 20–27 May under heavy German shelling in the area of Damloup village to the north of Fort Vaux, suffering numerous casualties in the process.[3]

Fort Vaux was commanded by forty-nine-year-old *Major* Sylvain-Eugene Raynal. Originally from the 7ᵉ *Régiment Tirailleurs Algeriens* and latterly the 96ᵉ *Régiment d'Infanterie*, Raynal was shot in the shoulder in September 1914 and was then hospitalised for ten months after a shell exploded in his *poste de commandement* in December. He was wounded for a third time on 1 October 1915, suffering shrapnel wounds to the legs, which left him with walking difficulties and reliant on a stick, and was medically discharged from the army as a result and promoted to the *Legion d'Honneur*. Raynal then volunteered when the *Ministére de la Guerre* opened the command of forts to invalided officers in order to free up able-bodied individuals for field service and, having stipulated service at Verdun, arrived to take command of Fort Vaux on 24 May 1916.[4] What he found was not encouraging. Despite Pétain's order at the end of February that all forts were to dig trenches and tunnels leading into their underground wartime entrances to protect troops entering and leaving, nothing had been done, and neither had measures been taken to repair the faulty gauge for the fort's 5,000-litre water reservoir, a problem Raynal does not appear to have been made aware of by his predecessor. He also found his new command crowded with troops 'in such numbers that it is extremely difficult to move, and I took a very long time to reach my command post ... If an attack materialised all the occupants would be captured before they could defend themselves.'⁵ The fort's normal garrison numbered four officers and 279 men drawn from infantry, artillery, engineer and other units and at the end of May the fort was protected by a detachment from the 7/51 *Compagnie du Génie* along with *Lieutenant* Alirol's 6ᵉ *Compagnie* and *Lieutenant* Bazy's 3ᵉ *Compagnie de Mitrailleuses* (machine gun company) from the 124ᵉ *Régiment d'Infanterie*.⁶ By this time German artillery fire had rendered the trenches protecting the fort untenable in daylight and the fort itself was thus hosting a variety of wounded, stretcher-bearers, signallers and stragglers from units stationed in the trenches around the fort including other elements of the 124ᵉ *Régiment d'Infanterie* and men from the 53ᵉ and 101ᵉ *Régiments d'Infanterie*. Attempts to clear these men out proved fruitless, because the evicted either returned or were rapidly replaced by others, all understandably seeking shelter from the incessant shelling outside. Thus, by the beginning of June, there were between 500 and 600 men crammed into Fort Vaux along with a lone spaniel named Quiqui belonging to a member of the 7/51 *Compagnie du Génie* and a small loft of four military carrier pigeons; one of these, Carrier Pigeon No. 787-15, was to play a leading role in the epic events shortly to unfold.⁷

On the German side MAY CUP was to be the heaviest German effort since the battle opened in February, involving the 1 *Königlich Bayerische* (Royal Bavarian) *Korps*, 10 *Reserve Korps* and 15 *Korps* commanded by *General der Infanterie* Oskar Ritter von Xylander, *Generalleutnant* Robert Kosch and *General der Infanterie* Berthold von Deimling respectively. The initial attack was to be carried out by five divisions spread across a frontage of just over 3 miles, rather than the 7 miles of the 21 February assault, with a troop density of one man per yard of front. Neither was there to be any finesse or infiltration tactics, just a head-on assault intended to batter its way through the French defences by sheer weight of numbers, with no regard for friendly casualties. To support the attack, von Knobelsdorf had amassed a total of 2,200 guns by the end of May versus 1,177 French pieces, although the advantage was not quite as clear cut as the bare numbers suggest, particularly with regard to the fort-busting German 420 mm howitzers. Their performance had become severely degraded by this point because the gun barrels were approaching the limit of their useful life, having had more shells put through them than the manufacturers had envisaged. At best this caused shells to 'keyhole' or tumble end-over-end after firing, with obvious implications for accuracy and penetration, while at worst shells could detonate prematurely in or as they emerged from the barrel, which happened to one gun firing on Fort Souville at the end of February.

The wear and tear problem was exacerbated by expending effort on non-vital targets such as the repeated targeting of Fort Moulainville, located south of the Verdun–Metz road. Moulainville thus sustained more structural damage than any other fort in the *Camp Retranché de Verdun*, even though from the German perspective it was of marginal relevance at best in comparison with Fort Souville or Fort Vaux. This diversion of effort also had unexpected consequences. After one 420 mm round failed to explode after hitting Fort Moulainville, French ballistic experts were able to swiftly back calculate the trajectory to pinpoint the gun and bring it under fire. The huge size and consequent immobility of the German 420 mm pieces rendered them especially vulnerable to increasingly effective French counter-battery fire too, which included a specially formed French naval artillery detachment; on one occasion a swift counter-fire mission destroyed a German ammunition dump containing almost half a million shells in the Bois de Spincourt. By the beginning of June a combination of French counter-battery fire and wear and tear had reduced the number of serviceable 420mm pieces to four from the thirteen with which the German artillery had started the battle.[8]

The preliminary phase of Operation MAY CUP, intended to eliminate Fort Vaux and the Damloup *Batterie*, commenced on Thursday 1 June 1916 with attacks by *Infanterie Division* 1 and *Reserve Infanterie Division* 7; both units appear to have been seconded to *General der Infanterie* von Deimling's 15. *Korps* from Falkenhayn's *Oberste Heeresleitung* reserve. The axis of the attack ran through the Bois de la Caillette south of Fort Douaumont and then south-east toward Fort Vaux, and was focussed primarily upon the strongpoints protecting Fort Vaux's flank and rear in the Bois de Fumin. Once again the intensity of the German preparatory bombardment did much of the assault troop's work for them. The 28ᵉ *Régiment d'Infanterie*'s 3ᵉ *Bataillon* manning the Ravin de Bazil sector of the front line was virtually wiped out in the course of the night for example, and the unrelenting shelling reduced the 1ᵉʳ *Bataillon* to just eight men when it attempted to counter-attack the position from the support trench line. The German attack also sidelined the remnants of the adjacent 5ᵉ *Régiment d'Infanterie* and pushed into the shattered remains of the Bois de la Caillette, although the defenders were able to hang on with the aid of reinforcements from the 119ᵉ *Régiment d'Infanterie*.[9]

The massed formations of attackers moving in the open were clearly visible from Fort Vaux, although the garrison were unable to effectively engage them as the fort's 75 mm turret had been destroyed by a sympathetic detonation. Undaunted, Raynal had *Lieutenant* Bazy set up two of his machine guns on the fort glacis which inflicted some casualties on the doubtlessly puzzled enemy by firing at extreme elevation to achieve a range of 2.5 kilometres. Both woods were swiftly overrun along with the R3 and then the R2 strongpoints, the latter falling at 14:30. In a matter of hours the German advance had pushed far into the French lines, again assisted by further manifestations of *défaillance* by the French defenders with some of those that survived the preparatory bombardment fleeing in disorder, while others simply surrendered. *Général* Lebrun, the commander of the affected 3ᵉ *Corps* sector reported that the units of *Général* Georges Tatin's 24ᵉ *Division d'Infanterie* assigned to defend the lost ground had simply disappeared. The commander of strongpoint R1, *Capitaine* Charles Delvert from the 101ᵉ *Régiment d'Infanterie*, had a grandstand view of the German advance sparking a disorderly retreat in the Bois de la Caillette after a brief grenade battle and saw a number of prisoners being marched back to the German lines and captivity before the German advance began to move in his direction.[10]

The 101ᵉ *Régiment d'Infanterie*, commanded by a *Lieutenant-Colonel* Lanusse had moved into the line near Vaux village on 19 May and *Capitaine* Delvert had been assigned to man R1 with his 8ᵉ *Compagnie* shortly thereafter. The strongpoint had been very badly damaged by shellfire and the best location Delvert could find for his *poste de commandement* was 'a niche under a slab of reinforced concrete torn up by a 380 shell'.[11] The main regimental location was targeted by a preparatory German attack on 31 May that overran part of the position and wiped out some of the defending elements. When the *Trommelfeur* barrage began falling on his sector *Colonel* Lanusse brought his reserve up into the Bois de Fumin and his machine guns reportedly slowed the German advance and stacked up German bodies all along the 101ᵉ *Régiment* line. The Germans responded with a violent attack in the early hours of 2 June that drove 7ᵉ *Compagnie* out of Besançon Trench to the west of Fort Vaux and obliged the survivors to seek shelter in the fort, leaving it and R1 virtually cut off from French lines. *Capitaine* Delvert's company was reduced to seventy-one men by Saturday 3 June, and was therefore unable to interfere effectively with German assaults on Fort Vaux. Attempts by two companies from the 101ᵉ *Régiment* to reinforce Delvert the same day were stymied by German shelling with only eighteen and twenty-five men respectively reaching the relative safety of the strongpoint. Delvert and his men beat off repeated German attacks, as well as weathering shelling by both enemy and French artillery and the constant torment of thirst. The last supplies of water, four containers totalling two gallons that reportedly 'smelt of corpses', had come into the strongpoint at around 22:00 on Friday 2 June to be shared among seventy-one men; a modicum of independent relief came on the night of 5 June when Delvert's men were able to catch rainwater in their groundsheets. On the night of 5/6 June 8ᵉ *Compagnie* was finally relieved, although German shelling and fire from enemy machine guns deployed in the R2 strongpoint reduced its strength to thirty-seven by the time they finally reached safety; they had inflicted an estimated 300 casualties on their German attackers. Their departure came none too soon, as a final German assault on 9 June finally overran R1, taking 500 French prisoners in the process.[12]

The Germans had scheduled four days to clear and secure the Bois de la Caillette, Bois de Fumin and the strongpoints in the latter, but the speed of the advance far outpaced expectations and *General der Infanterie* von Deimling moved swiftly to capitalise on the situation. Dismissing protests by his staff that there was insufficient time to complete preparations, von Deimling pushed the attack schedule forward and ordered *Generalmajor* George von Engelbrechten and *Infanterie Division* 50 to attack Fort Vaux at 03:00 on 2 June.[13] Inside the fort, Raynal had watched helplessly as the Germans overran his flank protection and, surmising that a direct attack on the fort would be next, he set about making preparations to meet it. Nine separate breaches in the fort's fabric were sealed with sandbags, including the large hole in the roof of the corridor to the twin north counterscarp gallery. More sandbags were used to erect defensive barricades at key points in the corridors, complete with loopholes for weapons and grenades, and a large stockpile was also created for emergency use. Above ground the pre-attack *Trommelfeur* pounded the fort's glacis and exposed structure, with shells falling at a rate of 1,500 to 2000 per hour according to Raynal.[14] *Lieutenant* Albert Cherel was stationed in Fort Vaux at the time:

> There were all sizes [of shells]: the 77, the 105, bursting tearing; the 210, the 380, the soldiers had nicknamed the 'North-South' because of the strident roar in its wake in the air, perhaps 420 because we found a base near the guardhouse. For the next day these shells at times fell at a rate of 6 per minute and it seemed we lived among … a terrible storm … The air was barely breathable, especially as the unceasing bursting of shells near windows or entries pushed their smoke into the hallways with the dust of earth and stone thrown up by the explosions. The dust had another disadvantage; it increased thirst and made it unbearable.[15]

Although *Lieutenant* Cherel had no way of knowing, thirst was to become the crucial factor in the struggle for Fort Vaux.

The German attack was heralded by the lifting of their bombardment just before dawn on Friday 2 June and as Raynal had expected, it came from the uncovered dead ground where the Meuse Heights dropped abruptly to the Woëvre Plain; a preparatory German assault had driven the 142e *Régiment d'Infanterie* out of Damloup village and thus opened the way to Fort Vaux from the north-east via the Ravin de la Horgne.[16] The attack on the fort was commanded by *Generalmajor* Erich Weber Pasha, who had earned the Ottoman honorific for service in the Dardanelles in 1915, and initially involved two *bataillons* drawn from *Infanterie Regiment* 53 and *Infanterie Regiment* 158 supported by a *Kompanie* from *Reserve Pionier Bataillon* 20 commanded by a *Reserve Leutnant* Ruberg. The attackers charged up the slope leading to the fort and spilled into the battered concrete moat where they came under mutually supporting machine gun fire from the counterscarp galleries set into the north and north-east corners of the moat, which inflicted heavy casualties. The attached elements from *Reserve Pionier Bataillon 20* concentrated their attention upon the north-eastern gallery, manned by a party of thirty-three men from 7ᵉ *Compagnie 142ᵉ Régiment d'Infanterie* commanded by *Capitaine* Georges Tabourot, initially unsuccessfully by attempting to swing bundles of grenades into the gallery's firing embrasures from above; the haste generated by von Deimling's accelerated attack order meant there had been no time to fabricate proper demolition charges. However, when the machine gun in the gallery suffered a stoppage the *Pioniers* seized their chance and forced an entry after cramming a number of hand grenades through the embrasure. There they found a dead crew with their jammed weapon, a 40 mm Hotchkiss *Modèle 1879* revolver cannon and a *Canon de 12* both missing their breech-blocks, and *Capitaine* Tabourot.[17] The latter kept the interlopers away from the entrance to the narrow tunnel linking the gallery to the fort proper with hand grenades long enough for a sandbag barrier to be erected part way along the passage; this held against three German attacks, by which time a more durable barrier had been erected at an iron dividing door. In the meantime Tabourot had been mortally wounded in the legs and kidneys by a German grenade and the survivors of his detachment surrendered at around 05:00.

Things proceeded less successfully for those attacking the twin counterscarp gallery at the northern corner of the moat commanded by a *Sous-Lieutenant* Denizet from the fort's artillery contingent. Lowering bundled grenades in front of the embrasures again proved ineffective but a blast from a *Flammenwerfer* with a modified end-tube silenced the machine guns long enough for a group of around thirty men from *Infanterie Regiment 158*, led by *Leutnant* Kurt Rackow, to scale the inner face of the moat and reach the fort's glacis, although they were then cut off when the smoke and fumes cleared and the machine guns came back into action. Both guns were eventually knocked out but the occupants rebuffed all German attempts to enter the gallery until the late afternoon, by which time at least fifteen of the defenders had been wounded including *Sous-Lieutenant* Denizet; as both NCOs in the detachment had been killed, command devolved to a nineteen-year old *Soldat* named Cahuzac. The end came at around 14:00 when the Germans on the glacis discovered and removed the sandbags plugging the breach in the roof of the corridor linking the gallery to the fort proper and began dropping grenades into it. At that point Raynal withdrew Cahuzac and the rest of the men manning the gallery into the fort and ordered the corridor sealed off. By 16:00 *Infanterie Regiment* 158 was thus in possession of the whole fort superstructure and *Leutnant* Rackow had assumed command as the ranking officer, establishing the defence of both counterscarp galleries and establishing a machine gun position to dominate the approaches to the fort and its glacis. He then ordered *Leutnant* Ruberg and a party from *Pionier Kompanie* 100 to penetrate into the fort via the corridor from the north-east counterscarp gallery. Coming up against a secured steel door Ruberg improvised a demolition charge from grenades but was blown off his feet by the resultant blast that unseated the door and almost killed *Major* Raynal, who was inspecting the effort to block the corridor. Further German progress was then stymied by a hastily deployed French machine gun and Ruberg and his men thus abandoned their efforts and withdrew back down the corridor to the north-eastern counterscarp gallery.[18]

While all this was going on inside the fort, the fighting continued with unabated intensity on the surface and in the surrounding area. An attempt to retake Damloup village in the early afternoon of Friday 2 June by the 142ᵉ *Régiment d'Infanterie* failed when the two *compagnies* involved were virtually wiped out by German artillery fire before reaching the German positions, and elements of six *régiments* from the 53ᵉ and 63ᵉ *Divisions d'Infanterie* had to be pushed into the line in the vicinity of Fort Vaux, the Damloup *Batterie* and the Tavannes Tunnel under protection of darkness to bolster the crumbling French line. Despite this the French also continued to attack through the early hours of Saturday 3 June, with the 75ᵉ *Régiment d'Infanterie* attacking in the Bois de Caillette west of Fort Vaux at 02:00 and 09:00 while the 119ᵉ *Régiment d'Infanterie* conducted a two-*bataillon* attack down the nearby Ravin de Bazil. For their part the Germans spent the early hours of 3 June encircling Fort Vaux in its entirety, cutting it off from the R1 strongpoint and French lines, in part by launching two violent counter-attacks against the 119ᵉ *Régiment*. With his telephone line cut, Raynal released the first of his four carrier pigeons to *Général* Lebrun's 3ᵉ *Corps'* headquarters, located at the *Citadelle* in Verdun, requesting artillery fire be directed onto the fort's superstructure and reporting that the 'losses of the enemy are appalling, but he constantly receives reinforcements of fresh troops who climb the fort, working on top and around the structure and occupy our old trenches armed with machine guns, and he has even managed to install one on top of the fort.' The appearance of the pigeon at the *Citadelle*, wounded and without its message tube, appears to have alerted the French senior command to the possibility that Fort Vaux remained in French hands. A French aircraft was despatched to overfly the fort at low level at 05:00 on Sunday 4 June, as witnessed by war correspondent Kurt von Raden from a trench near the fort's moat, who also noted heavy-calibre French shells falling just minutes later as Raynal serendipitously received the friendly artillery fire he had requested; contact was also re-established via signal lamp with Fort Souville, which had been ignoring Raynal's signals on the assumption the fort had fallen.[19]

Confirmation that Fort Vaux remained in French hands

immediately prompted Nivelle to apply pressure on *Général* Lebrun to address the situation by relieving the German siege. Lebrun responded by ordering *Général* Tatin and the 124ᵉ *Division d'Infanterie* to counter-attack immediately and lead the sortie in person if necessary, a tall order given that much of Tatin's *Division* had been destroyed in the initial German attack and the survivors were widely scattered. Back at Fort Vaux *Leutnant* Rackow's men holding the fort's superstructure came under increasingly heavy and accurate French artillery fire while the effort to penetrate the fort underground was resumed along both the gallery tunnels and continued through the day. As the tunnels were barely 3 feet wide at best and as little as 4 feet high in places, the attackers had no option but to employ the simple but costly tactic of rushing the French defences in single file; the latter consisted of a series of sandbag barriers manned by lone French grenadiers backed by a machine gun to protect men building the next barrier behind it. The fighting was hellish, with men struggling and clawing at one another hand-to-hand in pitch blackness punctuated with the mind-numbing sound and blinding flash of explosions and gunfire that filled the cramped tunnels with dust, smoke and fumes, while the concrete walls magnified the concussion and channelled the flying debris, shrapnel and ricocheting small arms rounds. The cost of fighting in such a cramped, subterranean arena was inevitably high; by midnight on 2 June the *bataillon* from *Infanterie Regiment* 53 had lost all but one of its officers and Rackow's *bataillon* from *Infanterie Regiment* 158 had suffered severe losses to French artillery fire to the extent that both units had to be relieved on the night of 3/4 June.

Dawn on Sunday 4 June also brought a brief period of hope for Raynal and his embattled garrison. *Général* Tatin had managed to rally sufficient elements of his badly damaged 124ᵉ *Division d'Infanterie* to launch the relief attack ordered by Lebrun, likely little more than a *bataillon* each from the 53ᵉ and 124ᵉ *Régiments d'Infanterie.*[20] Attacking in six separate waves, the attackers pushed through shelling and machine gun fire and reached the western edge of the fort before being driven off with a bayonet charge by *Oberstleutnant* Franz von Gottberg's *Fusilier Regiment 39*, which had relieved *Infanterie Regiments 53* and *158* during the night. Meanwhile the struggle underground had taken a new tack as the attackers decided to smoke Raynal and his men out by sealing off all openings into the fort apart from those for ten *Flammenwerfer* to simultaneously pump fire and thus spread the weapon's signature thick black smoke and fumes into the fort. In the event, the new tactic did not succeed as envisaged. Work to seal the fort was disrupted when the activity was spotted by the gunners manning Fort Moulainville's 155 mm turret, only six *Flammenwerfer* survived the French shellfire en route to the fort and an attempt to use two of them on the hitherto unmolested counterscarp gallery at the south-west corner of the moat was stymied when the defenders spotted and killed the *Flammenwerfer* operators while they were making their preparations; the French then mounted a rapid sally to seize the weapons which were used to keep the southern section of the moat clear of further German interlopers.

The attack on the fort proper began at 08:30 on 4 June with fire from up to four *Flammenwerfer* being directed into the 380 mm shell breach in the roof of the corridor from the north gallery. The blast of flame prompted a panicked retreat by the men holding the sandbag barricades to the fort's central gallery followed by thick clouds of choking black smoke that prompted cries of 'A vos masques!' The situation was saved by *Lieutenant* Girard who ran back up the north-west corridor as the flames died down, reaching an abandoned machine gun just in time to open fire on German troops entering the corridor via the roof breach. He continued to man the weapon despite being wounded several times until reinforcements organised by Raynal arrived on the scene, and was then evacuated after succumbing to the effects of the smoke and fumes. The resultant fighting continued through the day and gained the Germans another 25 yards of corridor that included the entrance to one of the fort's three observation domes. On the French side, the *Flammenwerfer* attack inflicted twenty-five serious burn casualties on the French defenders and Raynal ordered the sandbags plugging the vents and breaches in the fort's structure to be temporarily removed in an effort to clear the fumes, as recalled by stretcher bearer *Caporal* Vanier from the 101ᵉ *Régiment d'Infanterie*:

> The Germans sent the burning liquid and black smoke into the casemates … we cannot breathe … With great care, we gradually take away the sandbags … We were lucky not to see Germans in the ditch. Some pop out to breathe. But we must return: commander's order is to close all exits.[21]

The attack also prompted Raynal to issue another plea for relief at 11:30:

> We are still holding but are under very dangerous attack by gas and fumes. Relief is imperative. Do give us optical communication with Souville, which does not respond to our calls. This is our last pigeon.

It is unclear if the other two birds had succumbed to conditions in the fort or had been despatched with messages, but Raynal's final carrier pigeon was No. 787-15. Badly affected by the fumes generated by the *Flammenwerfer* attack, the bird was initially unable to fly and returned repeatedly to the release loophole in Raynal's *poste de commandement* until, presumably revived by the fresh air, it finally departed on the ten minute flight to Verdun's *Citadelle*, where it promptly expired after delivering its message.

Awarded a posthumous *Légion d'Honneur* for its dedication to duty, the only member of his species so honoured, carrier pigeon No. 787-15 was officially designated as *Mort Pour le France* (died for France) and preserved for posterity with the aid of a taxidermist; he later received a dedicated plaque from the *Société Française de Colombophiles* (The Society of French Pigeon Fanciers) which was mounted in the courtyard of Fort Vaux and remains there to this day. The arrival of Raynal's message prompted a supportive lamp signal from Fort Souville, which had again assumed Vaux had fallen into German hands, and at 14:00 a *bataillon* from the 298ᵉ *Régiment d'Infanterie* launched a relief attack planned for the previous day; the delay was presumably due to the assumption that the fort had fallen. The assault succeeded in retaking a section of trench north-west of the fort along with thirty German prisoners, but the attackers were then pinned down by German machine guns mounted atop the fort's counterscarp galleries and were unable to make any further progress.[22]

However, any morale boost from the re-establishment of communications was swiftly dissipated. As we have seen, thirst had been a problem for the fort's garrison from the outset but was about to assume a much more crucial role in the fight for Vaux. After despatching his last carrier pigeon on 4 June Raynal was approached by an NCO from 7/51 *Compagnie du Génie*:

> It was in the course of the afternoon that the sapper sergeant in charge of the stores came and asked to speak to me in private, and said in a hoarse voice: 'Mon commandant, there is practically no water left in the cistern.' I started, I made him repeat what he had said, I shook him. 'There has been dirty work here'. 'No, sir, we have only served out the ration you laid down. It is the marks on the register which have been wrong.' Then our agony began. I gave orders to hold back the little that remained and to make no further allowance today.[23]

According to one of the fort's two medical personnel, *Médecin Auxiliaire* Gaillard, the standard water ration at the beginning of MAY CUP on 2 June was a litre per man per day; this was reduced to three-quarters of a litre on 3 June and to half a litre on 5 June following a day with no ration at all.[24] Following a conference with his surviving officers at 22:00 Raynal also decided to evacuate non-essential personnel from the fort, which at this point numbered in the region of 300 men. Within four hours of the conference the surplus personnel had been identified and divided into small groups led by nineteen-year-old *Aspirant* (Officer Cadet) Léon Buffet from the 142ᵉ *Régiment d'Infanterie*; Buffet was tasked to lead the first group to scout a route for those following and to deliver a report on conditions in the fort on Raynal's behalf. Buffet's lead group also included a *Caporal* Guillantou:

> The moment of departure arrived. It was 01:30. Aspirant Buffet set out at the head. I followed him, and from then on, I went in front. The machine guns were crackling, the rockets lit our way; a violent gunnery barrage accompanied us, from 305s down to 77s; it was a deluge of shells ... our group of nine ... didn't get disheartened and continued its advance ... We reached a quarry that was part of the French lines. The cry 'Halt! Who goes there?' pulled us up sharp. Immediately several voices responded: '*France*!' Our task was almost ended; the break-out had been successful.[25]

Buffet and his men appear to have regained French lines in the vicinity of the Tavannes Tunnel due south of Fort Vaux and were eventually joined by around a hundred other escapees; the remainder were presumably killed or captured.[26]

Meanwhile the Germans had been busy tunnelling beneath the *Casemate de Bourges* at the south-western corner of the fort, intending to detonate a mine and then pour *Flammenwerfer* fire into the resultant breach. The mine performed as expected when detonated at dawn on Monday 5 June, blowing a large breach in the *Casemate*, but a strong and unexpected gust of air from within the fort blew the flames back onto the *Flammenwerfer* operators. The consequent confusion allowed the indefatigable *Lieutenant* Girard to lead a counter-charge with grenades that drove back the attackers and permitted defences to be hastily improvised to meet the new threat; Girard was wounded again in the process. Although the embattled defenders had no way of knowing, the *Flammenwerfer* mishap finally eliminated confidence in the weapons as siege implements and they were subsequently withdrawn from the fort, while Raynal was able to at least temporarily stymie further mining efforts. Alerted by the mine explosion, and observing other evidence of German digging at several points from one of the remaining armoured observation turrets, Raynal signalled Fort Souville for artillery support; shortly thereafter he reported the gratifying sight of French shells bursting on the fort's superstructure and 'German bodies [being] hurled into the moat. Work above us ceased at once.'[27] Subsequent developments were less morale-raising however. In the course of the day the Germans pushed along the north-east corridor to within 60 metres or so of the fort's central gallery and in the process secured the entrance to the fort's latrines, thereby imposing further difficulty and indignity on the hard-pressed defenders. Perhaps worse, just as it finished flashing a message to Fort Souville, Raynal's signalling station was hit by a shell that killed three men, wounded several more and destroyed the signalling equipment.[28] The incident effectively severed Raynal's sole communication link as four subsequent attempts to contact Souville with a jury-rigged replacement drew no response; the last two, at 21:45 and 23:00 on 5 June repeated the same message: 'I must be clear tonight, unless supplies of water reaches me immediately I will be at the end of my strength. The troops, officers and men, in all circumstances, have done their duty to the end.'[29] It was at this point that *Aspirant* Buffet reappeared at the fort. After reaching Tavannes Buffet had been rushed up the chain of command to *Général* Lebrun and then on to an audience with Nivelle himself who pinned a medal on Buffet's chest and informed him that a counter-attack to relieve the fort was scheduled to commence at 02:00 the following morning, Tuesday 6 June.[30] Depending on the source Buffet then either immediately volunteered or had it suggested that he retrace his steps to Fort Vaux to deliver news of the imminent counter-attack to Raynal. He began the return journey from Tavannes at midnight on 5 June accompanied by a *Sergent* Fretté who had accompanied him on the outward journey; Fretté was wounded en route, by friendly small-arms fire according to one source, but Buffet regained the dubious shelter of Fort Vaux unscathed.

Buffet's arrival and news of the imminent counter-attack raised morale in the fort visibly, although Raynal was less than impressed to learn that the attack was only to be in *bataillon* strength and referred to seeing the same reaction on the faces of his surviving officers. The reservations proved well founded. The units slated to carry out the attack, the 238ᵉ and 321ᵉ *Régiments d'Infanterie*, could only raise two *compagnies* apiece reinforced with elements of the 4ᵉ *Régiment du Génie* and had apparently been manning the line for several days. In the event, the preparatory artillery bombardment overshot the fort, although the attack did begin on schedule at 02:00. The 321ᵉ *Régiment d'Infanterie* attacked from the east, overran the German front-line trench and reached the edge of the moat before being stopped cold by fire from German troops dug in on the fort's glacis which killed or wounded all the attacking units' officers and half their men in a matter of minutes. Unable to progress further, the survivors withdrew to their jump-off positions after expending their ammunition and grenades. *Soldat* Jacques Ferrandon recalled crawling all the way back across no man's land:

How long does it took me, I cannot say, but what I saw was terrible: all the French and German corpses, pell-mell. I turned away from one to another; not a hole did not contain many dead or dying; it was terrible ... to realize such a massacre.

Events unfolded in a similar manner on the west side of the fort where the 238ᵉ *Régiment d'Infanterie* attacked from Besançon Trench near the R1 strongpoint. One *compagnie*, weighed down with machine guns, ammunition and ladders to scale the moat, was pinned down in shell holes just short of the moat until nightfall. The Germans pulled back to allow some of the other attackers to penetrate into the moat where they were trapped by fire from machine guns emplaced on the fort superstructure; thirty survivors, seventeen of them wounded, were captured by a German counter-attack at 04:00. Those sheltering outside the moat held in place under fire all day before retiring to Besançon Trench after nightfall. The 238ᵉ *Régiment*'s losses had been appalling; *Capitaine* Aillaud led two officers and 169 men into the attack from which only twenty-two men returned and *Soldat* Georges Quetin recalled a single emotionally distraught *Caporal* answering the roll call for his entire *compagnie* after being withdrawn from the line. Little of this was visible to the garrison of the fort, although the men manning one of the *Casemate de Bourges* watched helplessly as a party of attackers close to the moat were picked off one by one under the guttering light of parachute flares.[31]

The failure of the relief attack plunged morale in the fort to new depths, and events through Tuesday 6 June compounded the damage. The continued German attacks along the underground corridors were held but a large calibre German shell brought down a section of roof in the fort's main gallery, and the garrison was virtually at the end of its tether. The last of the fort's water, foul with the stench of corpses, had been issued and Raynal, himself suffering from a recurring bout of malaria, saw desperate men trying to lick condensation from the fort's concrete walls while others had reportedly resorted to drinking their own urine. Worst of all was the plight of the eighty to ninety wounded, some of whom were severely burned and all of whom had gone without more than basic treatment for days; the fifty or so French dead were stacked elsewhere in the fort. The tipping point for Raynal appears to have come in the evening of 6 June:

> I was in my command post with Sous-Lieutenant Roy ... The door suddenly opened. There stood a terrifying apparition. It was a wounded man, his naked chest swathed in bloody bandages. He leant with one hand against the door frame, and thrusting out a leg, went down on one knee. He held out to me his other hand in a supplicating gesture, and in a whisper, muttered: '*Mon commandant*, something to drink.' I went over to him and raised him up. 'I have no water my brave fellow' ... Still groaning, my wounded man dragged himself back to the aid post. I looked at Roy. Like my own his eyes were clouded.[32]

After a conference with his four surviving able-bodied officers Raynal decided that Fort Vaux and its garrison had done all that could be expected of them. At 03:00 on Wednesday 7 June he therefore despatched *Sous-Lieutenant* Farges from the 142ᵉ *Régiment d'Infanterie* to approach the Germans via the *Casemate de Bourges* at the south-western corner of the fort, carrying a white flag and a letter addressed to 'The Commander of the German Forces Attacking Fort Vaux'.[33] Raynal flashed a final signal to Fort Souville thirty minutes later and at 06:00 sent *Lieutenant* Benazet to escort a German delegation led by a *Leutnant* Müller-Werner from *Fusilier Regiment* 39 from the corridor leading to the north counterscarp gallery to Raynal's *poste de commandement* through a ragged but proud honour guard from the fort's garrison. The delegation's arrival in the fort's central gallery was witnessed by *Caporal* Edmond Patry:

> You could hear the sound of their boots, they climbed the stone stairs in single file, the officer at the head, wearing a cap followed

by telephonists and pioneers, lighting up the corridor with their flashlights. The French were arranged on each side of the centre aisle of the fort; the Germans passed up the middle and saluted.[34]

Raynal then accepted and signed the surrender and presented Müller-Werner with the ornate bronze key to Fort Vaux. The time was approximately 06:30 on Wednesday 7 June 1916. With the siege over, the surviving members of the fort's garrison, which included the somewhat bedraggled spaniel Quiqui, were evacuated from the Calvary they had inhabited for the past week; dog and men then bemused their captors by breaking ranks to slurp the foul water from the first shell crater they came upon. In another scene reminiscent of the eighteenth or nineteenth century, Raynal was taken to 5. *Armee* headquarters at Stenay on Thursday 8 June, where the Crown Prince presented him with a captured French officer's sword to replace his own, lost somewhere inside the reeking chaos of Fort Vaux. The German magnanimity toward their prisoners was highly creditable given the damage they had inflicted. The fighting for Vaux cost *Infanterie Division* 50 a total of 2,742 officers and men killed, wounded or missing, while the garrison of Fort Vaux lost around fifty dead and between eighty and ninety wounded; the number of men who accompanied Raynal into captivity is unclear.[35]

With Fort Vaux finally in German hands von Knobelsdorf and 5. *Armee* were able to authorise *General der Infanterie* Ewald von Lochow and *Angriffsgruppe Ost* to implement Operation MAY CUP and secure the ridge running south-east from the *Ouvrage de Thiaumont*, located just over a mile west of Fort Douaumont, through the village of Fleury to Fort Souville. Securing the ridge would finally place German guns in visual range of Verdun, and in so doing fulfil Falkenhayn's original intent for Operation GERICHT as envisioned back in February 1916.

9

THE TIDE EBBS: THE FINAL GERMAN EFFORT, 8 JUNE 1916 – 12 JULY 1916

Although lack of water had obliged *Major* Raynal to surrender Fort Vaux to *Fusilier Regiment* 39 in the early morning of Wednesday 7 June 1916, the tale of the fort's investment did not end quite there. Virtually all the counter-attacks to relieve Fort Vaux had been understrength, *ad hoc* affairs that owed more to an unholy alliance between the philosophy of *attaque à outrance* and manpower shortages than to sober and considered military planning. As a result they had attempted to accomplish tasks that required brigades or divisions by deploying *bataillons* or even *compagnies*. However, Nivelle was organising a more powerful effort in parallel with the piecemeal attacks, on the grounds that Fort Vaux had to be saved at all costs because the army's honour was at stake, although given his record, the prospect of damage to personal reputation was likely also a factor. Nivelle initially suggested finding the troops required for the new attack via a levy of units from formations manning the line on the west bank of the Meuse, before taking the opportunity to realise one of his pet projects. This was combining what he considered to be the two finest *régiments* in the French army, the 2ᵉ *Régiment de Zouaves* and the *Régiment d'Infanterie Coloniale du Maroc*, into a special *Brigade de Marche* for use as assault troops in shock actions. Obtaining the necessary troops was the least of the problem however, although Nivelle refused to acknowledge that fact. *Major* d'Alenson, his chief of staff, and the remainder of the normally acquiescent and enthusiastic staff at 2ᵉ *Armée* headquarters attempted to persuade him of the drawbacks and practical difficulties of his scheme, not least of which was getting the troops in position at such short notice. When this failed to make any impression d'Alenson hastily organised a conference for Nivelle to discuss the matter with a score of high-ranking officers but again to no avail; Nivelle remained adamant and the offensive was slated to begin at dawn on 8 June.[1] Dismissing German reports that Fort Vaux had fallen as disinformation and propaganda, Nivelle also interviewed the officer selected to command the *Brigade de Marche*, a *Colonel* Savy, to impress upon him that he and his men had been selected for 'the finest mission that any French unit can have, that of going to the aid of comrades in arms who are valiantly performing their duty under tragic circumstances'.[2]

Colonel Savy thus had only approximately twenty-four hours to move his new command into the sector held by *Général* Auguste Hirschauer's 63ᵉ *Division d'Infanterie*, from whence the attack was to be launched. Both regiments were carried in trucks to Houdainville in pouring rain, from where they marched forward to their jump-off positions before the fort. *Lieutenant-Colonel* Régnier and the *Régiment d'Infanterie Coloniale du Maroc* had a relatively straightforward approach march, complicated only by the effects of the rain as described by *Sergent-Major* César Méléra, who was tasked to bring up the rear of his *bataillon* to round up stragglers:

The clay is so slippery and so difficult to climb that one marches as much on one's knees as one's feet. Arrived in a sweat at Souville Plateau where the Battalion is awaiting its rearguard. Lost the Machine gun Company. Found them again after half an hour ... Have to hold on to the coat of the man in front so as not to lose oneself. Fall into hole. Arrive in a glade. Halt; the machine gunners lost again. Three-quarters of an hour's pause.[3]

Arriving at *Général* Hirschauer's *poste de commandement* near Fort Tavannes at 19:00 on 7 June, the *Régiment du Maroc* moved on to the sector east of the fort held by the 321ᵉ *Régiment d'Infanterie* which was to lend support if necessary, although *Sergent-Major* Méléra and his rearguard did not reach Fort Tavannes until 04:00. Things did not unfold so smoothly for *Lieutenant-Colonel* Bonnery and the 2ᵉ *Régiment de Zouaves'* move to the line west of the fort. Guides from the 238ᵉ *Régiment d'Infanterie* were reportedly unable to make it back to Fort Tavannes due to German shellfire, obliging the *Zouaves* to find their own way through the rainy darkness and as a result they only reached their jump-off positions shortly before daybreak.

The attack began on schedule at 04:00 on Thursday 8 June. On the west side of the fort the 2ᵉ *Régiment de Zouaves*, soaked and exhausted after their all-night approach march, ran into an intense barrage from German 210 mm howitzers almost immediately on leaving their jump-off trenches. The shelling killed and wounded many men along with all but one of the *Régiment*'s officers, including *Lieutenant-Colonel* Bonnery, and pinned the survivors down in no man's land. It was thus left to the sole surviving *Sous-Lieutenant* to order a withdrawal back to the relative safety of the 238ᵉ *Régiment*'s trenches. The *Régiment du Maroc*'s assault from the east initially met with more success, in part thanks to *Capitaine* Georges Aymé who urged his men on from a trench parapet in full view of the enemy and continued to command his unit for two days despite being severely wounded. The attackers got as far as the moat before running into heavy fire from German machine guns emplaced on the fort's superstructure that inflicted severe losses on the attackers; one *bataillon* lost seven of its eight officers in a matter of minutes for example, but the attack was pressed until the *Régiment*'s *compagnies* had been reduced to around twenty-five men apiece. At that point the survivors withdrew to the trenches and shell holes they had attacked from and went to ground. Despite his confidence Nivelle's attack to relieve Fort Vaux thus proved to be yet another bloody and fruitless debacle. By the time it was relieved on 17 June the 2ᵉ *Régiment de Zouaves* had lost a total of 900 men killed, wounded and missing, while the *Régiment d'Infanterie Coloniale du Maroc* had suffered a total of 1,137 casualties. Pétain was reportedly and indeed justifiably incensed at the scale of loss and invoked his authority as commander of the *Groupement des Armées du Central* to specifically forbid Nivelle and 2ᵉ *Armée* from making any more attempts to retake Fort Vaux.[4]

In the event, Nivelle's relief attack was too late, and not merely because it went in almost twenty hours after Major Raynal had been obliged to capitulate. The German artillery bombardment that almost annihilated the 2ᵉ *Régiment de Zouaves* as it left its start line was actually the opening phase of MAY CUP. The unfortunate *Zouaves* had thus run headlong into an attack by *Infanterie Division* 50 as *Generalleutnant* Robert Kosch's 10. *Reserve Korps* sought to consolidate its hold on the newly captured Fort Vaux. However, the main focus of the German attack lay just under 3 miles to the west of Fort Vaux, at the north end of the ridge running south-east from Thiaumont Farm through the village of Fleury to Fort Souville. The outer cordon of the *Région Fortifée de Verdun* stretched south-west from Fort Douaumont along the Côte de Thiaumont and Côte de Froideterre, the high points on a long interlinked ridge that dropped away suddenly at its western extremity where the *Ouvrage* de Froideterre overlooked the River Meuse. To the east of Froideterre the line included two hardened *Postes de Commandement* dubbed PC118 and PC119 which had been converted into ad hoc defence works, a 70-metre long combined brigade headquarters, storage and personnel bunker dug into the reverse slope popularly known as the *Quatre Cheminées* (four chimneys) after the four conical air vents that projected from its roof and, roughly midway between Froidterre and Fort Douaumont, the *Ouvrage* de Thiaumont.

Initially constructed between 1887 and 1893, the *Ouvrage* de Thiaumont began as a masonry infantry shelter and barracks topped with parapet artillery emplacements for eight guns surrounded by a moat containing two protective artillery casemates. It was extensively modified and expanded between 1902 and 1905, gaining special concrete sheathing, a *Casemate de Bourges* housing two 75 mm guns, an armoured observation dome and two armoured sentry posts, along with two GF4 retractable machine gun turrets, all enclosed in a dry moat protected by iron railings and an apron of barbed wire 30 metres deep. The total cost of all this came in at 410,000 francs. The *Ouvrage* was linked into the *Région Fortifée de Verdun*'s narrow gauge railway for artillery ammunition resupply, although plans to add a retractable 75 mm turret in 1914 were abandoned due to the outbreak of war. Thereafter the two 75 mm pieces and their ammunition were removed from the *Casemate de Bourges*, in line with the *Grand Quartier Général*'s edict of 5 August 1915 that stripped French forts and other fixed defences of their artillery for reissue to field units. Like the other works in the *Région Fortifée de Verdun*, the *Ouvrage* was also rigged for demolition in the event of capture in January 1916.[5] Unsurprisingly given its location, the *Ouvrage* was heavily shelled in the initial phase of the German attack between 21 and 28 February, which damaged the infantry barracks and moat and destroyed one of the armoured sentry posts and remained under more or less constant shellfire thereafter, which effectively stymied plans to reinstall two 75 mm guns in the *Casemate de Bourges*. *Médicin* Louis Maufrais, who served in the area with the 94ᵉ *Régiment d'Infanterie* between March and April 1916, described a particularly intensive bombardment on 18 March:

> I'll live the hardest day of my stay in this redoubt at Thiaumont. At five in the morning, shells begin to fall everywhere … We are not, I think, especially targeted. This is the same throughout the area: a deluge. In the redoubt, the door shakes and resonates on its hinges. From time to time, wind from the shells blow out the candles. Our heads feel like they are on fire. Everything vibrates, including us. This is not the time to put ones nose outside. According to the noise, it looks like it's the same thing as far as [Fort] Vaux … Then it seems that the bombing slows. Around noon, the attack is reduced to small arms.[6]

By 20 March the shelling had damaged one of the GF4 machine gun turrets and virtually destroyed the moat, along with its protective iron railings, barbed wire apron and barrack block and the decision was taken to withdraw the permanent garrison. Thereafter the *Ouvrage* served as a shelter for the infantry units manning that sector of the line.[7]

By the beginning of June the second machine gun turret had also been put out of commission, and the *Ouvrage* de Thiaumont was well on its way to attaining its unique status as the only modern defensive installation in the *Camp Retranché de Verdun* to be totally destroyed in the course of the battle. Nonetheless, its location at the north end of the spine of high ground running south-east to Fort Souville, alongside Thiaumont Farm and a number of smaller works including three 100-man infantry shelters dubbed FT1, 2 and 3, made it the key to achieving the first phase of MAY CUP. The Thiaumont section of the line was held at that time by *Général* Jean Boyer's 52ᵉ *Division d'Infanterie*, which was trucked into Verdun to join *Général* Lebrun's 3ᵉ *Corps* after serving in the Champagne sector. *Lieutenant-Colonel* André de Lamirault's 347ᵉ *Régiment d'Infanterie* moved into the area of the *Ouvrage* de Thiaumont from 18:30 on 4 June to discover that the line consisted of interconnected shell craters rather than proper trenches. Within twenty-four hours German artillery fire had killed eight and wounded thirty-one, followed by a further fifteen wounded on 6 June; according to one source the 347ᵉ *Régiment* was also alone in being ordered to hold its new positions at any cost.[8] The standard pre-attack *Trommelfeur* bombardment commenced at 06:00 on Wednesday 7 June, the effect of which was magnified by the lack of French trenches and accurate German target registration garnered through the constant shelling of the French line over the preceding months. In addition, the usually efficient French counter-battery fire was nullified by lack of observation, for the German seizure of Forts Douaumont and Vaux had secured the high ground overlooking the Côte de Thiaumont, and French aerial observation was precluded as the Germans had attained temporary air superiority over the battlefield. The German bombardment continued throughout 7 June and into Thursday 8 June with gas shells being added into the mix from 06:00, targeted on the French second line and support positions. German infiltration into the French line began the previous afternoon despite the bombardment, but the first major ground attack commenced at 09:00 on 8 June and continued through the day, with the Thiaumont area being caught in a pincer by attacks from Fort Douaumont and the Bois de la Caillette to the east and the Bois de Nawé and Ravin de la Dame to the north. Confused fighting went on, often in torrential rain, for two days and nights, and while the 52ᵉ *Division d'Infanterie* retained possession of the area it was at a heavy cost. The 291ᵉ *Régiment d'Infanterie* lost 89 dead, 254 wounded and 494 missing between 7 and 10 June for example, while the 347e *Régiment d'Infanterie* lost just over half its battle strength during its six-day stint in the line, which cost 98 dead, including its commander *Lieutenant-Colonel* de Lamirault, 276 wounded and 630 missing; the morale and performance of both these units in the early June fighting was to have far-reaching repercussions as a result.[9]

By the beginning of June German gains had thus effectively nullified their opponents observation abilities, removed their room for manoeuvre, achieved air and artillery superiority and quickly reduced the French reserve at Verdun to a single infantry unit.[10] This was due in part to Joffre's capping of 2e *Armée* to a maximum of twenty-four divisions during Pétain's term in command, while the supply of fresh German formations to feed into the maw seemed inexhaustible. Had the German level of effort been maintained then they might well have finally achieved the breakthrough they had been seeking since February 1916, and possibly provoked a collapse of French national morale due to the amount of French blood spilled in the city's defence. As Pétain pointed out to Joffre in a letter on 11 June:

Verdun is menaced and Verdun must not fall. The capture of this city would constitute for the Germans an inestimable success which would greatly raise their morale and correspondingly lower our own.[11]

Pétain was so concerned by the loss of Fort Vaux and the partial collapse of some French units that he telephoned *Grand Quartier Général* at Chantilly on 8 June and threatened to evacuate the east bank of the Meuse immediately in order to save the artillery assets deployed there. Joffre responded by despatching his chief of staff *Général* Édouard de Castelnau to Verdun on another fact-finding mission, from which he returned on the night of 13/14 June.[12]

The four-day period up to 12 June was thus the most severe of the crises faced by the French at Verdun since the battle began, but the gathering crisis was averted, as in 1914, by the Russians. On 4 June the Brusilov Offensive launched the four Russian armies against the Austro-Hungarian front in Galicia, which promptly collapsed over the next few days with the loss of nearly a quarter of a million prisoners. The Austro-Hungarian chief of staff, *Feldmarschalleutnant* Franz Conrad von Hötzendorf, contacted Falkenhayn at *Oberste Heeresleitung* for assistance on the evening of the same day, no easy task in itself as the two men loathed one another. Falkenhayn, unwilling to be drawn away from the Western Front, initially assumed the Austro-Hungarians were exaggerating and refused to assist, but revised his opinion as the gravity of the situation became apparent. He therefore despatched a full *Korps* to *Oberbefehlshaber Ost* on 7 June from the reserve he had been jealously guarding in anticipation of the coming British attack on the Somme, followed by a further two divisions after a face-to-face meeting with von Hötzendorf the following day.[13] More importantly for events at Verdun, Falkenhayn also ordered 5. *Armee* to suspend Operation MAY CUP and the fighting thus died away with the French still in possession of the *Ouvrage* de Thiaumont and permitted them a breathing space to bring up reinforcements and shore up their battered defences.

The respite also permitted the French to address increasing and disquieting examples of *défaillance* among the units of 2ᵉ *Armée* involved in the fighting at Verdun, which had spread to the east bank from the fighting on the *Mort-Homme* and Côte 304 from March 1916. In addition to capping the size of 2ᵉ *Armée*, Joffre's abolition of the *noria* system obliged French infantry formations to return to the front line at Verdun more frequently and for longer periods than hitherto, with predictable results. By June 1916 French divisions were losing an average of 4,000 men every time they went into the line. The *Grand Quartier Général* representative at 2ᵉ *Armée* headquarters noted the deleterious results of all this, which pre-dated the German attack on 8 June. Instances of troops from the 5e *Division d'Infanterie* bleating like sheep to signify they were mere lambs being led to the slaughter went back to at least April 1916 for example, and in mid-May 1916 fifty men from the 140e *Régiment d'Infanterie* were court-martialled for refusing point blank to re-enter the trenches; all were given relatively light or suspended sentences for the gravity of the offence, on the grounds that 'the best way to punish men who did not want to fight at Verdun was to make them fight at Verdun'.[14] On another occasion elements of the 21e *Division d'Infanterie*, notably the 64e *Régiment d'Infanterie*, organised protests at being ordered back into the line, and in the 12e *Corps* men held a sit down strike for the same reason.[15] The ubiquitous and worrying nature of the problem prompted Nivelle to issue instructions to all officers to employ the most severe measures against offenders that included an exhortation to 'Ne pas se rendre, ne pas reculer d'un pouce, se faire tuer sur place' (do not return, do not step back an inch, be killed in place).[16]

The response to the German attack on 8 June by the 291e and 347e *Régiments d'Infanterie* during the fighting in the vicinity of the *Ouvrage* de Thiaumont cast this problem in even sharper relief, and drew a draconian response from the French military hierarchy. In a smaller-scale echo of earlier events in the Bois de Corbeaux and the Bois d'Avocourt on the other side of the Meuse, large numbers of men from both *Régiments* surrendered as indicated by the high number of missing in their casualty figures, and a *bataillon* from the 291e *Régiment d'Infanterie* surrendered virtually intact after its commanding officer was killed. Events developed in a more deadly manner for two junior officers from the 347e *Régiment d'Infanterie*. On 10 June a party of between thirty-five and forty men led by *Lieutenant* Henri Herduin from 17e *Compagnie*, a career soldier and holder of the *Médaille Militaire*, and *Sous-Lieutenant* Pierre Millant from

19ᵉ *Compagnie*, a graduate of Saint-Cyr, were awaiting relief by the 49ᵉ *Bataillon de Chasseurs à Pied*. When the relief failed to materialise, Herduin, likely assuming his party had been simply overlooked in the routine confusion, led them back to a barracks in Verdun, from where they rejoined their unit bivouacked in the Bois de Fleury the following afternoon. However, the commander of the 347ᵉ *Régiment*'s parent 103ᵉ *Brigade d'Infanterie*, *Colonel* Joseph Bernard, decided that Herduin and Millant's behaviour was a flagrant breach of Nivelle's instructions and wasted no time in invoking his new powers. *Brigade Ordre* No. 1101 issued at 17:00 on Sunday 11 June 1916 accused the officers of abandoning the fight and leaving the battlefield without orders; *Ordre* No. 1102, issued thirty minutes later, sentenced both officers to summary execution and they were shot at 17:43 despite a hurried but unsuccessful appeal by their fellow officers to the commander of the 52ᵉ *Division d'Infanterie*, *Général* Boyer. The story provoked an understandable outcry when revealed by Herduin's widow after the war. Fernande Herduin went on to win civil damages for the illegal execution from *Ministre de la Guerre* Louis Barthou in 1921, and succeeded in having both men officially exonerated in 1926. In the meantime collective punishment was also extended to the 291ᵉ and 347ᵉ *Régiments d'Infanterie* which were disbanded, their surviving personnel dispersed to other units and their colours returned to their respective regimental depots in disgrace.[17]

By June 1916 concern over morale at Verdun had thus led to government-level questions about the casualty rates, and the part played in them by Joffre's leadership. Joffre himself had grudgingly admitted that the pressures of combat and scale of loss at Verdun were causing 'symptoms of lassitude and discouragement' among the troops serving there, although he considered the root of the problem to lie with press criticism of the army's leadership.[18] As we have seen, *Président* Poincaré had been aware of morale problems at Verdun since March, and his concern was heightened by his inability to verify the official casualty figures; this in turn prompted suspicion that the real figures were being suppressed because they were even higher. The upshot was the *Chambre des Députés* (Chamber of Deputies) beginning its own investigation on 16 June via *Comités Secrets* (secret committees); the sessions extended over several months and focussed increasingly on Joffre's conduct of the war, notably driven by André Maginot, a former *Sergent* in the 44ᵉ *Régiment Réserve Territoriale*, who had won the *Médaille Militaire* before being severely wounded in the left leg near Verdun in November 1914. Maginot was particularly critical of Joffre's tactic of *grignotage* (nibbling) at the enemy which he described as 'a war interrupted by partial offensives resulting in no significant strategic gain but, on the contrary, in the most murderous losses', and declared the battle at Verdun 'a huge failure' and 'proof of inadequacy and short-sightedness in our High Command'; he also cited *Colonel* Driant's letters of August 1915 to Paul Deschanel as further evidence. Unsurprisingly the *Comités Secrets* became something of a magnet for Joffre's political opponents and were instrumental in his removal in December 1916.[19]

Back at the fighting front on the Meuse, the MAY CUP hiatus lasted for ten days, and the French were not alone in making good use of the additional time. While Crown Prince Wilhelm engaged in further ineffectual lobbying to have GERICHT terminated, von Knobelsdorf was busy extending his artillery superiority to 2,200 guns over the 1,800 French pieces and readying the attack force of 30,000 men, which now included the elite *Alpendivision*, a specialist mountain warfare unit formed in 1915, commanded by *Generalleutnant* Konrad Krafft von Dellmensingen. The renewed attack, which was scheduled to commence on Friday 23 June, was to be another two-stage affair beginning with an advance on a three-mile frontage intended to secure the Côte de Thiaumont–Côte de Froideterre ridge and push south as far as Fleury. At two men per yard of frontage, the attack was also to have the highest density of men per yard of frontage of the battle so far, moreso than the initial attack in February or that on 8 June. Consequently it eschewed infiltration tactics or tactical finesse in favour of simply bludgeoning a path through the French defences with sheer weight of numbers. In addition, von Knobelsdorf also had a new chemical card up his sleeve, as German chemists had formulated a phosgene gas designed specifically to defeat French-issue respirators. The plan was therefore to knock out the French artillery during the pre-attack bombardment by saturating its gun positions with shells containing the new gas, nicknamed Green Cross after the markings painted on the shells. Phosgene was an especially deadly substance that killed anything it came into contact with, including insects and plants, and was a particularly insidious weapon. The effects of the gas were not apparent to the victim before irreversible harm had been inflicted on the respiratory system, and the victim then drowned in fluid produced by the damaged lungs. For his part, von Knobelsdorf was so confident of success that he invited the *Kaiser* to the 5. *Armee* headquarters at Stenay to witness the triumph and ordered up the regimental bands and colours of the units involved for the anticipated victory parade.

German shelling had remained heavy during the ten-day pause and appears to have been ramped up toward the end; the 39ᵉ *Régiment d'Infanterie* reported intense shelling that caused severe losses especially during daylight in the period 13–21 June for example, while the *Ouvrage* de Froidterre was pounded with shells of up to 380 mm calibre on 20 June and over 500 assorted projectiles the following day. The preparatory bombardment proper began with the mass firing of gas shells beginning at 20:30 in the evening of 22 June, as witnessed by *Lieutenant* Marcel Bechu, a staff officer with *Général* Paul Toulorge's 130ᵉ *Division d'Infanterie* who noted an uncanny cessation of the German shelling followed by:

Multitudinous soft whistlings, following each other without cessation, as if thousands and thousands of birds cleaving the air in dizzy flight were fleeing over our heads to be swallowed up in swarms in the Ravine des Hospices behind [Fort Souville]. It was something novel and incomprehensible.

Lieutenant Pierre de Mazenod, serving in a field artillery unit from the neighbouring 129ᵉ *Division d'Infanterie*, likened the sound of the gas shells to 'thousands of beads falling on a large carpet'.[20] In all the German guns delivered 116,000 Green Cross shells targeted overwhelmingly on French artillery positions which caused a total of 1,600 gas casualties as the unfortunates on the receiving end discovered their respirators no longer afforded protection.[21] By dawn on 23 June, the French guns had been largely suppressed; most of the gun crews in *Lieutenant* de Mazenod's unit were reduced to one or two men for example, and the gas also caused chaos among the horse-drawn transport maintaining the flow of ammunition and victuals to the front line. At around 04:30 the German bombardment switched back to high explosive *Trommelfeur* for the three hours leading up to the beginning of the ground assault, which was to be executed by elements of three *Korps*; *General der Infanterie* Oskar Ritter von Xylander's 1. *Königlich Bayerische Korps* on the right, *Generalleutnant* von Dellmensingen's corps-sized *Alpendivision* in the centre and 10. *Reserve Korps* commanded by *Generalleutnant* Robert Kosch on the left.

On the western end of the attack frontage *Generalleutnant* Albert Schoch's *Bayerische Infanterie Division* 1 left its trenches to attack the *Ouvrage* de Froidterre at 07:35. Similar in size and construction to the *Ouvrage* de Thiaumont, the Froidterre work consisted of a 100-man concrete barrack bunker mounting a retractable GF4 machine gun turret, augmented with a command bunker equipped with another GF4 turret, an artillery bunker mounting a twin-75 mm retracting turret and a *Casemate de Bourges* mounting two more 75 mm pieces, spread over a roughly polygonal compound measuring roughly 350 by 220 metres. As at Thiaumont, Froidterre's defensive moat, railings and barbed wire apron had been largely destroyed by the preceding months of shelling and the pre-attack bombardment had also jammed the machine gun turrets with debris. This allowed the attackers to reach the top of the barrack bunker, from where they proceeded to drop grenades into the bunker through a fissure in the roof created by a large calibre shell the previous day. The situation was saved by a signaller named Nayton Albert who ran across the open courtyard to the artillery bunker to alert the crew of the twin 75 mm turret, which promptly fired off 116 rounds with the fuses set so short due to the extremely close range that the shells barely left the barrel before detonating. The resulting deluge of shrapnel swept the German troops from the barrack's roof and gained the *Ouvrage* garrison a breathing space to bring the machine gun turrets back into action, which then proved to be sufficient to keep the attackers at bay.[22] The gap was partially plugged by the 106ᵉ *Bataillon de Chasseurs à Pied* and 359ᵉ *Régiment d'Infanterie*, which managed to hold the German advance near the south-western edge of the Bois de Nawé; the former also succeeded in retaking some of the trenches lost by the 121ᵉ *Bataillon de Chasseurs à Pied* adjacent to the *Ouvrage* de Thiaumont and an overrun artillery position, although an attempt to push further with the assistance of elements of the 63ᵉ and 297ᵉ *Régiments d'Infanterie* the following day was less successful.[23] In the meantime, more of *Generalleutnant* Schoch's men pressed on down the reverse slope of the Côte de Froideterre running south into the Ravin des Vignes, and besieged the *Quatre Cheminées* shelter. The latter was at this point housing elements of headquarters of four French units, and the German interlopers proceeded to drop hand grenades down its distinctively shaped ventilation shafts. The siege was lifted by 4ᵉ *Compagnie*, 114ᵉ *Bataillon de Chasseurs à Pied* which was ordered forward from its reserve position in the nearby Bois des Vignes by *Général* Adolphe de Susbielle. Despite losing a number of men to shelling and phosgene gas pooled in low-lying areas on the approach march, the *Chasseurs* drove the Germans back with a bayonet charge before establishing a 1,500-yard defensive line with the assistance of two *compagnies* from the 297ᵉ *Régiment d'Infanterie*, also on the orders of *Général* de Susbielle.[24]

On the left of the attack frontage *Generalmajor* Ludwig von Estorff's *Infanterie Division* 103 enjoyed less success attacking the French units holding the area west of Fort Vaux. The bulk of the 405ᵉ *Régiment d'Infanterie* was deployed near Fleury and the Chapelle-Sainte-Fine crossroads, but a party from the 2ᵉ *Bataillon* under a *Capitaine* Rosier were encircled in the Bois de Chapitre and overwhelmed after running out of ammunition. Rosier was seriously wounded in the fighting and the 405ᵉ *Régiment*'s losses were so severe that it was disbanded on 11 July, its three *bataillons* being assigned to other units in 130ᵉ *Division d'Infanterie*; given the glowing regimental eulogies from a number of senior officers including *Général* Toulorge, the disbandment does not appear to have been punitive.[25] Some survivors of the 2ᵉ *Bataillon* withdrew to the Ravine des Fontaines where they joined the 407ᵉ *Régiment d'Infanterie*, which succeeded in holding *Infanterie Division* 103's advance with concentrated machine gun fire followed by a spirited counter-attack led by the regimental colonel that employed every able-bodied man including cooks, pioneers, signallers and orderlies.[26] Events developed most favourably in the centre of the German attack frontage, where *Generalleutnant* von Dellmensingen's *Alpendivision*, spearheaded by *Generalmajor* Ludwig Ritter von Tutschek's *Jäger Brigade* 1, seamlessly picked up from the fighting at the beginning of June. *Jäger Regiment* 2 and *Oberstleutnant* Franz Ritter von Epp's *Bayerische Leib Regiment* overran the elements of the 121ᵉ *Bataillon de Chasseurs à Pied* holding the *Ouvrage* de Thiaumont in short order, taking nearly half the men prisoner, a number which included eighteen officers according to one report. The *Jägers* then pressed south along the spine of high ground toward Fleury, wiping out two *compagnies* from the 239ᵉ *Régiment d'Infanterie* en route. By 08:15 German troops were advancing into Fleury itself, almost a mile from their start line. There they became entangled in a day-long fight for every building with 19ᵉ *Compagnie* of the 239ᵉ *Régiment*, before the latter were finally overwhelmed, while the 39ᵉ *Régiment d'Infanterie* put up equally dogged resistance in the adjacent Bois de Fleury and around a large ammunition storage bunker known as the *Poudrière* to the west of the village. French resistance was assisted by resurgent French artillery; *Sous-Lieutenant* Tourtay, watching from an observation balloon, was 'overjoyed' to see effective French artillery fire landing on German-held locations from around 09:00. Nonetheless, by the afternoon the attackers had secured a good portion of Fleury and were lofting extreme-range machine gun fire over the Côte de Belleville into the streets of Verdun, just over 2 miles away. Fleury was fully secured by midnight but the fight had cost the *Leib Regiment* fourteen officers and 550 men killed, wounded or missing. The Germans established a defensive line along the railway embankment running south-west from the village, although this was in full view of French artillery observers who directed fire onto the slightest sign of German activity.[27]

The severity of the fighting on 23 June is clear from the casualty figures. By the time they were relieved on 25 June, the 39ᵉ *Régiment d'Infanterie* had lost a total of forty-eight officers and 1,633 men killed, wounded or missing, while the 239ᵉ *Régiment d'Infanterie* had been reduced to an effective strength of five officers and 150 men, for example.[28] Overall the French lost around 13,000 killed and wounded, with an additional 4,000 taken prisoner.[29] The

German advance also severely unsettled the French command. By the end of the day the Governor of Verdun was supervising the digging of trenches in the city in readiness for a last-ditch defence. According to the subsequent legend, Joffre and Nivelle prevented a rattled Pétain from evacuating the east bank of the Meuse, a view supported by Nivelle's famous Order of the Day that included the immortal line sometimes attributed to Pétain: 'Ils ne passeront pas!' (they shall not pass).[30] The charge against Pétain was based largely on a telephone exchange between him and de Castelnau in the afternoon of 23 June but Pétain had only been alerting *Grand Quartier Général* to the ramifications of a continued German advance. At the same time the supposedly resolute Nivelle was actually ordering the evacuation of guns from the area of Bras and Froideterre, while the allegedly unflappable Joffre was sufficiently concerned to redirect four divisions from his jealously guarded hoard for the upcoming Somme offensive to Verdun.

In the event, this buck-passing proved unnecessary because, although it was not immediately apparent from the French side, Operation MAY CUP had failed, and for largely the same reasons that had dogged previous attacks. Once again the attack frontage was not sufficiently wide to permit a clean breakthrough and once again the advance proved increasingly vulnerable to flanking fire. Consequently, the 23 June attack merely formed a narrow salient into French-held territory, and on a totally exposed forward slope open to French observation and fire from three sides. More importantly, the troops in the salient were obliged to maintain their disadvantageous positions because, in spite of von Knobelsdorf's best efforts, 5. *Armee* simply lacked the reserves to resume the attack on 24 June; in this regard the three divisions sent east by Falkenhayn to assist their Austro-Hungarian allies might thus have made all the difference. In addition, the stock of phosgene gas shells, which had only been sufficient to cover the central sector of the attack frontage in any case, had been virtually exhausted and the new gas had not performed as advertised either. French-issue respirators proved less susceptible than expected, and while French artillery positions tended to be on higher ground, the heavier-than-air phosgene gas tended to pool in hollows and low ground. The impact of the gas was reduced further by the return to conventional shelling three hours or more before the ground attack commenced, which permitted the French artillery a vital breathing space. Finally, the weather had also taken a hand as 23 June was one of the hottest days of the year, and the heat was exacerbated by the physical state of the battlefield, which constant shelling had ploughed into a cratered, milky brown desert bereft of foliage or shade. Water was therefore a key requirement but had to be brought forward by hand with all the limitations and risk that entailed; only twenty-eight of ninety-five water bearers from the *Bayerische Leib Regiment* despatched to Fleury during the night of 23/24 June got through, for example.[31]

With MAY CUP thus irretrievably stalled, the *Kaiser* returned disappointed to *Oberste Heeresleitung* headquarters at Charleville-Mézières while the regimental bands and colours gathered for the triumphal parade were quietly dispersed back whence they had come. Von Knobelsdorf however was still convinced that GERICHT was both viable and correct, and he was thus loath to admit that the operation had failed. In fact, he remained so certain that victory was attainable with just one more effort that he again bypassed Crown Prince Wilhelm and set about persuading Falkenhayn to grant him permission to continue with the operation. Falkenhayn, preoccupied with preparing to meet the coming *Entente* offensive on the Somme, resisting requests from *Oberbefehlshaber Ost* for reinforcements to meet the unexpectedly resilient Brusilov Offensive and expanding *Oberste Heeresleitung*'s strategic reserve, initially refused. On the contrary, he was looking to rein in offensive actions as indicated in an instruction to 5.

Armee issued on 24 June, albeit one that suggests he was unaware of 5. *Armee*'s success the previous day:

> The general situation makes it very desirable that the *Heeresgruppe* limit seriously the use of men, materiel, and munitions. The opinion is requested as to how this can be carried out after ... Thiaumont, Fleury, and a certain area of the foreground to Fort Vaux are taken.[32]

Von Knobelsdorf persisted however and Falkenhayn, presumably in the hope that his *Verblutung* experiment could be brought to a favourable conclusion, eventually gave his consent on the proviso that 5. *Armee* achieved its objective with its existing pool of units and von Knobelsdorf promptly set about preparing what was to be the ultimate German effort at Verdun. Matters on the Meuse had not been quiescent in the meantime as Nivelle had brought back *Général* Charles Mangin, who had been sacked after the costly failure to retake Fort Douaumont at the end of May 1916. Placed in charge of all operations on the east bank of the Meuse, *le boucher* immediately embarked on a sustained but unsuccessful effort to drive the Germans out of Fleury and retake the Côte de Thiaumont, launching eight separate attacks between 24 and 30 June interspersed with German counter-attacks. At the end of that period the respective lines were where they had been at midnight on 23 June and again the only progress had been in lengthening the casualty list on both sides.

The new German attack was scheduled to begin on 9 July, and was to be a two-pronged affair again focussed on Fort Souville. The drive south from Fleury was to be renewed, employing the *Alpendivision*, *Bayerische Infanterie Division 1* and *Infanterie Division 103*. These formations were already ensconced in the exposed salient and were badly depleted; *Jäger Regiment 3* from the *Alpendivision* had suffered 1,200 casualties in the fighting from 23 June, for example.[33] The second prong, provided by 5. *Reserve Korps*, was to approach Fort Souville from the area of Fort Vaux to the north-east. This line of advance was overlooked from the east by the Damloup *Batterie* however, a number of hardened gun pits and concrete bunkers located atop a 342-metre elevation a mile or so south of Fort Vaux. The *Batterie* therefore had to be eliminated before the main assault could be launched, and the task was assigned to the formation that had conquered Fort Vaux, *Generalmajor* George von Engelbrechten's *Infanterie Division* 50. Von Engelbrechten chose to accomplish his mission via an imaginative ruse involving a number of heavy-calibre *Minenwerfers*. The latter set a pattern of staging short but intense barrages on the Damloup *Batterie*, during which the defending French infantry developed the habit of withdrawing to the safety of their protective shelters. In the early hours of Monday 3 July German assault troops crept close to the *Batterie* under cover of such a bombardment and then waited until the *Minenwerfers* began firing bombs without fuses at 02:00; they then stormed the *Batterie* before the defenders realised what was afoot, capturing three machine guns and taking over a hundred prisoners.[34]

In the meantime preparations for the main attack had gone ahead apace, although the weather again took a hand on Friday 7 July, with torrential rain that was a mixed blessing for the *Bayerische Leib Regiment* clinging to its improvised front line behind the railway embankment at Fleury. While it alleviated thirst, the rain also swiftly turned the shell-churned battlefield into a milky swamp that swallowed men and equipment. This was less than ideal preparation for troops who had already been exposed to unceasing French artillery fire for three days under strict orders forbidding any movement during the hours of daylight in an effort to preserve the element of surprise; this included rendering assistance to the wounded, with obvious implications for morale. The bad weather resulted in a two-day postponement of the attack, which was therefore rescheduled for Tuesday 11 July, although it came close to being cancelled altogether. Falkenhayn, in one of his regular fits of vacillation, withdrew permission for the assault on 11 July but by that time the pre-attack bombardment was underway and it was too late to get the cancellation out to the various divisional headquarters in time.[35]

The pre-attack bombardment commenced at around midnight Monday 10 July with Green Cross gas again playing an important role in the fire plan. The latter had been modified to ensure gas shells continued to fall on French artillery positions until the assault infantry were on the move, to avoid giving the French a respite as had occurred on 23 June. According to the 167ᵉ *Régiment d'Infanterie* holding the line south of Fleury, the German bombardment commenced at 02:00 on Tuesday 11 July and the gas shelling began thirty minutes later, followed by the ground attack at 04:00.[36] Whatever the precise timings, the gas shelling was observed from afar by *Sergent* Marc Boasson from the 414ᵉ *Régiment d'Infanterie*:

> [It was] a gripping spectacle; – little by little, we saw the country disappear, the valley become filled with an ashy-coloured smoke, clouds grow and climb, things turn sombre in this poisoned fluid. The odour of the gas, slightly soapy, occasionally reached us despite the distance. And at the bottom of the cloud one heard the rumble of explosions, a dull noise like a muffled drum.[37]

However, the phosgene gas once again proved to be less effective than expected, not least because the French had issued an improved respirator that largely nullified its effects, and French gas casualties were consequently limited to a literal handful. Demonstrating admirable restraint, the French guns held their fire until the German assault troops were on the move before commencing their counter-battery and defensive fire plans. The effect was especially devastating along the exposed railway embankment running south-west from Fleury, which was smothered with fire as von Tutschek's *Jäger Brigade* 1 left the shelter of their rudimentary trenches and shell craters. Around half of the *Brigade*'s lead elements were killed or wounded in a matter of minutes, and the commander of 1. *Bataillon, Jäger Regiment* 3 despatched a message to his brigade commander declining responsibility for continuing the attack in the face of such fire and ordered his men to dig in.[38]

The same process occurred to the east of Fleury in the Bois Vaux-Chapitre where *Oberst* Hans Karl von Winterfeld's *Infanterie Brigade* 8 attacked out of the Bois Vaux-Chapitre toward Fort Souville; *Infanterie Regiment* 140 was stopped cold by the French artillery fire with its 2. *Bataillon* losing almost its entire complement of officers in a matter of minutes. Despite this, the 04:00 attack south from Fleury by *Jäger Brigade* 1 proceeded well once the unwelcome shock of the French artillery fire had been absorbed. The 167ᵉ *Régiment d'Infanterie*'s 2ᵉ *Bataillon*, holding the right of the *Régiment*'s line, was forced back at around 05:00, opening the way for the *Jägers* to seize Fleury station, the *Poudrière* and overrun its parent 255ᵉ *Brigade d'Infanterie* headquarter at 05:50. The *Brigade* commander, *Colonel* Coquelin de Lisle, having despatched a situation report via carrier pigeon and burned his confidential papers at the German approach, was killed fighting to protect his headquarters.[39] The attackers then pushed on to the edge of the Bois de Fleury where they were stopped by the 167ᵉ *Régiment*'s left *bataillon*, which had to be reinforced at 10:00 by the neighbouring 168ᵉ *Régiment d'Infanterie*.[40] The breach may have been the result of a further incident of *défaillance*, given that a neighbouring unit saw some elements of the 167ᵉ *Régiment* firing on erstwhile comrades moving to surrender.[41] Later in the day Mangin called up the 100ᵉ and 168ᵉ *Régiments d'Infanterie* to plug the gap, but they became lost in the darkness and failed to reach their allocated position between the *Poudrière* and the Chapelle-Sainte-Fine; eighty men from the 100ᵉ *Régiment* were taken prisoner after blundering into the German line on the railway embankment. The German attack also pushed back two sections of the line near the Chapelle-Sainte-Fine crossroads held by the 7ᵉ *Régiment d'Infanterie*, prompting several local counter-attacks to regain the lost terrain. In the course of the day the 7ᵉ *Régiment* was also obliged to detach a *bataillon* to support the 358ᵉ *Régiment d'Infanterie* fighting in the Bois de Fumin to the east, and despatched 3ᵉ *Compagnie* under *Lieutenant* Kléber Dupuy to reinforce 10ᵉ *Compagnie* defending Fort Souville; Dupuy and his men were shortly to play a leading role in the drama that unfolded at the fort.

Despite *Infanterie Regiment* 140's initial mauling by the French artillery, the eastern German advance from the Damloup *Batterie* was equally successful. The 217ᵉ *Régiment d'Infanterie*, occupying exposed positions on the forward slope of the Ravin de la Horgne in the Bois de Fumin, was overwhelmed by the weight and ferocity of the German attack, the shock being exacerbated by the presence of *Flammenwerfer* teams. One *bataillon* was wiped out and another surrendered virtually en masse after being encircled in another example of *défaillance*. The regimental commander, a *Lieutenant-Colonel* Leyrand was captured in his *poste de commandement*, although this turned out to be just the beginning of his adventures. Unwounded when a shell-burst killed the two Germans escorting him back to Fort Vaux, Leyrand returned to his *poste de commandement* where he was recaptured and incarcerated with a number of other French prisoners waiting to be escorted to the rear. He was liberated at around 19:00 when a counter-attack by the survivors of his *Régiment* retook the *poste de commandement*, capturing eighty of his erstwhile jailers in the process, although 2ᵉ *Compagnie* pushed too far into the German lines and were in turn surrounded and captured.[42] The precipitate withdrawal of the 217ᵉ *Régiment* exposed the right flank of the 6ᵉ *Bataillon*, 358ᵉ *Régiment d'Infanterie* in the adjacent Bois de Fumin. One *compagnie* was promptly encircled and wiped out and another was obliged to pull back and link up with a third to avoid the same fate; the line was then held against repeated German attacks up to *bataillon* strength until reinforcements arrived from the 7ᵉ *Régiment d'Infanterie*.[43] The German advance also came dangerously close to the entrance of the Tavannes Tunnel, which carried the Verdun–Metz railway line for a kilometre and a half under the Côte de Belleville. The French had been using the tunnel as a protective conduit to the eastern end of the Verdun frontage since early in the battle, and it had become home for a variety of headquarters, transport, supply, medical and signal units, as well as a great number of stragglers seeking shelter from the incessant shelling. It is unclear whether the Germans knew about the tunnel, possession of which would have allowed them to bypass Fort Souville and the forts on the Côte de Belleville and move straight to Verdun, although the fact that they did not make a serious effort to secure it suggests that they did not. The French were understandably disinclined to take the chance however, and made hasty arrangements for its demolition.

By nightfall on 11 July the Germans had penetrated 400 yards into the French front-line toward Fort Souville, taken 2,400 prisoners and inflicted heavy losses on the French.[44] The 358ᵉ *Régiment d'Infanterie* had lost over a third of its effective strength by midnight for example, and the 217ᵉ *Régiment d'Infanterie* had lost thirty-three officers and 1,300 men by the time it was relieved on 15 July.[45] The German bombardment continued all night, rising to a crescendo as the attack was resumed at 05:00, sparking confused fighting as the exhausted troops clashed along the poorly defined front line. French resistance was stiffening, but the German infantry were by now approaching exhaustion, and Falkenhayn's insistence that 5. *Armee* carry out the attack without reinforcement meant that once again there were no fresh troops to maintain the momentum of the attack. However, at around 06:00 an excited staff officer from the *Alpendivision* forward headquarters informed *Generalleutnant* von Dellmensingen that a group of men were visible on the glacis of Fort Souville waving a German flag in an effort to attract reinforcements and presumably deflect the German artillery fire falling on the fort. After verifying the report with his binoculars, von Dellmensingen immediately ordered the artillery to shell the area south of the fort to seal it off, although frustratingly there were no reserves available to push forward and complete the seizure.

The men waving the flag were from *Infanterie Regiment* 140, although their number is unclear. One source refers to a stray group of thirty or so who had been driven forward by French artillery fire commanded by an unknown ensign, while another numbered the interlopers in the hundreds. Whatever their numbers, the interlopers were able to see Verdun basking in the early morning summer haze less than 2 miles distant, and it fell to *Lieutenant* Kléber Dupuy and 3ᵉ *Compagnie*, 7ᵉ *Régiment d'Infanterie* to resolve the situation. Dupuy, it will be recalled, had been despatched to reinforce 10ᵉ *Compagnie* of his *Régiment* defending Fort Souville. After having his own party reduced to sixty by artillery fire and gas en route, Dupuy arrived to find his predecessors bereft of officers and largely suffering from gas poisoning. The arrival of the German party sparked an exchange of grenades with the garrison while Dupuy rounded up every able-bodied infantryman and led a sally out onto the fort's superstructure, a courageous move given that Dupuy had no idea how many intruders he was facing. A fierce, three-hour fight then ensued with grenades and machine guns until 09:00, when the German interlopers were driven off the glacis, leaving a number of dead and ten prisoners and the survivors taking shelter in the surrounding shell holes and fragments of trenches; both sides were then driven back to their start positions by fire from French and German guns, as the former had also begun shelling the fort on the erroneous assumption it had fallen into German hands. The intrepid Dupuy was reinforced at 11:00 by a platoon from the 14ᵉ *Régiment d'Infanterie* and relieved at 21:30 by the 25ᵉ *Bataillon de Chasseurs à Pied*.[46] Although it was not apparent at the time, the brief presence of the party from *Infanterie Regiment* 140 marked the high water mark of the German advance toward Verdun and, after 139 days of near constant bloodletting, the effective end of Operation GERICHT.

10

FULL CIRCLE: FRENCH COUNTER-ATTACKS AND WHAT CAME AFTER, 14 JULY 1916 – 2016

From the German perspective Operation GERICHT ended on 2 September 1916 when the newly installed head of the *Große Generralstab* ordered the cessation of all offensive operations at Verdun.[1] However, it could be argued that in practical terms the end for the German side came with the eviction of the party from *Infanterie Regiment* 140 from the glacis of Fort Souville by *Lieutenant* Kléber Dupuy in the morning of Wednesday 12 July. This contention is supported by the fact that *Oberste Heeresleitung* ordered 5. *Armee* to suspend operations at Verdun and remain 'strictly on the defensive' on Friday 14 July.[2] At that point both sides had fired an approximate total of 37,000,000 artillery shells, 22,000,000 by German guns alone and French ammunition expenditure actually increased; in the period 26–31 July French guns fired 77,000 rounds of 75 mm and 24,000 rounds of larger calibre ammunition per day.³ Despite its longevity and appalling cost in lives the German turn away from Operation GERICHT was abrupt, although support for the volte-face was not universal. Perhaps unsurprisingly, von Knobelsdorf remained convinced that success at Verdun remained within reach in spite of the failure of the 11 July attack, and he began trying to persuade von Falkenhayn to authorise a further effort at a conference on 15 July; this prompted Falkenhayn to issue a further, rather ambiguous order to 5. *Armee* to maintain an 'aggressive posture ... for home and enemy consumption'.

Crown Prince Wilhelm, sensing that a continuation of GERICHT was being prepared behind his back, responded by calling a conference of his own at Stenay with *General der Infanterie* Ewald von Lochow and the newly arrived *Generalmajor* Hermann von François, commanders of *Angriffsgruppe Ost* and *Angriffsgruppe West* respectively. The latter recommended continuing the offensive in order to avoid showing weakness, possibly because as a new arrival he had not been involved in the bloodletting of the *Mort-Homme* and Côte 304. Von Lochow however, who had served on the east bank of the Meuse since the beginning of GERICHT in February, was of the view that even seizing Fort Souville would merely provoke another round of costly and indeterminate fighting. He thus sided with the Crown Prince's view that the offensive should be curtailed in favour of consolidating existing positions. When the Crown Prince relayed the outcome of his discussion to Falkenhayn at *Oberste Heeresleitung*, he was informed that he should follow whatever course he considered appropriate. Crown Prince Wilhelm's next move was therefore to lobby his father, the *Kaiser*, once again and on this occasion his lobbying bore fruit, largely due to the *Kaiser*'s disillusionment with Falkenhayn, Knobelsdorf and the course of the war generally. On 20 August 1916 von Knobelsdorf was removed from his post as chief of staff to 5. *Armee* and appointed to the command of

10. *Armee Korps* on the Eastern Front, and departed Stenay the following day; he retired from the *Heer* on 30 September 1919 and disappeared into obscurity.[4]

The *Kaiser*'s disillusionment with von Knobelsdorf was matched by similar feelings toward von Falkenhayn within the *Heer*, elements of which had never been totally convinced of the efficacy of his *Ermattungsstrategie* in any case. The failure of GERICHT, in conjunction with events in the east, especially the entry of Romania into the war on the side of the *Entente* on 27 August 1916, which Falkenhayn had adamantly insisted was impossible at that time, gave his enemies the ammunition they needed to engineer his removal. He was obliged to tender his resignation as head of the *Oberste Heeresleitung* to the *Kaiser* on Monday 28 August 1916.[5] Appointed to command 9. *Armee* in Transylvania on 6 September, Falkenhayn fought a successful campaign against the Romanians before being posted to *Heeresgruppe F* in Palestine on 20 July 1917, and then back to the, by then quiescent, Eastern Front to command 10. *Armee* from 5 March 1918 to the end of the war. After leaving the *Heer* in 1919 he retired to the *Schloss* Linstedt at Potsdam, where he penned his autobiography, a number of works on strategy and his war memoirs, which were published in English in two separate editions. Despite reportedly insisting that German casualties at Verdun had been only a third of the French, Falkenhayn appears to have suffered from psychologically rooted illness and told a relative he was unable to sleep at night; he passed away on 8 April 1922 aged sixty-one.[6] He was replaced as head of the *Oberste Heeresleitung* on 28 August 1916 by the duo of *Feldmarschall* Paul von Hindenburg and his chief of staff *Generalmajor* Erich Ludendorff, who subsequently adopted the title of *Erste Generalquartiermeister* (First Quartermaster General). Both men visited Verdun shortly after being appointed and were appalled at what they found; while later describing the battle as 'a beacon light of German valour', at the time Hindenburg acknowledged that the fighting at Verdun had 'exhausted our forces like an open wound. Moreover, it was obvious that in any case the enterprise had become hopeless ... The battlefield was a regular hell and regarded as such by the troops'. Ludendorff's comments echoed those of his chief: 'Verdun was hell. Verdun was a nightmare for both the staffs and the troops who took part. Our losses were too heavy for us.'[7] It was Hindenburg's order that finally brought Operation GERICHT to a close on 2 September 1916.

However, Hindenburg's order did not bring the fighting on the east bank of the Meuse to an end. This was partly because the French were not privy to events at the top of their opponent's military hierarchy and thus had no way of knowing that the attack of 11/12 July was the final German effort, and partly because 5. *Armee* was too physically close to their objective of dominating and/or seizing Verdun for comfort. As we have seen, *Général* Pétain had ordered 2ᵉ *Armée* to address the situation in response to the German attack of 23 June and *Général* Nivelle had assigned the task to Mangin, who promptly applied himself with his customary disregard for friendly casualties. By 14 July he had pushed the Germans back to the start line of their final attack and continued to attack north along the transverse ridge straddled by Fleury toward the shattered remains of the *Ouvrage* de Thiaumont. The fighting for the nearby PC119 was especially heavy, and in the process Fleury was reduced from a village providing accommodation for around 500 to a brick-coloured smear in the finely churned soil; according to legend a damaged silver chalice from the village church was the only tangible relic recovered after the battle.[8] Pétain was again placed in the invidious position of watching the French casualty figures mount from his *Groupement des Armées du Central* headquarters at Bar-le-Duc as the aggressive Mangin repeatedly mounted poorly coordinated piecemeal attacks, and by mid-July was again obliged to rein in his impetuous subordinate. On 15 July *Général* Henri Niessel's North African 37ᵉ *Division d'Infanterie*, which was apparently looking to redeem its reputation after its failure in the early stages of the battle, was pitched into an attack on the remains of Fleury with little familiarisation and badly coordinated artillery. Predictably the *Division* suffered very heavy casualties as a result; as Alistair Horne put it, 'once again the Verdun slopes were carpeted with the khaki-clad figures of Tirailleurs and Zouaves.' The incident prompted Pétain to go over Nivelle's head and make his dissatisfaction known to Mangin in person via a long and critical letter, and to order 2ᵉ *Armée* to conserve its strength for a coordinated counter-offensive.[9] The tempo of French operations thus fell away, although there was little reduction in their artillery activity, a policy referred to as 'not burying the hatchet' by Mangin. The daily, routine losses thus continued, recorded under the chillingly dehumanised heading of 'wastage' while Pétain set about organising the counter-stroke he had envisioned ever since taking command at Verdun back in February 1916.

The French death toll was increased yet further during this relatively quiet period by an event that paralleled the accidental explosion in German-occupied Fort Douaumont on 8 May 1916. The Tavannes Tunnel, home to 1,400 yards of the Verdun–Metz railway line, was being used by the French military as a well-protected base and storage bunker, and offered relief from the relentless German shelling. By June 1916 it was sheltering up to 2,000 men reliant upon one small water source, with no proper latrines or ventilation system. The German approach on the north-east end of the tunnel prompted an evacuation in preparation for demolition on 22 June, but the tunnel rapidly reverted to its former state when the threat receded. The already unsanitary conditions were exacerbated by the constant German shell fire which prevented the occupants from leaving the tunnel; they were thus obliged to relieve themselves in the gutter channels that ran alongside the track, which had to be regularly sluiced out by fatigue parties with jocular calls of 'Attention la merde ... Otez les gamelles! La jus coule partout' (watch the shit ... take away the bowls! The sauce flows everywhere).[10]

At around 21:00 on Monday 4 September a fire broke out at the south-western entrance to the tunnel, possibly among a cargo of signal rockets being carried in by mules, and spread to a cache of grenades which in turn ignited the fuel stored for a nearby petrol generator. At 21:15 a tremendous explosion tore through the tunnel, blocking the south-western entrance and setting fire to the temporary wooden structures within, which rapidly filled the tunnel with thick, choking smoke that defeated respirators. Survivors attempting to escape from the north-eastern exit were driven back by the German bombardment, which was intensified on seeing the smoke from the explosion; many survivors had to be prevented from re-entering the tunnel by an officer wielding a pistol. The fire burned for two days, so fiercely that many bodies were totally consumed; investigators found piles of charred corpses gathered beneath the vertical ventilation shafts in the tunnel roof, where men had vainly sought escape. Only a third of the bodies recovered could be identified. The true number of casualties is not therefore known but may have been as high as 600, including, among others, an entire brigade headquarters, men from the 1e and 8e *Régiments du Génie* and medical personnel and wounded from the 346e, 367e, 368e and 369e *Régiments d'Infanterie*.[11]

In the meantime Pétain was preparing his counter-offensive with his customary efficiency and painstaking attention to detail. The planning was carried out in close cooperation with Nivelle and Mangin, with the latter being responsible for much of the operational detail albeit under close supervision. The objective of the offensive was to push the German line back to the Côte de Froideterre ridge and recapture Fort Douaumont in a single bound of over 2 kilometres, an unprecedented distance for the

Verdun fighting. Through August and September 1916 a force of eight divisions and the requisite guns, ammunition and stores were methodically gathered to accomplish the task, in some instances with the assistance of Joffre, who arranged for seven of the 2ᵉ *Armée*'s twenty-two divisions to be replaced by mid-October.[12] The attack was to be made on a 5–7-kilometre frontage with *Général* Joseph Guyot de Salins' North African 38ᵉ *Division d'Infanterie* on the left tasked to secure Douaumont village and retake Fort Douaumont; the latter mission was entrusted to a *bataillon* from *Lieutenant-Colonel* Régnier and his *Régiment d'Infanterie Coloniale du Maroc*. In the centre *Général* Fénelon Passaga's 133ᵉ *Division d'Infanterie* was to secure the remains of Fleury, the Ravin de Bazil and the Bois de la Caillette south of the fort while *Général* Charles de Lardemelle's 74ᵉ *Division d'Infanterie* recaptured the Bois de Fumin, the Ravin de la Horgne and Fort Vaux. The second wave of the attack was made up of the 7ᵉ, 9ᵉ and 36ᵉ *Divisions d'Infanterie*, with the 22ᵉ and 37ᵉ *Divisions d'Infanterie* in reserve. All the assault units were billeted in the area between Saint-Dizier and Bar-le-Duc at the end of *la Route*, 40 miles or so south-west of Verdun for at least a month prior to moving up to the start line. There they exhaustively practised their part in the attack on specially constructed replicas of their attack frontages, including a full-size outline of Fort Douaumont.[13] The existing *Section* organisation, equivalent to the platoon in British parlance, was also reorganised to include a mixture of riflemen, machine guns and grenadiers in order to increase the firepower available at the *compagnie* level, which became the standard French army organisation into the 1930s.[14] Other preparations included engaging a civilian engineer involved in constructing the Panama Canal to design and build a method of pumping water over the battlefield using a system of canvas pipes, and burying all telephone cables 2 metres deep to protect them from shellfire.[15]

Communications were especially important because close

coordination was a key point in the artillery fire plan drawn up by Nivelle. This envisaged dropping a *barrage roulant* (rolling barrage) between 75 and 150 metres in front of the advancing infantry, which moved steadily forward at a rate of 100 metres every four minutes; the assault units were introduced to the new technique and practised it during their pre-attack training.[16] To deliver the bombardment Pétain had amassed a total of 654 guns, including 300 guns of 120 mm and 220 mm calibre and twenty heavy guns of 370 mm calibre or larger. The latter included two brand-new Schneider-Creusot 400 mm railway guns, the heaviest guns deployed to date by the French army, which were brought up and deployed with the same tight security that attended the British deployment of tanks on the Somme in mid-September 1916. The new weapons were to be targeted upon Forts Douaumont and Vaux, one gun to each. From 16 September up to five trains per day ran into Baylecourt station, 5 miles south-west of Verdun, bringing in a total of 500,000 tons of materiel, including 15,000 tons of assorted artillery ammunition.[17] The pre-attack bombardment commenced on Thursday 19 October 1916, controlled by observation balloons augmented by spotter aircraft as the French had attained air superiority, and initially employed just the field and medium calibre guns as part of a gradually increasing tempo. In the afternoon of Sunday 22 October the French bombardment abruptly lifted and the German artillery began to fire its pre-planned defensive fire tasks, in the belief that the French ground attack had begun. In fact the pause was a ruse and the German guns were promptly smothered by French counter-battery fire that effectively knocked out 68 of the 158 German batteries involved before resuming the pre-attack bombardment.[18]

The intensity of the French artillery bombardment increased at 08:00 on Monday 23 October to include all the heavier pieces. Fort Douaumont had been under fire from the outset, with a hit likely from a 370 mm gun destroying the fort's observation dome on 21 October, but not from the new 400 mm railway gun.[19] At 12:30 a 400 mm shell penetrated the fort's concrete carapace, which had been weakened by months of bombardment that had stripped away most of the 4-metre layer of protective soil, and detonated in the infirmary killing the fifty casualties and medical personnel ensconced there. A second projectile ten minutes later also penetrated the carapace and buried a number of men in a casemate. The heavy shells continued to fall at roughly fifteen minute intervals thereafter, the fifth bursting in the fort's main gallery, bringing down a section of the vaulted ceiling that killed sixty-nine men and completely blocked the gallery, while the sixth pierced all the way down to an ammunition store in the fort's lower levels. This prompted a sympathetic detonation that killed fifty *Pioniers* and ignited a fierce fire that rapidly filled the interior of the fort with thick, choking smoke and fumes. A further hit at 14:00, extinguishing the electric lighting system. The fort's commander, a *Major* Rosendahl from *Infanterie Regiment* 90, ordered the garrison down to the lower levels after the hit in the main gallery and at 17:00 ordered the evacuation of non-essential personnel. By nightfall, when the 400 mm gun ceased fire, the fort's main gallery was blocked by roof debris, the infirmary and bakery had been devastated along with several casemates and the fire caused by the detonation of the ammunition store in the lower levels was spreading. The fort was thus left in the hands of a party of *pioniers* and a hundred men commanded by a *Hauptmann* Soltan from *Infanterie Regiment* 84 which fought the fire until the water supply ran out, including using a cache of bottled carbonated water normally reserved for the wounded. After unsuccessfully despatching runners for reinforcements and further orders, Soltan finally withdrew from the fort at some point between 04:00 and 05:00 on Tuesday 24 October 1916, braving a French gas bombardment targeting the exits. A number of stretcher-bound wounded were brought out by *Hauptmann*

Soltan's party, although two men in one of the outlying machine gun galleries did not receive the word and were left behind. Consequently when a small group of artillery signallers from *Feldartillerie Regiment* 108 under a *Hauptmann* Prollius arrived at the fort in dense fog at around 07:00 they found the fires still burning but the fort essentially habitable, but undefended. Prollius promptly deployed his twenty or so men in defensive locations and despatched a runner to summon reinforcements and machine guns in what proved to be a forlorn hope.[20]

The French ground attack was scheduled to begin at 11:40 on 24 October and the assault divisions spent the night moving up to their jump-off positions west and south of Fort Douaumont. The troops were heavily laden as part of Pétain's meticulous battle preparations. Each man was carrying three bandoliers of small-arms ammunition, a musette bag of grenades, two haversacks containing standard and emergency rations, an extra water bottle full of water or coarse issue *pinard* wine and two empty sandbags in addition to the not inconsiderable standard load routinely carried by *poilus*, totalling in excess of 80 lb in all.[21] By this point the preparatory bombardment had delivered between 250,000 and 300,000 shells onto the attack frontage over the five-day period from 19 October.[22] The intensity of the bombardment, in conjunction with days of heavy rain, had collapsed and churned the German front line into a series of glutinous, partly inundated craters at best. A regimental commander from *Reserve Infanterie Division* 25 in the vicinity of Thiaumont reported that every fighting position on his sector of the front line had been destroyed by the shelling and, in an echo of the fighting in the Bois des Caures back in February, many of the defenders were helpless as their rifles, machine guns and ammunition had been buried by the bombardment.[23] In some instances the incoming assault troops were greeted by German deserters who had taken advantage of the thick autumnal fog to escape the relentless shelling, some of whom claimed not to have eaten for six days due to the bombardment. According to *Général* Doreau, the commander of the 213ᵉ *Brigade d'Infanterie*, a captured *Oberleutnant* expressed surprise at finding a brigade headquarters a mere 300 yards behind the front-line trenches.[24] The French bombardment lifted briefly as the assault troops began to advance at 11:40 in order to re-lay the guns for the *barrage roulant* but, with their observers blinded by the thick fog, the German gunners held back for twelve minutes fearing another French ruse like that of 22 October. By the time they realised their error and began shooting their defensive fire tasks the French infantry were well on their way across no man's land in the fog, using compasses and the knowledge gained from training on the mock-ups for navigation, and inspired and coordinated by buglers. On the other hand Pétain's careful preparation was undone by enthusiasm in some instances, with eyewitnesses reporting that the battlefield was littered with abandoned packs and other equipment discarded by their owners in their eagerness to get to grips with the *Boche*, in a textbook example of *attaque à outrance*.[25]

In spite of the fog the French attack went like clockwork, although the degree of success varied across the attack frontage. On the 74ᵉ *Division d'Infanterie*'s front before Fort Vaux the 230ᵉ *Régiment d'Infanterie* captured its initial objectives, code-named Claudel and Garrand Trenches, within ten minutes of the attack beginning but then became pinned down by heavy German machine gun fire that prevented it from securing the Bois de Fumin, while the neighbouring 333ᵉ *Régiment d'Infanterie* suffered heavy losses while overrunning two trench lines and an *ouvrage* in an attempt to outflank Fort Vaux from the west. The objectives were secured by 12:15 but the attackers were then obliged to withdraw due to a misdirected bombardment by French guns. The 50ᵉ and 71ᵉ *Bataillons de Chasseurs à Pied* enjoyed better luck pushing into the Bois de Chênois and Bois de Fumin, and at 18:00 assisted the

229e *Régiment d'Infanterie* attacking two German strongpoints code-named Clausewitz and Seydlitz. A further assault was launched to clear stubborn pockets of resistance at 20:00, and both objectives were secured by midnight. In the centre of the attack frontage the 401e *Régiment d'Infanterie* and 107e *Bataillons de Chasseurs à Pied* from *Général* Passaga's 133e *Division d'Infanterie* also made good progress, securing the Chapelle-Sainte-Fine crossroads and pushing through the Bois de Vaux-Chapitre to occupy the Ravin de Bazil and area around the Étang de Vaux north-east of the crossroads. The 321e *Régiment d'Infanterie* overran two trenches north-east of Fleury and occupied the Bois de la Caillette by 12:35 and after pausing for an hour to regroup, continued the advance through the fog toward Fort Douaumont. Reaching the south-east corner of the ditch, the attackers pushed up onto the glacis of the fort with little resistance and secured the observation dome for the 155 mm gun turret at 15:30, before settling down to await the arrival of the unit tasked to secure the fort.

However, the most spectacular success was achieved by *Général* Guyot de Salins' 38e *Division d'Infanterie* on the left of the attack frontage. *Lieutenant-Colonel* de Partouneaux's 11e *Régiment d'Infanterie*, which left its jump-off positions two minutes early due to an incorrectly set watch, found its first objective unoccupied and then fought a fierce battle to clear and hold German positions in the Haudromont Quarries west of Douaumont village, that continued until 17:00. The 4e *Mixte Régiment de Zouaves et Tirailleurs* commanded by *Lieutenant-Colonel* Vernois lost around two hundred men to a German defensive fire barrage on its jump-off trenches just before the advance commenced, but despite this, overran the remains of the *Ouvrage* de Thiaumont that had been the scene of so much fighting in June in a matter of minutes. The nearby Thiaumont Farm was secured by 12:25 and Vernois' men penetrated into the Bois de Morchée before consolidating a defensive line just beyond the remains of Douaumont village in conjunction with *Colonel* Richaud's 4ᵉ *Régiment de Zouaves* by 14:45. Richaud's men, along with the 8ᵉ *Régiment de Tirailleurs* commanded by *Lieutenant-Colonel* Dufoulon, had achieved total surprise by moving at a run across no man's land and secured their objective without a fight, capturing a senior German commander in his underwear and a regimental postmaster delivering mail in the process. By midday the Bois de Nawé and Ravin de la Dame had been retaken and the North Africans were pushing along a ravine toward its rendezvous in Douaumont village by 14:00; an hour later a patrol from the 8ᵉ *Régiment*'s 17ᵉ *Compagnie* despatched to scout the Ravin de la Goulotte and the Ravin de Helley to their front overran a number of German shelters and took several prisoners.

Lieutenant-Colonel Régnier and the *Régiment d'Infanterie Coloniale du Maroc* had a less favourable start as their start line had been occupied by German troops seeking to escape the bombardment and a machine gun inflicted a number of casualties including the commander of the lead *bataillon*, a *Major* Modat, before being charged and knocked out by his deputy, *Capitaine* Alexander. In a rerun of the events of 25 February, the virtually undefended Fort Douaumont again exerted a magnetic attraction for a number of French units despite the fog, including a party from the 321ᵉ *Régiment d'Infanterie* led by a *Lieutenant* Megamont, *Capitaine* Dorey and a party from the *Régiment d'Infanterie Coloniale du Maroc*'s 1ᵉʳ *Bataillon*, in addition to the unit actually assigned to its capture, *Major* Nicolai's 8ᵉ *Bataillon*, which had been guided to its objective by a fortuitously captured German prisoner. The fort was technically surrendered to a Parisian sapper named Dumont from the 19ᵉ/2ᵉ *Compagnie du Génie*, who discovered the non-reinforced *Hauptmann* Prollius with four other officers and twenty-four men sheltering in the lower levels of the fort; he was awarded the *Légion d'Honneur* for his part in the recapture.[26] None of this was apparent from French lines due to the fog however, and Mangin and the other senior commanders spent several anxious hours watching the progress of the *barrage roulant* from the dust and detritus thrown above the fog, while French pilots in their *cages à poules* (chicken cages) swooped back and forth trying to ascertain what was happening on the ground. Twenty aircraft were lost on 24 October, several to shell splinters from the bombardment or crashing in the murk in addition to German fire, but finally their efforts began to bear fruit. In the late afternoon a machine dropped a section of map on *Général* Passaga's *poste de commandement* with the new French line marked upon and inscribed '*La Gauloise 16 heures 30. Vive la France!*'; *La Gauloise* was the nickname of his 133ᵉ *Division d'Infanterie*. At around the same time a section of the fog cleared to reveal the men of *Général* Guyot de Salins' 38ᵉ *Division d'Infanterie* firmly ensconced on the glacis of Fort Douaumont; one onlooker at Mangin's forward headquarters at Fort Souville likened the scene to a similar event at Austerlitz in 1805.[27]

By midnight on 24 October the French had advanced 3 kilometres, a distance it had taken their German opponents four and a half months to secure, capturing 6,000 prisoners, 164 machine guns and 15 artillery pieces in the process.[28] At least in part the French success was due to poor enemy morale as the German units involved had been in the line for a considerable period, some from the beginning of the battle, and they were exhausted, undermanned and short of supplies; many prisoners surrendered without a fight and some claimed to have had no rations for six days. After a weak counter-attack in the late afternoon of 24 October, *5. Armee* remained quiescent in the face of the French advance apart from maintaining heavy artillery fire on the new line. Mangin had intended to maintain the pressure by renewing the assault upon Fort Vaux the following day, but the assault units were still consolidating their new positions; a combination of battle losses and German shelling required them to be pulled out of the line between 26 and 31 October, although the French artillery continued to fire a pre-attack programme on the fort over the same period.[29] In the event the assault was not needed, for the Germans evacuated the fort during the night of 1 November. French signallers intercepted a German signal mentioning the fact in the early hours of 2 November, and two *compagnies* from the 118ᵉ and 298ᵉ *Régiments d'Infanterie* were detailed to verify the accuracy of the intercept during the coming night. Approaching the fort simultaneously from the north and south, the patrols reached the battered ditch at 01:00 and dug their way into the fort via the sandbag-plugged breach in the roof of the corridor linking the counterscarp gallery to the fort proper. Inside they found the corridors and chambers deserted but strewn with evidence of hurried flight in the shape of abandoned weapons, ammunition and bottled mineral water. Fort Vaux was declared officially liberated at 02:30 on Friday 3 November 1916, 152 days after *Major* Raynal had been obliged to surrender on 7 June.[30]

The success of the 24 October attack arguably made Verdun safe but the German line was still too close for the city to be considered secure from a German resumption of the offensive, and over the following six weeks preparations thus went ahead for another major French effort. These included constructing 18 miles of roadway and several miles of narrow gauge railway to help move and supply the 760 artillery pieces slated to support the attack, which began in freezing winter weather on Friday 15 December after an intensive five-day bombardment. Carried out on a 6 mile frontage by four divisions, the attack pushed the Germans back to the Côte du Poivre and Côte de Talou ridges on a line running west from Bezonvaux to Louvemont and then south-west to Vacherauville on the bank of the Meuse, all of which had been lost in the opening days of the battle. The attack cost 5. *Armee* over 11,000 prisoners and 115 guns, although in conjunction with the 24 October attack the offensive also added a further 47,000 casualties to the French butcher's bill.[31] With the front line once again 5 miles from Verdun, the threat to the city on the east bank of the Meuse was finally alleviated. The situation on the west bank was not addressed until the following year, when a French multi-division offensive launched on 20 August 1917 recaptured the calvaries of March and April 1916 at Côte 304, the *Mort-Homme*, the Côte de l'Oie and the Bois d'Avocourt, pushing the Germans back to their west bank start line and losing them a further 9,500 prisoners.[32] Matters came full circle on 26 September 1918 with a further French drive up both banks of the Meuse, in conjunction with the American Expeditionary Force. On the east bank the French finally recovered the Bois de Caures, where *Colonel* Driant and his valiant band of light infantrymen from the 56e and 59e *Bataillons de Chasseurs à Pied* had carried out their epic stand against the might of *General* von Schenck's 18. *Korps* two years and eight months earlier.

The recapture of the Bois de Caures in September–October 1918 may have brought the matter full circle, but the Battle of Verdun is commonly accepted to have extended between February and December 1916. Within those chronological parameters forty-eight German divisions, half the total for the entire Western Front, had served in the Mill on the Meuse along with sixty-six of the ninety-six French divisions deployed there. The disparity was due to Pétain's *noria* system, which spread the burden more equally across the French army. This varied from the German system of leaving divisions in the line and continually topping them up with replacements; the drawback of the latter system was starkly displayed during the French offensive on 24 October 1916.[33] Even with this spreading of the load the French army had paid a horrendous price. Precise figures are a vexed subject due to the differing accounting criteria and nature of the fighting but by 31 August 1916 the fighting at Verdun had cost the French between 315,000 and 423,000 casualties, equating to approximately 61,000 dead, 261,000 wounded and 101,000 missing; their opponents from 5. *Armee* lost between 281,333 and 329,000 men in total, equating to an upper limit of approximately 142,000 killed or missing and 187,000 wounded.[34] For all this horrendous price in human life and suffering, GERICHT failed to attain its overt objective, for the closest the Germans came to Verdun was the glacis of Fort Souville. Falkenhayn's experiment in *Ermattungsstrategie* and *Verblutung* also failed, for while the French army had certainly been bled, it also proved sufficiently resilient to absorb the punishment meted out by its opponent, albeit with a rising occurrence of incidents of *défaillance*. More pertinently, as the figures cited above show, the bleeding had turned into a mutual rather than one-way process, and the margin of difference was hardly economic even if it had been otherwise acceptable or indeed sustainable.

As with the German ending of Operation GERICHT in July 1916, the effective end of the French battle for Verdun in December 1916 brought radical change at the top of the French military hierarchy in its train. A combination of the cost of Verdun, the failure of the Somme offensive to deliver as advertised and a critical report suggesting that Joffre's power should be reined in by removing the French force in Salonika from his command by *Ministre de la Guerre Général* Pierre Roques gave his political enemies the leverage they had sought. On 13 December 1916 *Premier Ministre* Aristide Briand formed a new government with a seriously reduced majority and, in an effort to rally support, he replaced Roques with *Général* Hubert Lyautey and moved Joffre from his post as head of the army to a deliberately vague new post as a military 'technical adviser' to the government, using promotion to *Maréchal* as an inducement. On perceiving his new post was largely symbolic and without any real power or influence, Joffre resigned the day after his elevation to *Maréchal*, either 26 or 27 December depending on the account. He too then sank into obscurity, spending over a decade preparing his memoir before passing away on 3 January 1931; he was buried on his estate at Louveciennes in the western suburbs of Paris and his memoir was published the following year. The business of choosing a replacement as head of the army was dictated by French domestic politics. Of the available candidates Pétain had ruled himself out by exhibiting withering contempt for his political masters, having once commented to *Président* Poincaré that 'nobody was better placed than the President to know that France was neither led nor governed'. De Castelnau was tainted by his association with Joffre, and *Général Ferdinand* Foch by the failure on the Somme and his Catholicism, along with *Général* Louis Franchet d'Esperey. In the event, Pétain remained at his post as commander of the *Groupement des Armées du Central*, de Castelnau was *limogé*, Foch was given the technical adviser post rejected by Joffre and Franchet d'Esperey was given command of the *Groupement des Armées du Nord*. The winner of the reshuffle was therefore Nivelle due to the success of the French in October and December offensives at Verdun, allied to the fact he was a Protestant, and he was appointed *Commandant en Chef des Armées* in Joffre's stead on 15 December, albeit with reduced powers; his sidekick Mangin was also promoted to command the 6ᵉ *Armée* with effect from 19 December.[35]

The problem was that Nivelle did not fully appreciate how brittle an instrument the French army had become due to the cost of the fighting in the Artois, Champagne and especially at Verdun. More specifically, he drastically underestimated the significance of the overt acts of *défaillance* that marked the closing stages of the fighting at Verdun. When *Président* Poincaré visited Verdun in December 1916 to award decorations, for example, his car was stoned by *poilus* who heckled him with shouts of *'embusqués'*, a French military slang term for shirker. Graffiti was noted on the main route from Verdun to the front line directing troops along the *Chemin de l'Abattoir* (path to the abattoir), and a unit marching forward for the 15 December attack took to bleating like sheep.[36] The straw that finally broke the camel's back was Nivelle's much vaunted offensive on the River Aisne against the *Chemin des Dames* ridge in April 1917. Despite his grandiose claims to have invented a winning formula, on this occasion the *barrage roulant* that had performed so well at Verdun in October and December 1916 failed to work its magic. This was in part because, despite advice to the contrary, Nivelle insisted on attacking a heavily fortified section of the German line, and also partly due to another episode of unforgivably lax security, with full details of the attack plan being published in the Paris press before the event. The offensive began on 16 April, and within nine days the French army had lost 30,000 dead, 100,000 wounded and 4,000 missing or taken prisoner.[37] Units began to refuse to obey orders to attack on 17 April and the mutiny then spread rapidly, ultimately affecting sixty-eight divisions to varying degrees and involving around 40,000 men. Neither was this all, for although the mutiny peaked in May and June 1917, incidents of indiscipline continued until January 1918. Pétain replaced Nivelle at the end of April, an embarrassing process in which Nivelle had to be forcibly ejected from his office while vociferously laying blame for the *Chemin des Dames* debacle on his subordinates, and Mangin in particular. Banished to a command in North Africa, Nivelle retired from the army in 1921, died on 22 March 1924 and was buried at Les Invalides in Paris. For his part, Mangin went on to command the 10ᵉ *Armée* in the fighting in 1918 and after occupation duty in the Rhineland became inspector general of colonial troops. He suffered a stroke and became ill with appendicitis in his Paris home on 9 March 1925 and died three days later; he too was eventually interred at Les Invalides in 1932.

The unenviable task of clearing up the mess created by Nivelle fell, perhaps predictably, upon Pétain, and he approached the task of quelling the unrest, restoring order and rebuilding the army's morale with his customary thoroughness. In all, 499 men were tried by court martial and sentenced to death for disciplinary offences, although all but twenty-seven of the sentences were subsequently commuted to various periods of imprisonment. A further 515 men were sent to prison for between five and fifteen years, 742 receiving sentences ranging from fifteen days and five years, 650 were sentenced to forced labour for between three years and life, and a further 1,438 were sentenced to communal labour for one or two years.[38] Some complete units were disbanded, their members being dispersed across the army; others were stripped of their colours as a mark of disgrace. The burden did not fall solely on the rank and file; two *généraux* and nine *lieutenant-colonels* were relieved of their commands for poor performance or incompetence. The full price of restoring order has yet to be established, as the official documentation is not scheduled to be released by the French government archives until 2017. Pétain rebuilt the army's confidence by addressing the concerns of the common *poilu*, in the same way he had restored the faith of the troops at Verdun in February 1916. He visited ninety divisions to clarify their grievances which largely boiled down to arrangements and privileges that were routine provision in other contemporary armies. Thus for the first time since the conflict began, French soldiers were given an official entitlement to leave every four months, access to the requisite road and rail transport and the right to appeal if leave was delayed or denied. Special rest centres were set up for troops withdrawn from the line and regulations were enacted to ensure that they were actually allowed to rest, rather than being used as a convenient source of manual labour; these centres were also provided with field kitchens and properly trained cooks who ensured the troops were fed with fresh produce and especially green vegetables as a health measure. In addition, legislation was passed to spread the burden of conscription more equitably and financial arrangements were put in place to assist the families of soldiers killed in action. These measures proved popular with *poilu* and public alike, and Pétain was widely hailed as *le médecin de l'Armée* (the army's doctor).[39] Over time his treatment restored the French army's morale and effectiveness, and enabled it to weather the German offensives at the beginning of 1918 and then perform its own counterstrokes that ultimately obliged the Germans to accept the armistice in November 1918.

However, unlike his arguably less deserving contemporaries, Pétain was not destined to a quiet retirement. After serving as inspector general of the army and *Ministre de la Guerre*, he was again called into the breach in the summer of 1940 to take on the thankless task of heading the collaborationist Vichy regime after the French defeat. On this occasion his efforts were less well received after the event, and he fell victim to the French predilection for scapegoating. *Maréchal* Philippe Pétain was tried and sentenced to death for treason in August 1945, with the sentence being commuted to life imprisonment in view of his age. He died in 1951 aged ninety-five with his wish to be buried among his soldiers at Verdun being denied, despite numerous petitions and, in February 1973, the kidnapping of his body by activists seeking to have his wish fulfilled. He thus remains buried in the small military cemetery on the Île d'Yeu off the French Atlantic coast where he had been imprisoned.

The Battle of Verdun continued to exert its influence over the French army, not least through the passive, defensive mindset that created the Maginot Line, and played no small part in the military defeat of 1940. Arguably the greatest and longest lasting impact has been upon the ground over which it was fought, however. At the western and south-eastern extremities of the Verdun salient, the Butte de Vauquois and the Les Eparges ridge still bear the ineradicable marks of mine warfare of a concentration and scale arguably unmatched by the British efforts on the Somme and along the Messines Ridge in Belgium.

On the west side of the River Meuse, the villages of Avocourt, Chattancourt and the others devastated by the fighting between March and May 1916 have been rebuilt and the arable land surrounding them has been returned to productive use. Côte 304 and the *Mort-Homme* themselves defied rehabilitation however, and were finally sown with conifer trees in the 1930s that were witness to brief but bitter fighting in the German breakout from the Ardennes in 1940. Both summits are marked with numerous memorials, the *Mort-Homme* with a macabre representation of Death rising from the earth cradling a furled flag, mounted on a plinth inscribed '*Ils nont pas passe*' (They did not pass). Côte 304 has a tall, imposing column bearing names of the units that fought there along with a simple dedication to the 10,000 men who remain in the hill, approached by an arrow-straight road almost a full mile long flanked by shell craters and the remains of trenches meandering away in the gloom under the firs. Around the memorials too signs of the battle remain clearly evident, the outlines of the ravaged ground blanketed but unaltered by a century's worth of pine needles and the occasional selective timber harvesting with heavy machinery. Unexploded ordnance can often be seen casually piled for the attention of French army bomb disposal teams, and the timber-harvesting machinery also routinely throws up rusted barbed wire, mouldering pieces of equipment, shrapnel and even human remains. The scale of harvesting has been seriously increased over the past few years, and how well the preserved battlefield will fare once shorn of its protective conifer covering remains to be seen. Writing in 1962, Alistair Horne noted a paucity of visitors to the west bank heights and referred to them thus:

One of the eeriest places in this world ... [where a] grown man will not willingly repeat the experience of getting lost in the labyrinth of firecuts that crisscross the deserted plantations.[40]

The *Mort-Homme* now boasts a metalled road, dedicated coach parking and a large information board rather than the rough, rutted farm track that existed into the 1990s, but having visited both sites on a number of occasions the present author would concur with Horne's view as both the *Mort-Homme* and Côte 304 have a desolate, slightly menacing air.

Be that as it may, the most indelible evidence of the battle can be found on the east bank of the Meuse. There the ground had been poisoned even more badly by the combination of poison gas, chemical explosive and corrupted human and animal flesh, and the topsoil itself had been scorched away by the constant artillery fire and resolutely resisted all attempts to turn it back to arable usage. Even if that were not the case, the population of the villages and hamlets in the area where the fighting had been heaviest had been dispersed as refugees, and there was little for them to return to had they been so inclined. Nine villages there had been totally erased, traceable only as a different coloured smear in the churned earth or through the odd brick or shards of roof tile. Eight of the disappeared villages are commemorated only with marker stones. The exception is Fleury which, chosen as an overall memorial due to its central location, still boasts a symbolic mayor and has had its street plan laid out for posterity as a series of woodland paths. Further memorials can be found in what the French refer to as the *Coeur du Champ de Bataille* (heart of the field of battle). The high point of the German advance is marked with a larger-than-life sculpture of a wounded lion roaring defiance on the Chapelle-Sainte-Fine crossroads. The site of Fleury railway station was until recently occupied by a two-storey memorial museum that boasted a life-size diorama of a section of the battlefield, although the grim 1960s concrete structure had been demolished and was being redeveloped on the present author's last visit in early 2014. Most impressive of all is the huge Ossuary opened in 1932, almost two hundred yards in length, constructed atop the Thiaumont Ridge.

Semi-cylindrical in shape and surmounted by a tower designed to represent an artillery shell, the Ossuary contains the remains of 130,000 unidentified French soldiers gathered from across the battlefield; a further 15,000 identified men are interred in the *Cimetière National* to its front.

The memorials exist cheek by jowl with more immediate evidence of the fighting. West of the Ossuary the battered remains of the *Ouvrage* de Thiaumont, PC118 and PC119 can be seen just off the minor road running down to the Meuse. The intact *Ouvrage* de Froideterre has gained a car park, information board and benches for visitors, as has the *Quatre Cheminées* shelter with its *horizon-bleu* painted ventilation covers across the road to the south. To the east of the Ossuary the courtyard of Fort Douaumont has also been turned into a car park, and visitors can follow in the footsteps of the men from *Infanterie Regiment* 24, the 321ᵉ *Régiment d'Infanterie* and the *Régiment d'Infanterie Coloniale du Maroc* via footpaths worn along the rim of craters, between the turrets and observation domes on the glacis and along the defensive ditches. Fort Vaux has received similar treatment, and the back wall of the fort boasts large memorial plaques to Major Raynal and his most celebrated subordinate, *Légion d'Honneur*-winning carrier pigeon No. 787-15, souvenir brass replicas of whom can be purchased from a small shop within. For a small fee visitors can also prowl the dank interior corridors of both forts and marvel at the courage and fortitude of men like *Capitaine* Tabourot and *Lieutenant* Girard who endured, fought and in many instances died in the fumes and flame-torn darkness. The remains of other, less well preserved forts can also be found nestling quietly in the greenery. The entrance to Fort Souville, complete with signs warning the unwary of the dangers of venturing within, can be found just off one of the wide bridle paths that criss-cross the *Champs de Bataille*, and the badly battered remains of Fort Tavannes lie a few yards beyond another sign marking the boundary of a French military reservation. A good deal of the battlefield is still used by the French army as a training area. Fort Douaumont overlooks an anti-tank firing range, for example, and it is not uncommon to come across the blue plastic remains of training grenades, discarded ration cans and hastily filled in slit trenches amongst the deadfall and undergrowth; it can be a jarring and surreal experience to come unexpectedly face to face with *Sections* of French soldiers, bristling with weapons and field radios, practising their craft on the ground where so many of their forebears died. And everywhere off the metalled roads and unmade tracks are the craters and trenches, softened only slightly by light underbrush and a century's worth of deadfall and pine needles, undulating and snaking away in all directions like the surface of a petrified sea.

In 1987, following a formal reconciliatory meeting on the battlefield between the French President and German Chancellor three years earlier, the United Nations bestowed the title of World Capital of Peace, Freedom and Human Rights on Verdun. It is interesting to speculate on what the *poilus* and their German opponents who fought there in 1916 would make of this development but be that as it may, the attempt to utilise Verdun's now not quite so recent heritage as an awful exemplar of the horrific reality of modern industrialised warfare is commendable. Only time will tell whether the effort expended yields the desired result.

APPENDIX 1: MAPS AND BATTLE PLANS

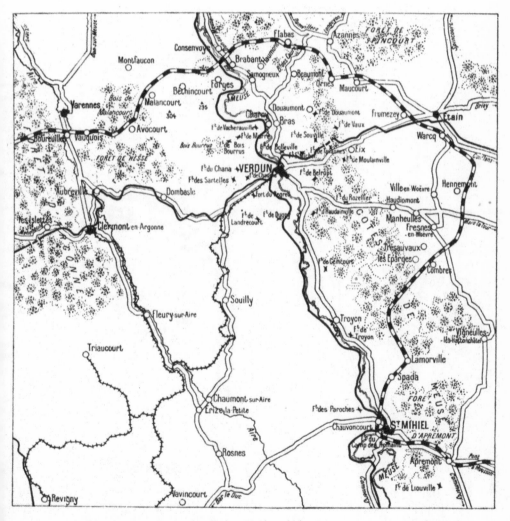

43. The Verdun front, from the Battle of the Marne in 1914 to Operation GERICHT in February 1916. Note the flanking heights of Les Eparges to the south-east and Vauquois to the north-west.

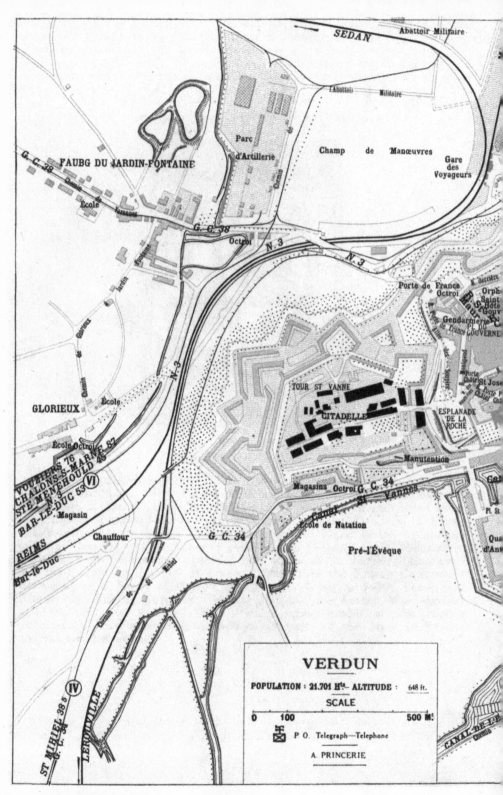

44. Map of Verdun before 1914, showing the geometric Vauban defence works.

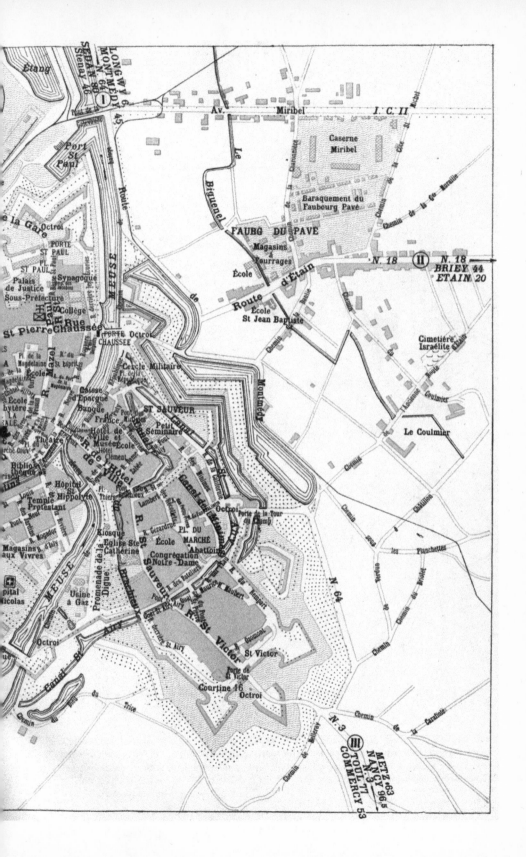

Étang

LONGWY 62
MONTMÉDY
N. 64
SEDAN 46
Stenay 46

Port
St
Paul

Av.   Miribel   I. C. II

Caserne
Miribel

Baraquement du
Faubourg Pavé

FAUBG DU PAVE

Magasins
à
Fourrages

École

N. 18   Ⓘ   N. 18
BRIEY 44
ETAIN 20

e de la Gare   Octroi
PORTE
ST PAUL
PL.
ST PAUL
Palais
de Justice
Sous-Préfecture

Synagogue

Collège

St Pierre   Rue   Chaussée

PORTE Octroi
CHAUSSÉE

Cercle Militaire
Pl. de la
République

École
St Jean Baptiste

Route   d'Étain

Cimetière
Israélite

Caisse
d'Épargne
Banque

Pl. de la
Magdelaine

École
bytère

A
Madeleine
La
LE

Théâtre

Hôtel de
France
Hôtel de
Ville et
Musée
ÉcoleHôtel
Clément

ST SAUVEUR

Petit
Séminaire

R. de Ville

Biblio
isbèque
lind

Hôpital
St Hippolyte

Temple
Protestant

Pl.
Thiers

Le Coulmier

Kiosque

Pl. DU
MARCHÉ
École

Octroi   Porte de la Tour
du Champ

Magasins
aux Vivres

Église Ste
Catherine

Congrégation
Notre-Dame
Abattoir

Usine
à Gaz

pital
Nicolas

Promenade de la Digue

R. St Sauveur

R. St Victor

St Victor

Octroi

Courtine 16   Octroi

Porte de
St Victor

Canal St Airy

MEUSE

N. 64

les   Planchettes

Ⓘ
N. 3
METZ 63
NANCY 96.5
TOUL 77
COMMERCY 53

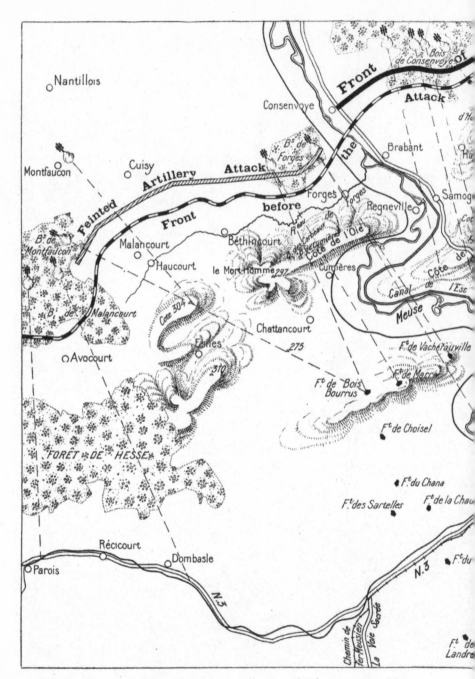

45. The Verdun sector before the German offensive of February 1916. Note the location of the forts and the German artillery positions with fields of fire.

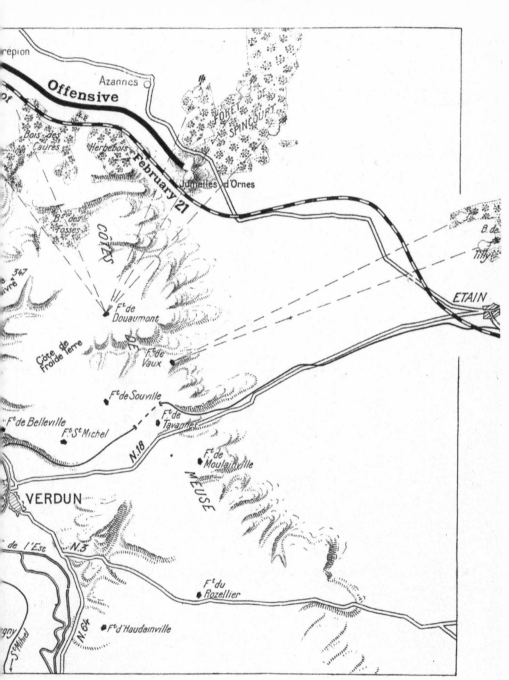

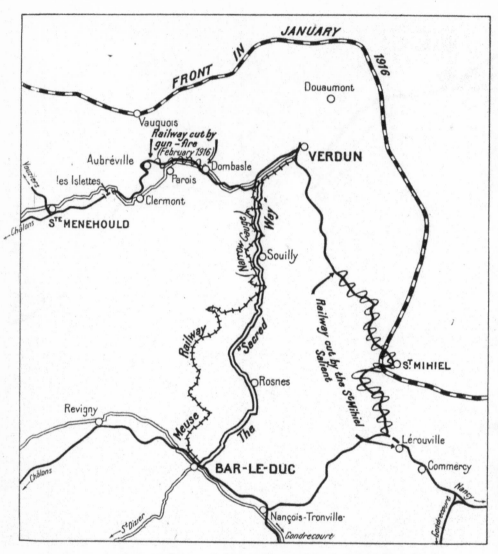

46. La Route: the vital supply route linking Verdun and Bar-le-Duc, later dubbed the Voie Sacrèe (the Sacred Way).

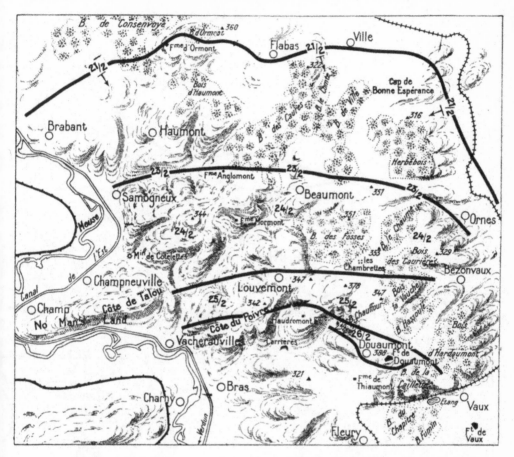

47. The initial German attack on the east bank of the River Meuse, 21–26 February 1916. Attacking from the top of the map, the bold lines depict the four stages of the attack on 21, 22, 23, 24 and 25 February.

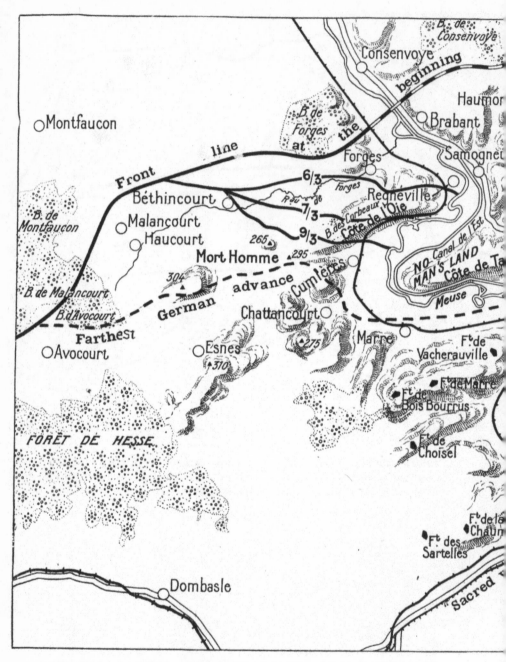

48. The Verdun battlefield on both banks of the River Meuse; bold lines with dates show the progress of the German attacks on both banks in the first half of March 1916.

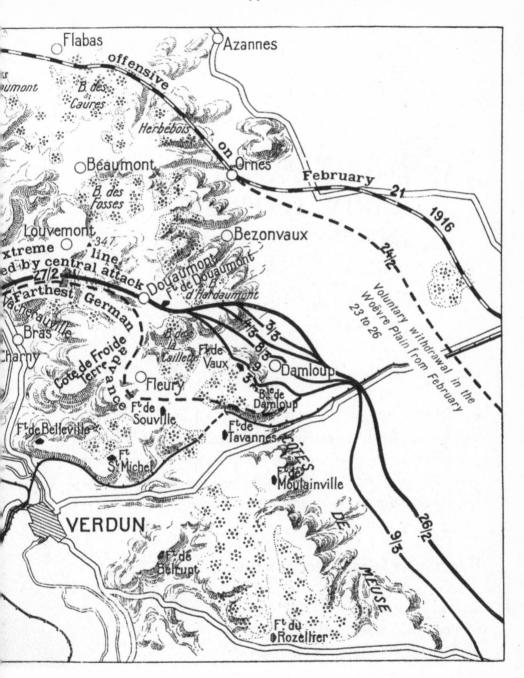

APPENDIX 2: APPROXIMATE GUIDE TO FRENCH AND GERMAN ARMY ORGANISATIONS & STRENGTHS

The following is intended to provide background context by clarifying the size and strength of units and their organisational relationship. The numbers are very approximate as they varied between units and were subject to official reorganisations over the course of the war, and are only provided for rough comparison purposes.

French Army Infantry Organisation:

Section: *c.* 50 men
Compagnie: (4 x Sections) *c.* 250 men
Bataillon: (4 x *Compagnies*) *c.* 1,200 men
Regiment: (3 x *Bataillons*) *c.* 3,500 men
Brigade: (2 x *Regiments*) *c.* 8,000 men
Division: *c.* 15,000 men

German Army Infantry Organisation:

Platoon: *c.* 60 men
Kompanie: (3x *Platoons*) *c.* 260 men
Bataillon: (5 x *Kompanies*) *c.* 1,400 men
Regiment: (3 x *Bataillons*) *c.* 4,200 men
Brigade: (2 x *Regiments*) *c.* 8,500 men
Division: *c.* 17,000 men

NOTES

1 'Virodunum: The Fortress That Controls the River Crossing', Verdun 450 BC – AD 1873

1. For a contemporary diagram see the 'Fortified Places' website entry on 'Verdun' at http://www.fortified-places.com/verdun. html, accessed 02/09/2014
2. Quoted from Victor Lucien Tapié, *France in the Age of Louis XIII and Richelieu* (Cambridge: Cambridge University Press, 1984), pp. 236–7; see also A. Lloyd Moote, *Louis XIII, the Just* (London: University of California Press, 1991), pp. 226–8
3. See Jean-Denis G. G. Lepage, *Vauban and the French Military Under Louis XIV: An Illustrated History of Fortifications and Strategies* (Jefferson, North Carolina: McFarland & Company, 2010), pp. 177–8; for another contemporary map/plan see the 'Fortified Places' website entry on 'Verdun' at http://www. fortified-places.com/verdun.html, accessed 02/09/2014
4. Quoted from Alistair Horne, *The Fall of Paris: The Siege and the Commune 1870–71* (London: Papermac, 1989), p. 38
5. Quoted from Léonce Patry, *The Reality of War: A Memoir of the Franco-Prussian War 1870–1871*, translated by Douglas Fermer (London: Cassell & Co., 2001), p. 45

6. ibid., pp. 58–9
7. See Horne, *The Fall of Paris*, p. 44; and Michael A. Palmer, *German Wars: A Concise History 1859–1945* (Minneapolis: Zenith Press, 2010), p. 30
8. Châlons-sur-Marne was renamed Châlons-en-Champagne in 1998
9. See Patry, pp. 72–9 and map 'From Thionville to Metz', p. 60
10. Roughly 'We are in a chamber pot and we will be shat on'; see for example Horne, *The Siege of Paris*, p. 52
11. Figures from Martin van Creveld, *Supplying War: Logistics from Wallenstein to Patton* (Cambridge: Cambridge University Press, 1977), p. 102; cited in Patry, p. 12
12. Figures cited in Horne, *The Siege of Paris*, p. 62; for details of the *Garde Mobile* see Patry, pp. 30–1
13. See Horne, *The Siege of Paris*, p. 62; and Patry pp. 33–4
14. See Horne, *The Siege of Paris*, p. 62
15. ibid., pp. 348–9
16. ibid., p. 314
17. ibid., p. 414
18. Figures cited in Patry, pp. 359–60

2 Fortresses and *Pantalon Rouge*: Verdun and the French Army, 1873 – 1914

1. Sometimes rendered Serré de Rivière
2. See Neil J. Wells, *Verdun: An Integrated Defence* (Uckfield, East Sussex: Naval & Military Press, 2009), pp. 22–4
3. See ibid., pp. 25–7; and Map 2 'The First Two Groups of Fortifications' between pp. 106–107
4. Figures cited in ibid., pp. 29–30; and Map 1 'France's Frontier Defences Regions', between pp. 106–107
5. See Robert A. Doughty, *Pyrrhic Victory: French Strategy and Operations in the Great War* (London: Belknap Press of Harvard University, 2005), pp. 12–13; and Wells, pp. 28–31

6. See 'Fortiff Sere: L'association Séré de Rivière' [French language website], section on 'Trouée des Charmes', 'Le Fort de Manonviller' page, especially diagram 'Plan du Fort Manonviller en 1885' at http://fortiffsere.fr/troueedecharmes/index_fichiers/Page4590.htm, accessed 01/12/2014

7. See 'Fortiff Sere: L'association Séré de Rivière' [French language website], section on 'Trouée des Charmes', 'Le Fort de Manonviller' page, especially diagrams 'Plan du Projet de Renforcement du Fort de Manonviller en 1892' and 'Plan du Fort de Manonviller en 1914' at http://fortiffsere.fr/troueedecharmes/index_fichiers/Page4590.htm, accessed 02/12/2014; and Clayton Donnell, *Breaking the Fortress Line 1914* (Barnsley: Pen & Sword Military, 2013), pp. 117–19. For details of the Galopin and Bussière turrets see 'Fortiff Sere: L'association Séré de Rivière' [French language website], section on 'La Tourelle Galopin de 155L Modèle 1890' at http://www.fortiffsere.fr/cuirassements/index_fichiers/Page2539.htm, accessed 01/12/2014 and 'La Tourelle Bussière pour Canons de Gros Calibre' at http://www.fortiffsere.fr/cuirassements/index_fichiers/Page1318.htm, accessed 01/12/2014

8. See Wells, p. 40

9. See Clayton Donnell, *The Fortifications of Verdun 1874–1917* (Oxford: Osprey Publishing, 2011), p. 8; for details of road construction and the development of the French military narrow gauge railway system see Wells, p. 53 and Appendix 16: 'The système Péchot – French Military Railways', pp. 176–83

10. See Wells, p. 40; and Donnell, *The Fortifications of Verdun*, pp. 10–11; for details of construction period, cost, personnel and armament see ibid., Table 'Initial Project and the "Forts de la Panique", December 1874 to February 1875', p. 10; for locations and distances from Verdun see also Map 'The Fortifications of Verdun', p. 9

11. See Wells, p. 40

12. See Donnell, *The Fortifications of Verdun*, p. 11; cost and

personnel figures calculated from figures cited in Tables 'Initial Project and the "Forts de la Panique", December 1874 to February 1875', 'Return to the Initial Project, July 1875', and 'New Exterior Line – Threats from the Alliance between Germany, Austria-Hungary and Italy', pp. 10, 12–13

13. See ibid., pp. 12–14
14. See ibid., pp. 14–16
15. See Wells, p. 53
16. See Donnell, *The Fortifications of Verdun*, Tables 'Torpedo-shell Crisis, 1886' and 'Final Generation – All Concrete', pp. 13, 15; see also 'Fortiff Sere: L'association Séré de Rivière' [French language website], section on 'La Place Forte ou du Camp Retranché de Verdun', 'Le Fort de Vacherauville' page, especially diagram 'Plan du Fort de Vacherauville en 1914' at http://www.fortiffsere.fr/verdungauche/index_fichiers/Page4602.htm, accessed 23/01/2015
17. See Donnell, *The Fortifications of Verdun*, p. 23
18. See ibid., p. 23; and Wells, Appendix 10 'Manpower Requirements for the Principal Fortifications of *Le camp retranché de Verdun*', pp. 157–8, especially Footnote 35, p. 158
19. For details of the development of the defences and their specifics see Wells, pp. 39–91; for personnel numbers and numbers and types of fortifications see ibid., Appendix 10 'Manpower Requirements for the Principal Fortifications of *Le camp retranché de Verdun*', pp. 157–8 and Appendix 15 'Summary of *Le camp retranché de Verdun*' p. 175; for details of the narrow gauge railway system see ibid., Appendix 16 'The système Péchot – French Military Railways', pp. 176–83. See also 'Fortiff Sere: L'association Séré de Rivière' [French language website], section on 'La Place Forte ou du Camp Retranché de Verdun', map 'Carte de la place forte de Verdun en 1914' at http://fortiffsere.fr/verdun/, accessed 23/01/2015
20. 820 million francs figure cited in Donnell, *The Fortifications*

of Verdun, p. 23; for 60–78 million francs see Wells, pp. 90–1; and Appendix 9 'Total Costs of the Principal Fortifications of *Le camp retranché de Verdun*', pp. 155–6

21. The motto was inscribed in all Verdun's forts; see Ian Ousby, *The Road to Verdun* (London: Pimlico, 2003), p. 53

22. For details see 'Fortiff Sere: L'association Séré de Rivière' [French language website], section on 'La Place Forte ou du Camp Retranché de Verdun' Section, 'Le Fort de Douaumont ou Fort Gérard' page at http://fortiffsere.fr/verdun/index_fichiers/Page11436.htm, accessed 26/01/2015

23. For costings see Wells, Appendix 'Total Costs of the Principal Fortifications *of Le camp retranché de Verdun*', pp. 155–6

24. Quoted from French official report, source unclear; cited in Doughty, p. 4

25. For a detailed discussion of the evolution of this system see Doughty, pp. 6–10

26. For details see for example Paul-Marie de la Gorce, *The French Army: A Military-Political History* (London: Weidenfeld and Nicolson, 1963), pp. 80–3; Hew Strachan, *The First World War, Volume I: To Arms* (Oxford: Oxford University Press, 2001), pp. 190–1; and *151 Régiment d'Infanterie de Ligne* [French language website], 'The System of National Conscription of France, 1873–1914' page at http://www.151ril.com/content/history/french–army/11#ThreeYears, accessed 05/02/2015

27. Cited in de la Gorce, pp. 9–10

28. See for example ibid., p. 83

29. See Anthony Clayton, *Paths of Glory: The French Army 1914–18* (London: Cassell, 2003), p. 38; and Ian Sumner and Gerry Embleton, *The French Army 1914–18, Osprey Men-At-Arms Seies No. 286* (London: Reed International Books, 1995), pp. 13–14

30. Quoted in Ian Ousby, *The Road to Verdun* (London: Pimlico, 2003), p. 28

31. See Strachan, p. 187; and Ousby, p. 28

32. See for example Terence Zuber, *The Battle of the Frontiers:*

Ardennes 1914 (Stroud: The History Press, 2009), pp. 75–6; and Strachan, p. 187

33. Quoted in Clayton, p. 38
34. See Strachan, pp. 186–7
35. See Clayton, p. 38; and Alistair Horne, *The Price of Glory: Verdun 1916* (London: Penguin, 1964), p. 21
36. See Wells, p. 31
37. See Strachan, pp. 185–6
38. See Doughty, p. 10
39. See Strachan, pp. 185–7, 189
40. See ibid., pp. 189–190; and Doughty, pp. 14–15
41. See Doughty, pp. 26–7
42. See Horne, *The Price of Glory*, p. 32
43. See Doughty, pp. 18–19, 37
44. See for example James Joll, *The Origins of the First World War* 2nd Ed. (London: Longman, 1992), p. 98; and Doughty, pp. 19–22
45. See Doughty, pp. 27–8; and Clayton, p. 37
46. Quoted in Ousby, pp. 28–9
47. See Horne, *The Price of Glory*, p. 19
48. See ibid., pp. 19–20

3 The Belfort Gap and *Plan XVII*: Setting the Scene, August 1914 – February 1915

1. See Doughty, *Pyrrhic Victory*, pp. 46–53
2. Figures cited in Doughty, p. 53; and Strachan, *The First World War, Volume I*, p. 206
3. See Strachan, p. 155
4. See Clayton, *Paths of Glory*, p. 19; Horne, *The Price of Glory*, p. 24; and Strachan, p. 206
5. See Doughty, pp. 18–19, 37; see also Clayton, pp. 17–19; for a detailed account of the evolution of Plan XVII see Strachan, pp. 180–95

6. See Clayton, pp. 19–20

7. See Doughty, pp. 59–60

8. Figures cited at 'Association de Réservistes de la Marine Alsace' [French language website], 'La Charge Héroïque du 19ᵉ Dragons le 19 Août 1914 à Brunstatt' at http://www.arm–asso.fr/2013/09/la-charge-heroique-du-19e-dragons-le-19-aout-1914-a-brunstatt/, accessed 29/03/2015

9. For a detailed and iconoclastic account of the Battle of the Ardennes see Terence Zuber, *The Battle of the Frontiers: Ardennes 1914* (Stroud: The History Press, 2009)

10. Figures cited in Strachan, p. 219; and Clayton, p. 29

11. Quoted from Clayton, p. 29

12. See Doughty, pp. 66–8; Strachan, pp. 218–19; and Clayton, pp. 28–9

13. Figures cited in David Stevenson, *1914–1918: The History of the First World War* (London: Penguin, 2004), p. 54

14. Figures cited in Horne, *The Price of Glory*, p. 26

15. Quoted in ibid., p. 25–6

16. For Ruffey's order see Doughty, pp. 75–6

17. De Gaulle comment cited in Clayton, p. 30, source uncertain

18. Figures cited in Holger H. Herwig, *The Marne 1914: The Opening of World War I and the Battle that Changed the World* (New York: Random House, 2011), p. 101

19. Figures cited in ibid., pp. 217–18

20. See ibid., p. 100

21. *Chasseurs à Pied*: literally hunters on foot, the French term for light infantry

22. See 'Fortiff Sere: L'association Séré de Rivière' [French language website], section on 'Trouée des Charmes', Le Fort de Manonviller' page, especially 'Etat du Fort Pendant la Première Guerre Mondiale' at http://fortiffsere.fr/troueedecharmes/index_fichiers/Page4590.htm, accessed 17/04/2015

23. See Herwig, *The Marne 1914*, p. 103; and 'Fortiff Sere: L'association Séré de Rivière' [French language website], section on 'Trouée des Charmes Section, Le Fort de Manonviller'

page, especially 'Etat du Fort Pendant la Première Guerre Mondiale' at http://fortiffsere.fr/troueedecharmes/index_ fichiers/Page4590.htm, accessed 17/04/2015

24. See Herwig, *The Marne 1914*, p. 103

25. Quote cited in ibid., p. 103

26. For French details see 'Fortiff Sere: L'association Séré de Rivière' [French language website], section on 'Trouée des Charmes', 'Le Fort de Manonviller' page, especially 'Etat du Fort Pendant la Première Guerre Mondiale' at http:// fortiffsere.fr/troueedecharmes/index_fichiers/Page4590.htm, accessed 17/04/2015

27. See Herwig, *The Marne 1914*, p. 103

28. Figures cited at 'Fortiff Sere: L'association Séré de Rivière' [French language website], section on 'Trouée des Charmes', 'Le Fort de Manonviller' page, especially 'Etat du Fort Pendant la Première Guerre Mondiale' at http://fortiffsere. fr/troueedecharmes/index_fichiers/Page4590.htm, accessed 17/04/2015

29. Quotes cited in Herwig, *The Marne 1914*, p. 103

30. See 'Fortiff Sere: L'association Séré de Rivière' [French language website], section on 'Trouée des Charmes', 'Le Fort de Manonviller' page, especially 'Etat du Fort Pendant la Première Guerre Mondiale' at http://fortiffsere.fr/troueedecharmes/ index_fichiers/Page4590.htm, accessed 17/04/2015

31. See 'Fortiff Sere: L'association Séré de Rivière' [French language website], section on 'Trouée des Charmes', 'Le Fort de Manonviller Page, 'Etat du Fort Pendant la Première Guerre Mondiale' and diagram 'Plan du Fort de Manonviller en 1918' at http://fortiffsere.fr/troueedecharmes/index_fichiers/ Page4590.htm, accessed 20/04/2015

32. See James Joll, *The Origins of the First World War* 2nd Ed. (London: Longman, 1992), p. 98

33. See Herwig, *The Marne 1914*, p. 34

34. For the argument that the Schlieffen Plan was not intended as an operational concept see for example Terence Zuber,

Inventing the Schlieffen Plan: German War Planning, 1871–1914 (Oxford: Oxford University Press, 2003); id., *The Real German War Plan 1904–1914* (Stroud: The History Press, 2011); and David Fromkin, *Europe's Last Summer: Why the World Went to War in 1914* (London: William Heinemann, 2004)

35. See Herwig, *The Marne 1914*, pp. 40–1
36. See Herwig, *The First World War: Germany and Austria-Hungary 1914–1918* (London: Arnold, 1998), pp. 56–7
37. Figures cited in Herwig, *The Marne 1914*, p. 48
38. See Herwig, *The First World War*, pp. 60–2
39. See Herwig, *The Marne 1914*, pp. 50–1; and id., *The First World War*, p. 60
40. Quoted from Herwig, *The First World War*, p. 68
41. Forty-day period cited in ibid., p. 58
42. For a detailed account see for example Strachan, pp. 316–35
43. See Herwig, *The Marne 1914*, pp. 107–17; Strachan, pp. 208–12; and Clayton Donnell, *The Forts of the Meuse in World War One* (Oxford: Osprey Publishing, 2007), especially pp. 42–51
44. See Strachan, p. 243
45. See Herwig, *The Marne 1914*, p. 262
46. Division numbers cited in Strachan, p. 243
47. Figures cited in Herwig, *The First World War*, p. 119
48. Figures cited in Strachan, p. 278
49. See Strachan, p. 278; and Horne, *The Price of Glory*, p. 27
50. See Clayton, p. 58
51. Figures cited in ibid., pp. 67–73
52. See Richard Holmes, *Fatal Avenue: A Traveller's History of the Battlefields of Northern France and Flanders, 1346–1945* (London: Jonathan Cape, 1992), p. 220
53. See Horne, p. 56
54. See 'Fortiff Sere: L'association Séré de Rivière' [French language website], section on 'Les Hauts de Meuse', 'Le Fort de Troyon'

page, at http://fortiffsere.fr/hautsdemeuse/index_fichiers/
Page10763.htm, accessed 11/05/2015

55. See ibid., section on 'Les Hauts de Meuse', 'Le Fort du Camp
des Romains' page at http://www.fortiffsere.fr/hautsdemeuse/
index_fichiers/Page10760.htm, accessed 12/05/2015

56. See Doughty, pp. 113–14

57. See Holmes, pp. 221–2; and *Verdun and the Battles for
its Possession: A Panoramic History and Guide* (Clermont-
Ferrand: Michelin & Cie, 1920), p. 4

4 Mine Warfare at the Shoulders: Framing the Battlefield and the Evolution of Operation GERICHT, February 1915 – February 1916

1. Figures cited in *Verdun: Vision and Comprehension*, 6th
Edition (Drancy: Editions Mage, 1989), pp. 47–8

2. Quoted from Holmes, *Fatal Avenue*, p. 222

3. Cited in Ousby, *The Road to Verdun*, p. 55

4. See *Verdun and the Battles for its Possession*, p. 5; and Horne,
The Price of Glory, p. 56

5. See 'Fortiff Sere: L'association Séré de Rivière' [French
language website], section on 'Place de Verdun', 'Le Fort de
Douaumont' page at http://fortiffsere.fr/verdun/index_fichiers/
Page11436.htm, accessed 17/5/2015; and 'Le Fort de Vaux'
page at http://fortiffsere.fr/verdun/index_fichiers/Page11439.
htm, accessed 17/5/2015; and Horne, *The Price of Glory*, p.
119

6. See Clayton, *Paths of Glory*, p. 37

7. For details see 'Fortiff Sere: L'association Séré de Rivière' [French
language website], section on 'Trouée des Charmes', 'Le Fort
de Manonviller' page at http://fortiffsere.fr/troueedecharmes/
index_fichiers/Page4590.htm, accessed 17/04/2015; and
Clayton, p. 26

8. See for example Ousby, pp. 54–5

9. See Horne, *The Price of Glory*, p. 59

10. See ibid., pp. 58–9; Clayton, pp. 99–100; and Wells, *Verdun: An Integrated Defence*, pp. 98–9; the latter refers to Fort Vaux losing its 75 mm turret to a sympathetic detonation of the demolition charge in the autumn of 1915, but this appears to have occurred in February or March 1916 during Operation GERICHT

11. See Ousby, pp. 55–6

12. See Herwig, *The First World War: Germany and Austria-Hungary 1914–1918*, p. 105; and Strachan, *The First World War, Volume I*, p. 262

13. See Robert T. Foley, *German Strategy and the Path to Verdun: Erich von Falkenhayn and the Development of Attrition, 1870–1916* (Cambridge: Cambridge University Press, 2007), p. 92

14. See Herwig, *The First World War*, p. 114

15. See Foley, pp. 106–8

16. See Herwig, *The First World War*, pp. 130–34; and Foley, pp. 109–23

17. Figures cited in Herwig, *The First World War*, p. 179

18. See Foley, pp. 156–7

19. For details see ibid., pp. 163–7

20. See ibid., pp. 168–69, 171–2

21. Figures cited in Herwig, *The First World War*, p. 172

22. See Foley, p. 171

23. Figures cited in ibid., p. 177, Footnote 96

24. French figures cited in Doughty, *Pyrrhic Victory*, pp. 201–2; German figures cited in Foley, p. 178

25. For details see for example Foley, pp. 38–55

26. See Herwig, *The First World War*, p. 180; and Foley, pp. 189–91

27. See Herwig, *The First World War*, pp. 180–2

28. For details see Foley, pp. 193–203

29. See ibid., pp. 195–6

30. See ibid., pp. 196–7

31. See ibid., pp. 204–5

32. Figures cited in Herwig, *The First World War*, p. 183

33. Quoted from ibid., p. 182

34. See Horne, *The Price of Glory*, p. 47; and Foley, p. 197

35. For kill ratio see Herwig, *The First World War*, p. 182; for alternative translation of *Gericht* see Horne, *The Price of Glory*, p. 47

36. See Foley, p. 210

37. See Horne, *The Price of Glory*, p. 50

38. 1,201 figure cited in Foley, p. 15; 1,220 in Horne, *The Price of Glory*, p. 51

39. See Foley, p. 215

40. See Horne, *The Price of Glory*, pp. 53–4

41. See Foley, p. 214

42. Quoted in Horne, *The Price of Glory*, p. 52

43. For details see 'Les Canons de l'Apocalypse' [French language website], 'Langer Max 38cm SKL/' page at http://html2.free.fr/canons/canmax.htm, accessed 25/05/2015; and 'Traces of WW1' website, 'Gun Emplacement German 380mm Gun' page on 'Max', at http://en.tracesofwar.com/article/47308/Gun-Emplacement-German-380-mm-Gun-Max.htm, accessed 25/05/2015

44. Quoted from Horne, *The Price of Glory*, pp. 61–2

45. Quoted from Ousby, pp. 59–60

46. See Horne, *The Price of Glory*, p. 62

47. See ibid., p. 63

48. See Doughty, pp. 266–7

49. See Horne, *The Price of Glory*, pp. 67–8

50. See Ousby, p. 63; and Horne, *The Price of Glory*, p. 77

51. See Horne, *The Price of Glory*, p. 77

5 With *Stollen*, *Flammenwerfer* and *Artillerie*: The First Phase of the Battle, 21 February 1916 – 28 February 1916

1. Quoted from Horne, *The Price of Glory*, p. 53

2. Figures cited in William Martin, *Verdun 1916: 'They Shall Not Pass'* (London: Praeger, 2004), p. 27

3. See 'Les Canons de l'Apocalypse' [French language website], 'Langer Max 38cm SKL/' page, especially table 'Tableau des positions pour les pièces de 38cm SLK45, 35/38cm, 35.5cm et 21/35cm' at http://html2.free.fr/canons/canmax.htm, accessed 02/06/2015

4. See Horne, *The Price of Glory*, pp. 79, 84

5. See Donnell, *The Forts of the Meuse in World War One*, p. 43

6. See Ousby, *The Road to Verdun*, p. 64

7. Quoted from Jacques Péricard, *Verdun 1916* (Paris: Nouvelle Librairie de France, 1992); cited in Malcolm Brown, *Verdun 1916* (Stroud: Tempus Publishing, 1999), pp. 45–6

8. See Foley, *German Strategy and the Path to Verdun*, p. 218

9. See Horne, *The Price of Glory* pp. 84–5; for details of Capitaine Pujo see Elizabeth Greenhalgh, *Foch in Command: The Forging of a First World War General* (Cambridge: Cambridge University Press, 2014), p. 148

10. See Horne, *The Price of Glory* p. 84

11. See Péricard; quoted in Brown, p. 46

12. See Martin, p. 33; and Horne, *The Price of Glory* p. 87

13. See Ousby, p. 71; and Horne, *The Price of Glory*, pp. 87, 90–2

14. For a detailed 3D graphic representation of the Bois des Caures positions see Martin, 'Colonel Driant's Last Stand', pp. 30–1

15. See Ousby, pp. 68–9; and Horne, *The Price of Glory*, pp. 82–3, 88

16. See Horne, *The Price of Glory*, pp. 89–90

17. See Ousby, p. 70; and Horne, *The Price of Glory*, p. 91

18. Figures cited in Brown, p. 47; and Horne, *The Price of Glory* pp. 88, 92

19. See 'Au Fil des Mots et de l'Histoire' [French language website], 'La 72e division á Verdun (21–24 février 1916) (5ème partie)' page, at http://aufildesmotsetdelhistoire.unblog.

fr/2012/03/29/la-72e-division-a-verdun-21-24-fevrier-1916-5eme-partie/, accessed 06/06/2015

20. See Horne, *The Price of Glory* pp. 94–6
21. Figure cited in ibid., p. 100
22. See ibid., p. 98
23. Quoted in Ousby, p. 73
24. See Horne, *The Price of Glory* p. 98; and Martin, pp. 35–6
25. See Ousby, p. 74
26. Figures cited in Horne, *The Price of Glory* p. 100; and Ousby, p. 75
27. See Martin, p. 40
28. See Ousby, p. 79
29. See ibid., pp. 93–4
30. Figures cited in Horne, *The Price of Glory* p. 110
31. For details see ibid., pp. 111–13
32. See ibid., pp. 114–15
33. See ibid., pp. 111, 112
34. See Clayton, *Paths of Glory*, pp. 85–6
35. See Horne, *The Price of Glory*, pp. 113–14
36. See Ousby, p. 94
37. See Doughty, *Pyrrhic Victory*, p. 70
38. See Ousby, pp. 94–5; and Doughty, p. 272
39. For a detailed account see Horne, *The Price of Glory*, pp. 120–33; and Ousby pp. 86–7
40. Quoted in Horne, *The Price of Glory*, p. 135
41. Quoted in ibid., p. 133
42. See Henry Bordeaux, *Douleur et gloire de Verdun, 21 fevrier 1916–2 janvier 1917* (Paris: Librairie Plon, 1957–1959); cited in Ousby, p. 62
43. Figure cited in Doughty, p. 275
44. See Horne, *The Price of Glory*, pp. 135–6
45. See H. Warner Allen, Special Correspondent of the British Press with the French Armies, *The Times*, 8 March 1916; cited in Malcolm Brown, *Verdun 1916* (Stroud: Tempus, 1999), p. 120
46. See Doughty, pp. 270–1

47. Quoted from Ousby, p. 95; see also Doughty, pp. 271–2; and Horne, *The Price of Glory*, p. 142
48. Quotes from Doughty, p. 272; and Horne, *The Price of Glory*, p. 141
49. See Doughty, pp. 272–3
50. Quote from Horne, *The Price of Glory*, p. 146; and Martin, p. 44
51. See Horne, *The Price of Glory*, p. 156
52. Quoted in ibid., p. 157
53. See Martin, p. 44; for a detailed account see Horne, *The Price of Glory*, pp. 155–7
54. Quoted in Foley, p. 219
55. See Horne, *The Price of Glory*, pp. 162–3, 166–7
56. Figures cited in ibid., p. 166
57. See Foley, p. 219
58. See Horne, *The Price of Glory*, p. 165
59. For a detailed account see 'Leben und Tod des Generalmajor Wilhelm von Lotterer, 1857–1916' [German language web page] at http://www.dffv.de/Verdun/Lotterer/Lotterer.htm, accessed 15/06/2015
60. See Doughty, p. 274; and Horne, *The Price of Glory*, pp. 166–7
61. Figures cited in Horne, *The Price of Glory*, p. 159
62. See Doughty, p. 275
63. Figures cited in ibid., p. 275
64. Cited in Brown, p. 84
65. Figures cited in Horne, *The Price of Glory*, pp. 159–61

6 *Le Mort-Homme* and *Côte* 304: The Battle Expands to the West Bank of the River Meuse, 6 March 1916 – 29 May 1916

1. Figure cited in Foley, *German Strategy and the Path to Verdun*, p. 20

2. See Horne, *The Price of Glory*, p. 169

3. See Foley, p. 223

4. See Horne, *The Price of Glory*, p. 168

5. See ibid., p. 169–70

6. See Foley, footnote 77, p. 224

7. See ibid., pp. 224–5

8. See Martin, *Verdun 1916*, pp. 45–6; Foley, pp. 224–5; and Horne, *The Price of Glory* pp. 174–5

9. See Horne, *The Price of Glory* pp. 173–4

10. Figures cited in Martin, p. 47

11. Figures cited at 'Les Francais à Verdun 1916' [French language website], section on 'Les Régiments d'Infanterie et les Bataillons de Chasseurs qui ont participé à la Bataille de Verdun', '401–450 RI' page, entries for 408e *Régiment d'Infanterie* and 409e *Régiment d'Infanterie* at www.lesfrancaisaverdun-1916. fr/regiment-ri401.htm, accessed 21/06/2015

12. See Martin, p. 49; and Horne, *The Price of Glory* pp. 173–4

13. Figure cited in Foley, footnote 90, p. 226

14. For attack timings see 'Les Francais à Verdun 1916' [French language website], section on 'Les Régiments d'Infanterie et les Bataillons de Chasseurs qui ont participé à la Bataille de Verdun', '101–150 RI' page, entry for 111e *Régiment d'Infanterie* at www.lesfrancaisaverdun-1916.fr/regiment-ri101.htm#ri111, accessed 22/06/2015; for figures see Horne, *The Price of Glory*, pp. 177–8

15. Testimony from *Sergent* Richard Thoumin, 26e *Régiment d'Infanterie*, 11e *Division d'Infanterie*; cited in Brown, *Verdun 1916*, p. 76

16. Figures cited in Horne, *The Price of Glory*, p. 178

17. See Foley, p. 226; and Horne, *The Price of Glory*, p. 179; for timings and French attack details see 'LesFrancais à Verdun 1916' [French language website], section on 'Les Régiments d'Infanterie et les Bataillons de Chasseurs qui ont participé à la Bataille de Verdun', '101–150 RI' and '191–200 RI' pages,

entries for 157ᵉ and 210ᵉ *Régiments d'Infanterie* at http://
www.lesfrancaisaverdun-1916.fr/, accessed 22/06/2015

18. Figure cited in Foley, p. 226
19. Quoted from a letter by *Leutnant* Christian Bordeching; cited in Brown, p. 107
20. Testimony from *Caporal* Pierre Teilhard de Chardin, 4ᵉ *Régiment Mixte Zouaves et Tirailleurs*, 38ᵉ *Division d'Infanterie*; cited in Brown, p. 75
21. See Horne, *The Price of Glory*, p. 180
22. Entry from the diary of *Feldwebel* Karl Gartner, *Infanterie Regiment 243*; cited in Brown, p. 71
23. See Martin, p. 48
24. See Clayton, p. 106; quote cited in Horne, *The Price of Glory*, p. 161
25. Quoted from Raymond Jubert, *Verdun (mars-avri-mai 1916)* (Paris: Payot, 1918); cited in Brown, p. 87
26. See *Horne, The Price of Glory*, pp. 224–6; and Doughty, *Pyrrhic Victory*, pp. 277–8
27. See Foley, p. 228
28. For timing see Ousby, *The Road to Verdun*, p. 198; for ammunition trains see Horne, *The Price of Glory*, p. 181; for 37ᵉ *Régiment d'Infanterie* details see 'Les Francais à Verdun 1916' [French language website], section on 'Les Régiments d'Infanterie et les Bataillons de Chasseurs qui ont participé à la Bataille de Verdun', '1-50 RI' page, entry for 37ᵉ *Régiment d'Infanterie* at www.lesfrancaisaverdun-1916.fr/regiment-ri1.htm, accessed 29/06/2015
29. Quoted in Ousby, p. 198
30. Timing cited in Ousby, p. 199; for details of 94ᵉ and 162ᵉ *Régiments d'Infanterie* see 'Les Francais à Verdun 1916' [French language website], section on 'Les Régiments d'Infanterie et les Bataillons de Chasseurs qui ont participé à la Bataille de Verdun', '51-100 RI' and '151-200 RI' pages, entries for 94ᵉ and 162ᵉ *Régiments d'Infanterie* at http://www.lesfrancaisaverdun-1916.fr/regimentintro.htm, accessed 29/06/2015

31. See Ousby, pp. 197–8
32. Testimony from *Sous-Lieutenant* Raymond Jubert, 151ᵉ *Régiment d'Infanterie*; quoted in Brown, pp. 77–8
33. Order quoted in full in Brown, pp. 78–9
34. Quoted in Horne, *The Price of Glory*, p. 182
35. See 'Les Francais à Verdun 1916' [French language website], section on 'Les Régiments d'Infanterie et les Bataillons de Chasseurs qui ont participé à la Bataille de Verdun', '251-300 RI' page, entry for 251ᵉ *Régiment d'Infanterie* at www.lesfrancaisaverdun-1916.fr/regiment-ri251.htm, accessed 03/07/2015
36. See Foley, pp. 230–1

7 More on Both Banks: Reappraisals and Renewed Effort, 29 April 1916 – 1 June 1916

1. Extract from report from von Mudra to 5. *Armee* headquarters, dated 21/04/1916; cited in *German Strategy and the Path to Verdun*, p. 229
2. See Horne, *The Price of Glory*, pp. 14–15
3. Quoted in Foley, p. 229
4. See Foley, pp. 229–30; and Horne, *The Price of Glory*, pp. 215–17
5. See Horne, *The Price of Glory*, pp. 182–3
6. Testimony from *Soldat* Pierre Rouquet, 151ᵉ *Régiment d'Infanterie*; quoted in Brown, *Verdun 1916*, p. 106
7. See 'Les Francais à Verdun 1916' [French language website], section on 'Les Régiments d'Infanterie et les Bataillons de Chasseurs qui ont participé à la Bataille de Verdun', '51-100 RI' page, entry for 68ᵉ *Régiment d'Infanterie* at www.lesfrancaisaverdun-1916.fr/regiment-ri51.htm#ri68, accessed 04/07/2015
8. For details see 'Les Francais à Verdun 1916' [French language website], section on 'Les Régiments d'Infanterie et les Bataillons

de Chasseurs qui ont participé à la Bataille de Verdun', '101-150 RI' and '250–300 RI' pages, entries for 114ᵉ, 125ᵉ, 268ᵉ, 290ᵉ and 296ᵉ *Régiments d'Infanterie* at http://www. lesfrancaisaverdun-1916.fr/, accessed 04/07/2015

9. Figures cited in Clayton, *Paths of Glory*, p. 108

10. See 'Les Francais à Verdun 1916' [French language website], section on 'Les Régiments d'Infanterie et les Bataillons de Chasseurs qui ont participé à la Bataille de Verdun', '101-150 RI' and '250-300 RI' pages, entries for 173ᵉ and 296ᵉ *Régiments d'Infanterie* at http://www.lesfrancaisaverdun-1916.fr/, accessed 04/07/2015

11. Testimony from *Leutnant* W. Weingartner, *Minenwerfer Kompanie* 38, *Jäger Division* 38; cited in Brown, pp. 107–8

12. See 'Les Francais à Verdun 1916' [French language website], section on 'Les Régiments d'Infanterie et les Bataillons de Chasseurs qui ont participé à la Bataille de Verdun', '250-300 RI' page, entry for 296ᵉ *Régiment d'Infanterie* at www.lesfrancaisaverdun-1916.fr/regiment–ri251.htm#ri268, accessed 04/07/2015

13. See Horne, *The Price of Glory*, p. 182

14. Quoted from Charles F. Horne (Ed.), *Records of the Great War*, (National Alumni, 1923); cited at http://www.firstworldwar. com/diaries/verdun_lemorthomme.htm, accessed 04/07/2015

15. See 'Les Francais à Verdun 1916' [French language website], section on 'Les Régiments d'Infanterie et les Bataillons de Chasseurs qui ont participé à la Bataille de Verdun', '250-300 RI' page, entry for 267ᵉ *Régiment d'Infanterie* at www.lesfrancaisaverdun-1916.fr/regiment-ri251.htm#ri267, accessed 04/07/2015

16. Quoted from interview with *Soldat* Pierre Rouquet; cited in Brown, p. 106

17. See 'Les Francais à Verdun 1916' [French language website], section on 'Les Régiments d'Infanterie et les Bataillons de Chasseurs qui ont participé à la Bataille de Verdun', '250-300 RI' page, entry for 287ᵉ *Régiment d'Infanterie* at

www.lesfrancaisaverdun-1916.fr/regiment-ri251.htm#ri287, accessed 04/07/2015

18. See Ousby, *The Road to Verdun*, pp. 210–11; and Horne, *The Price of Glory*, pp. 226–30

19. See 'Les Francais à Verdun 1916' [French language website], section on 'Les Régiments d'Infanterie et les Bataillons de Chasseurs qui ont participé à la Bataille de Verdun', '51-100 RI' age, entry for 74ᵉ *Régiment d'Infanterie* at www.lesfrancaisaverdun-1916.fr/regiment–ri51.htm#ri74, accessed 06/07/2015

20. Quoted from Ousby, pp. 210–11

21. See 'Les Francais à Verdun 1916' [French language website], section on 'Les Régiments d'Infanterie et les Bataillons de Chasseurs qui ont participé à la Bataille de Verdun', '51–100 RI' page, entry for 74ᵉ *Régiment d'Infanterie* at www.lesfrancaisaverdun-1916.fr/regiment-ri51.htm#ri74, accessed 06/07/2015

22. Quoted in Horne, *The Price of Glory*, p. 231

23. Quoted in ibid., p. 231

24. See for example ibid., p. 239

25. Diary of *Lieutenant* Henri Desagneaux, 106ᵉ *Régiment d'Infanterie*, entry for Thursday 15 June 1916; cited in Brown, p. 125

26. René Arnaud, *Tragédie Bouffe, A Frenchman in the First World War*, translated by J.B. Donne (London: Sidgewick and Jackson, 1966); cited in Brown, p. 126

27. Figures cited in *Verdun: Vision and Comprehension*, p. 32

28. Quoted in Horne, *The Price of Glory*, p. 232

29. See Brown, pp. 113–14

30. See Martin, *Verdun 1916*, p. 55; and Horne, *The Price of Glory*, p. 216

31. See for example Doughty, *Pyrrhic Victory*, p. 287

32. See Ousby, p. 214

33. See Martin, p. 56; and Horne, *The Price of Glory*, p. 233

34. See Horne, *The Price of Glory*, pp. 234–5

35. See Ousby, pp. 215–16; and 'Les Francais à Verdun 1916' [French language website], section on 'Les Régiments d'Infanterie et les Bataillons de Chasseurs qui ont participé à la Bataille de Verdun', '51-100 RI' and '250-300 RI' pages, entries for 74ᵉ and 274ᵉ *Régiments d'Infanterie* at http://www.lesfrancaisaverdun-1916.fr/, accessed 09/07/2015

36. See Ousby, pp. 215–16; and 'Les Francais à Verdun 1916' [French language website], section on 'Les Régiments d'Infanterie et les Bataillons de Chasseurs qui ont participé à la Bataille de Verdun', pages '51-100 RI' and '250-300 RI', entries for 74ᵉ and 274ᵉ *Régiments d'Infanterie* at http://www.lesfrancaisaverdun-1916.fr/, accessed 09/07/2015

37. See 'Les Francais à Verdun 1916' [French language website], section on 'Les Régiments d'Infanterie et les Bataillons de Chasseurs qui ont participé à la Bataille de Verdun', '1-50 RI' page, entry for 36ᵉ *Régiment d'Infanterie* at www.lesfrancaisaverdun-1916.fr/regiment-ri1.htm, accessed 09/07/2015

38. See Horne, *The Price of Glory*, pp. 232–4

39. See ibid., pp. 235–6; and Ousby, p. 215

40. See Ousby, pp. 216–17; and 'Les Francais à Verdun 1916' [French language website], section on 'Les Régiments d'Infanterie et les Bataillons de Chasseurs qui ont participé à la Bataille de Verdun', '51-100 RI' page, entry for 74ᵉ *Régiment d'Infanterie* at www.lesfrancaisaverdun-1916.fr/regiment-ri51.htm#ri74, accessed 09/07/2015

41. For details see 'Les Francais à Verdun 1916' [French language website], section on 'Les Régiments d'Infanterie et les Bataillons de Chasseurs qui ont participé à la Bataille de Verdun', '1-50 RI' and '200-250 RI' pages, entries for 18ᵉ, 34ᵉ, 49ᵉ and 218ᵉ *Régiments d'Infanterie* at http://www.lesfrancaisaverdun-1916.fr/, accessed 09/07/2015

42. Quoted in Ousby, p. 217

43. See Horne, *The Price of Glory*, p. 237

44. Figures cited in Ousby, p. 217; Horne, *The Price of Glory*, p. 237; and 'Les Francais à Verdun 1916' [French language

website], section on 'Les Régiments d'Infanterie et les Bataillons de Chasseurs qui ont participé à la Bataille de Verdun', '101-150 RI', entry for 129ᵉ *Régiment d'Infanterie* at www.lesfrancaisaverdun-1916.fr/regiment-ri101.htm#ri129, accessed 09/07/2015

45. See Horne, *The Price of Glory*, p. 237
46. Figures cited in Ousby, pp. 221–3

8 Clearing the Way for the Final Push: The Fight for Fort Vaux, 1 June 1916 – 8 June 1916

1. See 'Fortiff Sere: L'association Séré de Rivière' [French language website], 'La Place Forte ou du Camp Retranché de Verdun Section, Le Fort de Vaux ou Fort Dillon' page at http://fortiffsere.fr/verdun/index_fichiers/Page11439.htm, accessed 14/07/2015
2. Quote cited in 'Les Francais à Verdun 1916' [French language website], section on 'Fortifications', 'Le Fort de Vaux' page at www.lesfrancaisaverdun-1916.fr/fortifications-vaux.htm, accessed 15/07/2015
3. See 'Les Francais à Verdun 1916' [French language website], section on 'Les Régiments d'Infanterie et les Bataillons de Chasseurs qui ont participé à la Bataille de Verdun', pages '101-150 RI' and '151-200 RI' pages, entries for 124ᵉ and 142ᵉ *Régiments d'Infanterie* at www.lesfrancaisaverdun-916.fr/regiment-ri101.htm#ri124, accessed 18/07/2015
4. See Martin, *Verdun 1916*, pp. 60–1
5. Quote from Raynal cited in Horne, *The Price of Glory*, p. 248
6. For details of normal Fort garrison see 'Fortiff Sere: L'association Séré de Rivière' [French language website], section on 'La Place Forte ou du Camp Retranché de Verdun', 'Le Fort de Vaux ou Fort Dillon' page at http://fortiffsere.fr/verdun/index_fichiers/Page11439.htm, accessed 18/07/201; for details

of garrison from 31/05/1916 see 'Les Francais à Verdun 1916' [French language website], section on 'Les Régiments d'Infanterie et les Bataillons de Chasseurs qui ont participé à la Bataille de Verdun', '101-150 RI' page, entry for 124ᵉ *Régiment d'Infanterie* at www.lesfrancaisaverdun-1916.fr/regiment-ri101.htm#ri124, accessed 18/07/2015

7. See Horne, *The Price of Glory*, p. 248; and Martin, pp. 60–1

8. See Horne, *The Price of Glory*, pp. 241–4

9. See 'Les Francais à Verdun 1916' [French language website], section on 'Fortifications', 'Le Fort de Vaux' page at www.lesfrancaisaverdun-1916.fr/fortifications-vaux.htm, accessed 27/07/2015

10. See Horne, *The Price of Glory*, pp. 244–5

11. Quoted in ibid., p. 245

12. See 'Les Francais à Verdun 1916' [French language website], section on 'Les Régiments d'Infanterie et les Bataillons de Chasseurs qui ont participé à la Bataille de Verdun', '101-150 RI', entry for 101ᵉ *Régiment d'Infanterie* at www.lesfrancaisaverdun-1916.fr/regiment–ri101.htm#, accessed 22/07/2015; and Horne, *The Price of Glory*, pp. 245–6, 252–4, 255–6

13. See Horne, *The Price of Glory*, p. 244

14. See ibid., p. 249

15. Quote cited in 'Les Francais à Verdun 1916' [French language website], section on 'Fortifications', 'Le Fort de Vaux' page at www.lesfrancaisaverdun-1916.fr/fortifications-vaux.htm, accessed 27/07/2015

16. See 'Les Francais à Verdun 1916' [French language website], section on 'Fortifications', 'Le Fort de Vaux' page' at www.lesfrancaisaverdun-1916.fr/fortifications-vaux.htm, accessed 28/07/2015

17. The *Canon de 12* was a bronze 1853-pattern 122 mm bronze smooth-bore cannon modified with a locking breech and a traversable two-wheeled carriage deployed as a short-range defence weapon in many Serré de Rivière fortifications. For

details see 'Fortiff Sere: L'association Séré de Rivière' [French language website], page on 'Le Canon de 12 de Place ou de Campagne Mle. 1853–59', L'Obusier de 12 et le Canon de 12 Culasse Mle. 1884' page at http://www.fortiffsere.fr/artillerie/index_fichiers/Page907.htm, accessed 28/07/2014

18. See Martin, pp. 61–2; and Horne, *The Price of Glory*, pp. 249–51

19. For French attack details and quote of Raynal's report see 'Les Francais à Verdun 1916' [French language website], section on 'Fortifications', 'Le Fort de Vaux' page at www.lesfrancaisaverdun-1916.fr/fortifications-vaux.htm, accessed 10/08/2015; for von Raden details see Martin, p. 62

20. See 'Les Francais à Verdun 1916' [French language website], section on 'Les Régiments d'Infanterie et les Bataillons de Chasseurs qui ont participé à la Bataille de Verdun', '50-100 RI' and '100–150 RI' pages, entries for 53ᵉ & 124ᵉ *Régiments d'Infanterie* at www.lesfrancaisaverdun-1916.fr/regiment-intro.htm, accessed 28/07/2015

21. See 'Les Francais à Verdun 1916' [French language website], section on 'Fortifications', 'Le Fort de Vaux' page at www.lesfrancaisaverdun–1916.fr/fortifications–vaux.htm, accessed 10/08/2015

22. See Horne, *The Price of Glory*, p. 254; and 'Les Francais à Verdun 1916' [French language website], section on 'Les Régiments d'Infanterie et les Bataillons de Chasseurs qui ont participé à la Bataille de Verdun', '251–300 RI' page, entry for 298ᵉ *Régiment d'Infanterie* at www.lesfrancaisaverdun-1916.fr/regiment-ri251.htm#ri298, accessed 10/08/2015

23. Quoted from Brown, *Verdun 1916*, pp. 115–16

24. See 'Le Francais á Verdun 1916' [French language website], 'Fortifications' Section, 'Le Fort de Vaux' page at www.lesfrancaisaverdun-1916.fr/fortifications-vaux.htm, accessed 10/08/2015

25. Quote cited in Brown, pp. 116–17

26. For conference timing and final total reaching safety see

'Les Francais à Verdun 1916' [French language website], section on 'Fortifications', 'Le Fort de Vaux' page at www.lesfrancaisaverdun-1916.fr/fortifications-vaux.htm, accessed 10/08/2015

27. Quoted in Horne, *The Price of Glory*, p. 256

28. See ibid., pp. 256–7

29. For timings and text of all messages see 'Les Francais à Verdun 1916' [French language website], section on 'Fortifications', 'Le Fort de Vaux' page at www.lesfrancaisaverdun-1916.fr/fortifications-vaux.htm, accessed 10/08/2015

30. Interestingly the 'Les Francais à Verdun 1916' website refers to Buffet being informed by Nivelle that the attack was scheduled to begin at 06:00, but Horne refers to Buffet informing Raynal of a 02:00 start and to the fort's garrison standing to for the latter time, and the 02:00 start time is also cited in the accounts of the infantry units involved; see 'Les Francais à Verdun 1916' [French language website], section on 'Fortifications', 'Le Fort de Vaux' page at www.lesfrancaisaverdun-1916.fr/fortifications-vaux.htm and the section on 'Les Régiments d'Infanterie et les Bataillons de Chasseurs qui ont participé à la Bataille de Verdun', '201-250 RI' and '301-350 RI' pages, entries for 238e and 321e *Régiments d'Infanterie* at www.lesfrancaisaverdun-1916.fr/regiment-intro.htm, accessed 10/08/2015; see also Horne, *The Price of Glory*, pp. 256–7

31. See 'Les Francais à Verdun 1916' [French language website], section on 'Les Régiments d'Infanterie et les Bataillons de Chasseurs qui ont participé à la Bataille de Verdun', '201–250 RI' and '301–350 RI' pages, entries for 238e and 321e *Régiments d'Infanterie* at www.lesfrancaisaverdun–1916.fr/regiment–intro.htm, accessed 10/08/2015; Horne, *The Price of Glory*, pp. 258; and Martin, p. 63

32. Quoted in Brown, p. 117

33. In some accounts *Lieutenant* Farges name is rendered Fargues

34. See 'Les Francais à Verdun 1916' [French language website], section on 'Fortifications', 'Le Fort de Vaux' page at www.

lesfrancaisaverdun-1916.fr/fortifications-vaux.htm, accessed 10/08/2015

35. See Horne, *The Price of Glory*, pp. 259–60

9 The Tide Ebbs: The Final German Effort, 8 June 1916 – 12 July 1916

1. For a detailed record of the conference by an anonymous attendee referred to as 'Commander P' see 'Les Francais à Verdun 1916' [French language website], section on 'Fortifications', 'Le Fort de Vaux' page, entry headed '*6 juin – Pression allemande sur le fort de Vaux (rive droite)*' at www. lesfrancaisaverdun-1916.fr/fortifications-vaux.htm, accessed 12/08/2015; see also Horne, *The Price of Glory*, pp. 260–1

2. Quoted in Horne, *The Price of Glory*, p. 261

3. Quoted in ibid., p. 261

4. See 'Les Francais à Verdun 1916' [French language website], section on 'Fortifications', 'Le Fort de Vaux' page at www. lesfrancaisaverdun-1916.fr/fortifications-vaux.htm, accessed 12/08/2015; and Horne, *The Price of Glory*, p. 262

5. See 'Fortiff Sere: L'association Séré de Rivière' [French language website], section on 'La Place Forte ou du Camp Retranché de Verdun', 'L'ouvrage B de Thiaumont' page at http://fortiffsere. fr/verdun/index_fichiers/Page11442.htm, accessed 12/08/2015

6. Quoted from Les Francais à Verdun 1916 [French language website], section on 'Fortifications', 'L'ouvrage de Thiaumont' page at www.lesfrancaisaverdun-1916.fr/fortifications-thiaumont.htm, accessed 12/08/2015. *Médicin* is a medical rank equivalent to *Capitaine*; for details of Maufrais' service see 'Temoignages de 1914–1918' [French language website], page on 'Maufrais, Louis (1889–1977)' at 'http://www. crid1418.org/temoins/2010/11/04/maufrais-louis-1889-1977/, accessed 14/08/2015

7. See 'Fortiff Sere: L'association Séré de Rivière' [French language

website], section on 'La Place Forte ou du Camp Retranché de Verdun', 'L'ouvrage B de Thiaumont' page at http://fortiffsere. fr/verdun/index_fichiers/Page11442.htm, accessed 14/08/2015

8. See 'Les Francais à Verdun 1916' [French language website], section on 'Les Régiments d'Infanterie et les Bataillons de Chasseurs qui ont participé à la Bataille de Verdun Section, '301–350 RI' page, entry for 347ᵉ *Régiment d'Infanterie* at www.lesfrancaisaverdun-1916.fr/regiment-ri301.htm#ri347, accessed 15/08/2015

9. Figures cited at 'Les Francais à Verdun 1916' [French language website], section on 'Les Régiments d'Infanterie et les Bataillons de Chasseurs qui ont participé à la Bataille de Verdun', '251–300 RI' page, entry for 291ᵉ *Régiment d'Infanterie* at www.lesfrancaisaverdun-1916.fr/regiment-ri251.htm#ri293, accessed 15/08/2015

10. See Doughty, *Pyrrhic Victory*, p. 288

11. Quoted in Horne, *The Price of Glory*, pp. 269–70; see also p. 273

12. See ibid., p. 272

13. See for example Foley, *German Strategy and the Road to Verdun*, pp. 243–5

14. See Ousby, *Verdun*, pp. 224–5

15. See Horne, *The Price of Glory*, pp 266–7

16. Quoted in ibid., p. 267

17. See ibid., p. 267–8; and Ousby, pp. 226–7

18. Quote cited in Ousby, p. 222

19. For details see ibid., pp. 221–3

20. Quotes cited in Horne, *The Price of Glory*, pp. 282–83

21. Figures cited in Ousby, p. 229

22. See 'Fortiff Sere: L'association Séré de Rivière' [French language website], section on 'La Place Forte ou du Camp Retranché de Verdun', 'L'Ouvrage A de Froidterre' page at http://fortiffsere. fr/verdun/index_fichiers/Page4551.htm, accessed 18/08/2015

23. See 'Les Francais à Verdun 1916' [French language website], section on 'Les Régiments d'Infanterie et les Bataillons de Chasseurs qui ont participé à la Bataille de Verdun', 'B.C.P.'

page, entries for 106ᵉ *Bataillon de Chasseurs à Pied* and 359ᵉ *Régiment d'Infanterie* at http://www.lesfrancaisaverdun-1916. fr/, accessed 18/08/2015

24. See 'Les Francais à Verdun 1916' [French language website], section on 'Les Régiments d'Infanterie et les Bataillons de Chasseurs qui ont participé à la Bataille de Verdun', 'B.C.P.' page, entry for 114ᵉ *Bataillon de Chasseurs à Pied* at www. lesfrancaisaverdun-1916.fr/regiment-bcp.htm#bcp121, accessed 18/08/2015

25. For details see 'Historique du 405e Régiment d'Infanterie' [French language website], pp. 6–7 at http://tableaudhonneur. free.fr/405eRI.pdf, accessed 19/08/2015

26. See Brown, *Verdun 1916*, p. 129

27. See Horne, *The Price of Glory*, pp. 285–6; and 'Les Francais à Verdun 1916' [French language website], section on 'Les Régiments d'Infanterie et les Bataillons de Chasseurs qui ont participé à la Bataille de Verdun', entries for 39ᵉ and 239ᵉ *Régiments d'Infanterie* at http://www.lesfrancaisaverdun-1916. fr/, accessed 18/08/2015

28. Figures cited at 'Les Francais à Verdun 1916' [French language website], section on 'Les Régiments d'Infanterie et les Bataillons de Chasseurs qui ont participé à la Bataille de Verdun', entries for 39ᵉ and 239ᵉ *Régiments d'Infanterie* at http://www. lesfrancaisaverdun-1916.fr/, accessed 19/08/2015

29. Figures cited in Horne, *The Price of Glory*, p. 289

30. See Ousby, footnote p. 231

31. Figure cited in Horne, *The Price of Glory*, p. 289

32. For details see Foley, pp. 246–8

33. See Horne *The Price of Glory*, p. 289

34. See ibid., pp. 294–5

36. See 'Les Francais à Verdun 1916' [French language website], section on 'Les Régiments d'Infanterie et les Bataillons de Chasseurs qui ont participé à la Bataille de Verdun', entry for 167ᵉ *Régiment d'Infanterie* at www.lesfrancaisaverdun-1916. fr/regiment-rii51.htm#rii67, accessed 19/08/2015

37. Quoted in Horne, *The Price of Glory*, pp. 295–96

38. See ibid., p. 296

39. See Martin, *Verdun 1916*, p. 78

40. See 'Les Francais à Verdun 1916' [French language website], section on 'Les Régiments d'Infanterie et les Bataillons de Chasseurs qui ont participé à la Bataille de Verdun', entries for 167e & 168e *Régiments d'Infanterie* at www.lesfrancaisaverdun-1916. fr/regiment-intro.htm, accessed 19/08/2015

41. See Horne, *The Price of Glory*, p. 297

42. See 'Le Francais á Verdun 1916' [French language website], section on 'Les Régiments d'Infanterie et les Bataillons de Chasseurs qui ont participé à la Bataille de Verdun', entry for 271e *Régiment d'Infanterie* at www.lesfrancaisaverdun-1916. fr/regiment-ri201.htm#ri217, accessed 19/08/2015; and Horne, *The Price of Glory*, pp. 296–97

43. See 'Les Francais à Verdun 1916' [French language website], section on 'Les Régiments d'Infanterie et les Bataillons de Chasseurs qui ont participé à la Bataille de Verdun', entry for 358e *Régiment d'Infanterie* at www.lesfrancaisaverdun-1916. fr/regiment-ri351.htm#ri358, accessed 19/08/2015

44. Figure cited in Horne, *The Price of Glory*, p. 297

45. Figures cited at 'Les Francais à Verdun 1916' [French language website], section on 'Les Régiments d'Infanterie et les Bataillons de Chasseurs qui ont participé à la Bataille de Verdun' Section, entries for 271e and 358e *Régiments d'Infanterie* at www.lesfrancaisaverdun-1916.fr/regiment-intro.htm, accessed 19/08/2015

46. See Horne, *The Price of Glory*, pp. 297–98; and 'Les Francais à Verdun 1916' [French language website], section on 'Les Régiments d'Infanterie et les Bataillons de Chasseurs qui ont participé à la Bataille de Verdun', entries for 7e and 14e *Régiments d'Infanterie* and 25e *Bataillon de Chasseurs à Pied* at www.lesfrancaisaverdun-1916.fr/regiment-intro.htm, accessed 19/08/2015

10 Full Circle: French Counter-Attacks and What Came After, 14 July 1916 – 2016

1. See Foley, *German Strategy and the Path to Verdun*, p. 258; and Horne, *The Price of Glory*, pp. 302–3
2. See Foley, pp. 254, 256–57
3. Figures cited in; and Doughty, *Pyrrhic Victory*, p. 298
4. See Horne, *The Price of Glory*, p. 301–2
5. For details of Falkenhayn's unseating see for example Herwig, *The First World War*, pp. 195–97; and Foley, pp. 256–58
6. See Horne, *The Price of Glory*, p. 334–35
7. For beacon quote see Herwig, *The First World War*, p. 184; cited in Foley, p. 259; other Hindenburg and Ludendorff quotes cited in Horne, *The Price of Glory*, pp. 302–3
8. See Horne, *The Price of Glory*, p. 300
9. Quote from ibid., p. 303; see also Ousby, *The Road to Verdun*, pp. 233–34
10. Quote cited in Horne, *The Price of Glory*, p. 304
11. For details see 'Fortiff Sere: L'association Séré de Rivière' [French language website], section on 'La Place Forte ou du Camp Retranché de Verdun', 'Le Tunnel de Tavannes' page at fortiffsere.fr/verdun/index_fichiers/Page589.htm, accessed 02/09/2015; 'Le Francais á Verdun 1916' [French language website], section on 'Fortifications', 'Le Fort et le Tunnel de Tavannes' page at www.lesfrancaisaverdun-1916.fr/fortifications-tavannes.htm, accessed 02/09/2015; and Horne, *The Price of Glory*, pp. 303–6
12. See Doughty, p. 306
13. See 'Les Francais à Verdun 1916' [French language website], section on 'Fortifications', 'Le Fort de Douaumont' page at www.lesfrancaisaverdun-1916.fr/fortifications-douaumont.htm, accessed 02/09/2015
14. See Doughty, p. 306
15. See Horne, *The Price of Glory*, pp. 308–9
16. See ibid., p. 308
17. Figures cited in 'Les Francais à Verdun 1916' [French language

website], section on 'Fortifications', 'Le Fort de Douaumont' page at www.lesfrancaisaverdun-1916.fr/fortifications-douaumont.htm, accessed 02/09/2015; and Horne, *The Price of Glory*, p. 308

18. See Ousby, p. 249

19. For destruction of the observation dome see Horne, *The Price of Glory*, p. 311

20. For details see ibid., pp. 310–12; Martin, *Verdun 1916*, pp. 81–2; and 'Les Francais à Verdun 1916' [French language website], section on 'Fortifications', 'Le Fort de Douaumont' page at www.lesfrancaisaverdun-1916.fr/fortifications-douaumont.htm, accessed 02/09/2015

21. See 'Les Francais à Verdun 1916' [French language website], section on 'Fortifications', 'Le Fort de Douaumont' page at www.lesfrancaisaverdun-1916.fr/fortifications-douaumont. htm, accessed 02/09/2015

22. Former figure cited in Horne, *The Price of Glory*, p. 313; latter figure cited in Clayton, *Paths of Glory*, p. 109

23. See Martin, p. 82

24. See 'Les Francais à Verdun 1916' [French language website], section on 'Fortifications', 'Le Fort de Douaumont' page at www.lesfrancaisaverdun-1916.fr/fortifications-douaumont. htm, accessed 02/09/2015

25. See Horne, *The Price of Glory*, p. 314

26. See Martin, pp. 82–3; Horne, The Price of Glory, pp. 314–15; and 'Les Francais à Verdun 1916' [French language website], section on 'Fortifications', 'Le Fort de Douaumont' page and various specific *Régiment* pages at www.lesfrancaisaverdun-1916.fr/fortifications-douaumont. htm, accessed 02/09/2015

27. See Horne, *The Price of Glory*, pp. 315–16

28. Figures cited at 'Les Francais à Verdun 1916' [French language website], section on 'Fortifications', 'Le Fort de Douaumont' page at www.lesfrancaisaverdun-1916.fr/fortifications-douaumont.htm, accessed 02/09/2015

29. See 'Le Francais á Verdun 1916' [French language website], section on 'Fortifications', 'Le Fort de Vaux' page at www. lesfrancaisaverdun-1916.fr/fortifications-vaux.htm, accessed 02/09/2015

30. See 'Le Francais á Verdun 1916' [French language website], section on 'Fortifications', 'Le Fort de Vaux' page at www. lesfrancaisaverdun-1916.fr/fortifications-vaux.htm, accessed 02/09/2015; and also the section on 'Les Régiments d'Infanterie et les Bataillons de Chasseurs qui ont participé à la Bataille de Verdun', '101-150 RI' and '251-300 RI' pages, entries for 118ᵉ and 298ᵉ *Régiment d'Infanterie* at www.lesfrancaisaverdun-1916.fr/regiment-intro.htm, accessed 02/09/2015

31. Figures cited in Horne, *The Price of Glory*, p. 317

32. Figures cited in *Verdun and the Battles for its Possession*, p. 20

33. Figures cited in Martin, p. 84

34. Figures cited in Foley, p. 256; Horne, *The Price of Glory*, p. 298; and Martin, p. 84

35. For details see Doughty, pp. 318–21; and Horne, *The Price of Glory*, pp. 319–20

36. See for example Clayton, p. 122; Horne, *The Price of Glory*, pp. 317–18; and Ousby, pp. 234–5

37. Figures cited in Horne, *The Price of Glory*, p. 322

38. Figures cited in Clayton, p. 134

39. See ibid., pp. 134–5

40. Quoted from Horne, *The Price of Glory*, p. 351

BIBLIOGRAPHY

Books

Brown, Malcolm, *Verdun 1916* (Stroud: Tempus Publishing, 1999)

Clayton, Anthony, *Paths of Glory: The French Army 1914–1918* (London: Cassell, 2003)

Donnell, Clayton, *The Forts of the Meuse in World War One* (Oxford: Osprey Publishing, 2007)

The Fortifications of Verdun 1874-1917 (Oxford: Osprey Publishing, 2011)

Breaking the Fortress Line 1914 (Barnsley: Pen & Sword Military, 2013)

Doughty, Robert A., *Pyrrhic Victory: French Strategy and Operations in the Great War* (London: Belknap Press of Harvard University, 2005)

De la Gorce, Paul-Marie, translated by Kenneth Douglas, *The French Army: A Military-Political History* (London: Weidenfeld & Nicolson, 1963)

Foley, Robert T., *German Strategy and the Path to Verdun: Erich von Falkenhayn and the Development of Attrition, 1870–1916* (Cambridge: Cambridge University Press, 2007)

Fromkin, David, *Europe's Last Summer: Why the World Went to War in 1914* (London: William Heinemann, 2004)

Greenhalgh, Elizabeth, *Foch in Command: The Forging of a First World War General* (Cambridge: Cambridge University Press, 2014)

Herwig, Holger H., *The First World War: Germany and Austria-Hungary 1914–1918* (London: Arnold, 1998)

The Marne 1914: The Opening of World War I and the Battle That Changed the World (New York: Random House, 2009)

Holmes, Richard, *Fatal Avenue: A Traveller's History of the Battlefields of Northern France and Flanders, 1346–1945* (London: Jonathan Cape, 1992)

Horne, Alistair, *The Price of Glory* (London: Penguin 1964)

The Fall of Paris: The Siege and the Commune 1870–71 (London: Papermac, 1989)

Joll, James, *The Origins of the First World War* 2nd Ed. (London: Longman, 1992)

Martin, William, *Verdun 1916 "They Shall Not Pass"* (London: Praeger, 2004)

Moote, A. Lloyd, *Louis XIII, the Just* (London: California University Press, 1991)

Ousby, Ian, *The Road to Verdun* (London: Pimlico, 2003)

Palmer, Michael A., *German Wars: A Concise History, 1859-1945* (Minneapolis: Zenith Press, 2010)

Patry, Léonce (translated by Douglas Fermer), *The Reality of War: A Memoir of the Franco-Prussian War 1870-1871* (London: Cassell & Co., 2001)

Stevenson, David, *1914-1918: The History of the First World War* (London: Penguin Books, 2004)

Strachan, Hew, *The First World War, Volume I: To Arms* (Oxford: Oxford University Press, 2001)

Sumner, Ian & Gerry Embleton, *The French Army 1914-18, Osprey Men-At-Arms Series No. 286* (London: Reed International Books, 1995)

Tapié, Victor Lucien, *France in the Age of Louis XIII and Richelieu* (Cambridge: Cambridge University Press, 1984)

Verdun and the Battles for its Possession: A Panoramic History and Guide (Clermont-Ferrand: Michelin & Cie, 1920)

Verdun: Vision and Comprehension, 6th Edition (Drancy: Editions Mage, 1989)

Wells, Neil J., *Verdun: An Integrated Defence: An Outline of the French Fortifications of the Great War Based on a Detailed Review of the Defences of Verdun* (Uckfield, East Sussex: Naval & Military Press, 2009)

Zuber, Terence *Inventing the Schlieffen Plan: German War Planning, 1871-1914* (Oxford: Oxford University Press, 2003)

The Battle of the Frontiers: Ardennes 1914 (Stroud: The History Press, 2009)

The Real German War Plan 1904-1914 (Stroud: The History Press, 2011)

Websites

'Association de Réservistes de la Marine Alsace' [French language website] at http://www.arm-asso.fr/

'Au Fil des Mots et de l'Histoire' [French language website] at http://aufildesmotsetdelhistoire.unblog.fr/

'Firstworldwar.com; A Multimedia History of World War One' at http://www.firstworldwar.com/

'Fortiff Sere: L'association Séré de Rivière' [French language website] at http://www.fortiffsere.fr/

'Fortified Places' at http://www.fortified-places.com/

'Historique du 405e Régiment d'Infanterie' [French language website] at http://tableaudhonneur.free.fr/405eRI.pdf

'Les Francais à Verdun 1916' [French language website] at http://www.lesfrancaisaverdun-1916.fr/

'Leben und Tod des Generalmajor Wilhelm von Lotterer, 1857-1916' [German language web page] at http://www.dffv.de/Verdun/Lotterer/Lotterer.htm

'Les Canons de l'Apocalypse' [French language website] at http://html2.free.fr/canons/

'151 Régiment d'Infanterie de Ligne' [French language website] at http://www.151ril.com/

LIST OF ILLUSTRATIONS AND MAPS

1. Damage inflicted by the German bombardment of Verdun on the Rue Mazel east of the cathedral. (Author's collection)
2. The underground citadel had 4 kilometres of passageways and could feed and accommodate 6,000 men. This casemate has been pressed into service as a barrack room. Note the vaulted brick roof, electric lighting and ceramic insulators on the power cable in the upper right. Contemporary accounts suggest that accommodation was much more crowded and the atmosphere much less clear and wholesome, which might explain the rather unnatural stiffness of the 'relaxing' soldiery. (Author's collection)
3. Aerial photograph of Fort Douaumont taken in May 1916, three months after it was captured by *Infanterie Regiment* 24 on 25 February. (Author's collection)
4. Fort Douaumont was retaken on 23 October 1916 by North African soldiers after a preparatory bombardment that used a quarter of a million shells. This picture shows men of the *Régiment d'Infanterie Coloniale du Maroc* sheltering in the moat of the fort on the morning of 25 October. (Author's collection)
5. Fort Vaux retaken by the French during the Battle of Verdun. (Courtesy of Jonathan Reeve)
6. The view over the barbed wire entanglement from the lines held by *Lieutenant-Colonel* Bonviolle's 165ᵉ *Regiment d'Infanterie* just north of the Bois d'Haumont at the northern edge of the Verdun salient. *General*

der Infanterie Hans von Zwehl's 7. *Reserve Korps* attacked from out of the woods and folds in the ground in the background in the late afternoon of 21 February 1916. (Author's collection)

7. Contemporary colour poster of soldiers marching beside a river and over a bridge into a shelled Verdun. (Courtesy of Jonathan Reeve)

8. Shells bursting on the *Mort-Homme* during the fighting in May 1916. (Author's collection)

9. French aid post like that occupied by *Caporal* Pierre Teilhard de Chardin, located in a dugout on Côte 304. (Author's collection)

10. Fully manned French trench on the *Mort-Homme* after its recapture in August 1917. Note the dugout entrance on the left. (Author's collection)

11. Ghastly mementos of battle at Verdun – a pile of human bones exhumed from a mass burial pit, post war. (Courtesy of Jonathan Reeve)

12. *Général* Robert Nivelle, Commander of the French 3ᵉ *Corps*, which arrived at Verdun at the end of March 1916. He was later promoted to command the French 2ᵉ *Armée* when Pétain moved on to take command of Army Group Centre in April 1916. (Author's collection)

13. Trench on the *Mort-Homme*. The sparse manning and relatively shallow depth suggests a communication trench on the lower slopes of the hill. (Author's collection)

14. *Général* Philippe Pétain, commander of the French 2ᵉ *Armée*, on the steps of his HQ at the Mairie at Souilly, 15 miles south-west of Verdun. The officer in the dark uniform is *Général* Joseph Joffre, Commander in Chief of the French army. (Author's collection)

15. One of the storm centres around Verdun. French troops in reserve in the Caillette Wood, June 1916. (Courtesy of Jonathan Reeve B2000p232)

16. *Le Boucher* (the butcher): *Général* Charles Mangin, commander of the 5ᵉ *Division d'Infanterie* and subsequently the 3ᵉ *Corps* comprising all French units on the east bank of the River Meuse. Technically competent, ruthless and courageous to the extreme, Mangin was as careless with the lives of his men as he was about his personal safety.

17. Contemporary colour poster of a soldier standing on a battlefield wearing a gas mask around his neck. The phrase 'they shall not pass' is said to have originated with *Général* Robert Nivelle at the Battle of Verdun. (Courtesy of Jonathan Reeve)

18. The German effort to reduce Fort Vaux began by dealing with French supporting positions to the north-west which included the village of Vaux. This picture shows the village in April 1917, after the German

attacks at the beginning of March and June 1916 had virtually wiped the village from the face of the earth. (Author's collection)

19. The *Ouvrage* de Thiaumont and access trench in May 1916, before the German offensive of early June. (Author's collection)

20. French troops in a trench running through the remains of Fleury, pictured in October 1916, just after the village had been retaken. The Germans held Fleury from 24 June 1916 and launched one thrust of their final attack toward Verdun from the village on 10–12 July 1916; the consequent French counter-attacks between July and October literally erased Fleury from the map. Note the use of bricks and stonework from destroyed buildings to shore up the trench sides. (Author's collection)

21. French soldiers in a front line trench nearing zero hour, Western Front. (Courtesy of Jonathan Reeve)

22 & 23. The main target of the final German attack on 11–12 July 1916 was Fort Souville, which guarded the last ridge of high ground between the Germans and Verdun. Only a small party of German troops managed to reach the fort's glacis on 12 July, and they were driven off by a counter-attack by the fort's garrison. The picture of the fort's main gate was taken in September 1916, and the snowy view of the inner entrance in March 1917. Both views show the damage inflicted by several months of sustained German bombardment. (Author's collection)

24. German shock troops training for an attack. German stormtroopers were first used in the Verdun battle. (Courtesy of Jonathan Reeve B119fp93)

25. Verdun's defences, French guns in Fort Souville, 1916. (Courtesy of Jonathan Reeve B2000p235)

26. German dead at Dead Man's Hill or *Mort-Homme*, the notorious elevation on the left bank of the Meuse fought over during the Battle of Verdun. (Courtesy of Jonathan Reeve)

27. A German soldier in no man's land throwing a grenade. (Courtesy of Jonathan Reeve B119fp93)

28. French machine gunners. (Courtesy of Jonathan Reeve B603p64)

29. The toll of the artillery, German dead in their pulverized trench. (Courtesy of Jonathan Reeve B119fpxvii)

30. Another recaptured stronghold, French troops in possession of the Haudremont Quarries, 1916. (Courtesy of Jonathan Reeve B2000p240)

31. Concrete emplacement for one of the three German 380 mm SK L/45 *Lange Max* (long Max) naval gun deployed by *Marine-Sonderkommando* 1 in the Bois de Warphémont north-east of Verdun; the other weapons

were located at the nearby Sorel Farm and Bois de Muzeray. Originally designed for heavy warships and with a range of 25 miles, each gun weighed in excess of 200 tons with a barrel length of over 50 feet; the emplacement included fire control equipment and a crane for loading. (Author's collection)

32. 380 mm round of the type fired by the *Lange Max* guns from *Marine-Sonderkommando* 1 on display at the Bois de Warphémont emplacement. Rounds like this opened the German bombardment at 04:00 on Monday 21 February 1916, with one of the first landing in the yard of the Bishop's Palace in Verdun Cathedral. (Author's collection)

33. Entrance tunnel to one of several underground ammunition storage bunkers on the Bois de Warphémont site, with one of the light railway carriages used for moving the ammunition to the hoist for loading. Each round weighed approximately 1,650 lb, although it is unclear if this includes the propellant charges. (Author's collection)

34. Shell craters and the remains of trenches in the western side of the Bois des Caures still clearly evident almost a century after the event; note the corrugated metal used for revetting and as overhead in dugouts. (Author's collection)

35. The underground battle entrance to Fort Tavannes, remarkably intact after almost a century. (Author's collection)

36. Built between 1888 and 1894, the *Batterie de Tavannes* is located midway between Fort Tavannes and the southern entrance to the Tavannes railway tunnel. Of masonry construction, the *Batterie* was not included in the concrete-hardening programme initiated from the late 1890s as a response to the 'Torpedo-shell Crisis' of 1885. (Author's collection)

37. The guardhouse and alternative entrance to the right of the main gateway into Fort Souville. The doorway and windows are a separate ablutions room for the guard; the narrower entrance to the left accesses a narrow passage leading into the fort proper, guarded by an internal firing embrasure. (Author's collection)

38. View down the glacis of Fort Vaux toward the dry moat, up which *Leutnant* Rackow and his men from *Infanterie Regiment* 158 stormed on Friday 2 June 1916. Picture taken near the crater created by the destruction of the retractable 75 mm gun turret; note the footpaths created by visitors around the craters and the mounting for an observation cupola at the left. (Author's collection)

39. The Douaumont Ossuary, erected near the site of the *Ouvrage de*

Thiaumont. Inaugurated on 7 August 1932 by Président Albert Lebrun, the Ossuary houses the unidentified remains of 130,000 men recovered from across the battlefield, fronted by the largest *Cimetière Nationale* in the world containing a further 16,142 graves; this lies beyond the trees left and right of the flagpole. (Author's collection)

40. One of the Mardi Gras *Batterie*'s central shelters. Consisting of eight emplacements for field guns atop ammunition storage chambers and two personnel shelters, the *Batterie*'s emplacements are arranged on a north-south axis facing east to cover the Woëvre Plain. (Author's collection)

41. Hardened sentry position with armoured observation dome located in the centre of the *Batterie* line. Close to the front line, the *Batterie* was extensively shelled during the 1916 battle and acted as a shelter and ammunition dump for troops serving in the area. (Author's collection)

42. The main entrance to Fort Souville. Constructed in 1875–77 and hardened with concrete from 1888, the fort marked the high water mark of the German advance on the east bank of the River Meuse in July 1916. Note the firing embrasures flanking the entrance; although not visible, there is also a small moat in front of the entranceway which would have been accessed via a drawbridge. Contemporary photographs suggest there may also have been a narrow gauge railway track leading up to the entrance. (Author's collection)

43. Map of Verdun before 1914, showing the geometric Vauban defence works. (Author's collection)

44. The Verdun front, from the Battle of the Marne in 1914 to Operation GERICHT in February 1916. Note the flanking heights of Les Eparges to the south-east and Vauquois to the north-west.

45. The Verdun sector before the German offensive of February 1916. Note the location of the forts and the German artillery positions with fields of fire. (Author's collection)

46. La Route: the vital supply route linking Verdun and Bar-le-Duc, later dubbed the Voie Sacrèe (the Sacred Way). (Author's collection)

47. The initial German attack on the east bank of the River Meuse, 21–26 February 1916. Attacking from the top of the map, the bold lines depict the four stages of the attack on 21, 22, 23, 24 and 25 February. (Author's collection)

48. The Verdun battlefield on both banks of the River Meuse; bold lines with dates show the progress of the German attacks on both banks in the first half of March 1916. (Author's collection)

INDEX

Index

Index

Index

317

First World War Books from Amberley

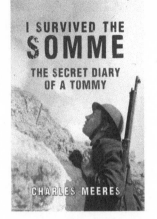

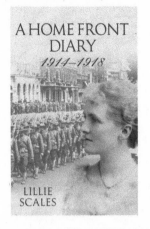

I SURVIVED THE SOMME

Charles Meeres

£16.99 HB

978-1-4456-0681-7

224 pages, 85 illustrations

A HOME FRONT DIARY 1914–1918

Lillie Scales ed. Peter Scales

'Utterly amazing...this is a riveting, inspiring read that will have you in tears one moment and cheered up the next.' *BOOKS MONTHLY*

£9.99 PB

978-1-4456-1896-8

96 pages, 40 illustrations

THE BEST 500 COCKNEY WAR STORIES

£9.99 PB

978-1-4456-0866-2

224 pages, 66 illustrations

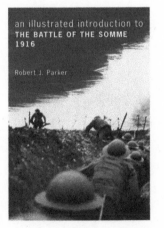

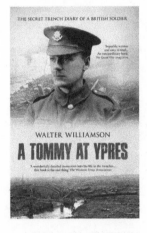

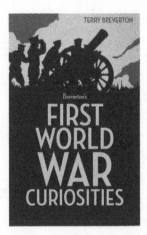

AN ILLUSTRATED INTRODUCTION TO THE SOMME

Robert J. Parker

£9.99 PB

978-1-4456-4442-4

96 pages, 70 illustrations

A TOMMY AT YPRES

Walter Williamson & Doreen Priddey

'Superbly written and easy to read... an extraordinary book.' *THE GREAT WAR MAGAZINE*

£12.99 PB

978-1-4456-1368-0

352 pages, 25 illustrations

BREVERTON'S FIRST WORLD WAR CURIOSITIES

Terry Breverton

£9.99 PB

978-1-4456-3341-1

320 pages

ALSO AVAILABLE AS EBOOKS

Available from all good bookshops or to order direct

Please call **01453-847-800**

www.amberleybooks.com

First World War Books from Amberley

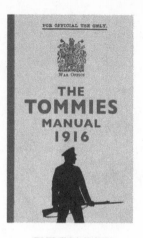

VERDUN
William F. Buckingham
£20 HB
978-1-4456-4108-9
320 pages, 40 illustrations

**THE TOMMIES
MANUAL 1916**
Hannah Holman
£9.99 PB
978-1-4456-3822-5
320 pages, 80 illustrations

**THE GREAT WAR
COOK BOOK**
May Byron
£9.99 PB
978-1-4456-3388-6
240 pages, 20 illustrations

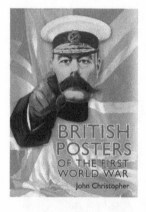

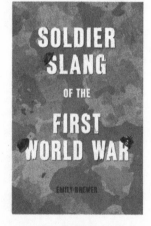

**FIRST WORLD WAR IN
THE AIR**
Phil Carradice
£14.99 PB
978-1-4456-0512-8
192 pages, 100 illustrations

**BRITISH POSTERS OF THE
FIRST WORLD WAR**
John Christopher
£20 HB
978-1-4456-3316-9
192 pages, 259 illustrations

**SOLDIER SLANG OF THE
FIRST WORLD WAR**
Emily Brewer
£12.99 PB
978-1-4456-3783-9
224 pages